How to In Size-Up Strangers Like Sherlock Holmes

Mark A. Williams, Sr.

Real Deal Publishing

How To Instantly
Size-Up Strangers Like
Sherlock Holmes

ISBN: 978-0-9907180-0-0
eISBN: 978-0-9907180-1-7

All the Sherlock Holmes quotes and excerpts in this book came from the 56 short stories and 4 novels that Sir Arthur Conan Doyle created.

Grateful acknowledgment to the Conan Doyle Estate Ltd. for the use of the Sherlock Holmes characters and stories created by Sir Arthur Conan Doyle.

Professional Cartoonist Royston Robertson created the cover illustration. Copyright © 2014 by Mark A. Williams, Sr. All rights reserved. Mr. Robertson can be reached at www.roystoncartoons.com.

Library of Congress Control Number: 2014954021

Library of Congress Cataloging-In-Publication Data

Williams, Sr., Mark A.

How To Instantly Size-Up Strangers Like Sherlock Holmes, 1st Edition

1. Self-Help 2. Psychology 3. Logic 4. Body Language

Published in the United States of America by: Real Deal Publishing, 124-20 Liberty Avenue, Suite 756, South Richmond Hill, NY 11419.

If you are unable to locate this book at your local bookstore, you may order it through www.realdealpublishing.net or www.amazon.com.

DISCLAIMER:

The author wrote this book only for entertainment and informational purposes. Sir Arthur Conan Doyle created the fictional character Sherlock Holmes in the late 19th century. The methods Holmes used may not always apply exactly to real people in modern times. The author and publisher believe the questions; principles, tips, exercises and techniques within this book are accurate, practical and scientifically based. They do not, however, guarantee any results, either directly or indirectly. Each person must develop and adapt the tips, suggestions and techniques to their own individual personality and situation. You should do your own research to determine if any of the tips, techniques or recommendations the author makes in this book would work for you.

The author has made every effort to provide accurate information, such as Internet addresses, at the time of publication. Neither the publisher nor the author, however, assumes responsibility for errors or changes that occur after publication. Additionally, the author does not have any control over websites listed in this book. The author also has no control over the content of those websites. The author has made every effort to include the most current and correct information possible. Nonetheless, inadvertent errors can occur. New research is constantly revising our understanding of people. The information in the book is intended to afford general guidelines on matters of interest to its' readers. The application of that information, however, can vary widely from person to person.

Accordingly, the author and publisher do not intend for the information in this book to serve as legal, medical, psychological or professional advice. If professional assistance is required, the services of a competent professional should be sought. The author and publisher disclaim any responsibility for any actions readers of this book take. In addition, they disclaim responsibility for any misunderstandings of the readers of this book. They disclaim all liability for any direct or indirect loss, damage or injury arising out of the use of this book. They also disclaim any liability even if someone advises the party involved of the possibility of such damages. Furthermore, the reader indemnifies and agrees to hold the author and publisher of this book harmless from such claims. By purchasing and reading this book, you agree to be bound to the statements above.

To my granddaughter
Lauren Loretta Gray
The Joy of my Life

*"...The Science of Deduction and Analysis
is one which can only be acquired
by long and patient study..."*
Sherlock Holmes, A Study in Scarlet

Table of Contents

What This Book Can Do For You

"What ineffable twaddle!" I cried....

"What is it?" asked Sherlock Holmes.

"Why this article." I said, "...it is evidently the theory of some armchair lounger who evolves all these neat little paradoxes in the seclusion of his own study. It is not practical. I should like to see him clapped down in a third class carriage on the underground, and asked to give the trades of all his fellow travellers. I would lay a thousand to one against him."

"You would lose your money." Sherlock Holmes remarked calmly. "As for the article I wrote it myself."

Sherlock Holmes, A Study in Scarlet

Renowned author and physician Sir Arthur Conan Doyle created the great fictional detective Sherlock Holmes. Dr. John H. Watson, *Holmes's* fictional friend and sidekick, chronicled 4 novels and 56 short stories in which Sherlock Holmes appeared.[1]

The inspiration for Holmes's fictional character came from Doyle's association with Professor Joseph Bell. Mr. Bell was a highly respected doctor in the late 19th Century. Doctor Bell's ability to instantly size-up his students inspired Doyle. Doyle then gave Holmes' one of his greatest detective skills. In several stories, Doyle uses Holmes's ability to size up strangers to astonish and fascinate his readers.

---

[1] Watson narrated 56 stories, Holmes narrated two stories and two stories were narrated in the third person.

Over a hundred years later, readers remain fascinated with the Sherlock Holmes stories and his ability to instantly size up strangers. What person upon meeting a stranger would not want to instantly tell if he or she is lying? Or know his or her background, job, age or other personal traits? Or tell where he recently came from or know his prior activities? Sizing up a stranger, as defined in this book, is the ability to discover facts and details about a person with just a glance.

Authors have written many articles and books about Holmes's investigative methods. Few, however, have focused in depth on his amazing skill in evaluating people. This is the first book, which will show readers, step by step, how to use the Holmes method to instantly size up strangers in everyday life. It will answer critics who believe that the average person cannot apply Holmes's method in the real world.

These critics claim that Holmes's method is not practical in the 21st Century. They argue the world has changed and Holmes would not find it as easy to size up strangers today. They say class distinctions no longer limit people as in Victorian times. They contend Holmes is a fictional character and you cannot do what he did in real life. They allege that Doyle created fictional stories designed to always make Holmes's methods work. They assert it is much harder today to interpret clues as Holmes did when meeting strangers. They state the average person is not a genius like Holmes and cannot follow his methods. This book takes the position that anyone can use the Sherlock Holmes Method to size up strangers. All you need to know is the *'secret'* upon which Holmes based his method.

The secret to the Sherlock Holmes Method is so obvious most people have overlooked it. Yet, the book does not tell you the secret upfront. Why? The answer is because *for some strange reason the secret works better when you discover it for yourself.* Holmes' himself realized this fact after he explained to his shocked clients how he knew things about them. His clients then downplayed his great skill once he revealed how he did it. This book will not make that same mistake. Instead, the book will challenge you to find the secret and recognize it for yourself.

The book will help you find and recognize the secret by providing you with several clues. In *A Case of Identity*, Sherlock Holmes said, "It has long been an axiom of mine that the little things are infinitely the most important." This first clue may help you recognize the secret when it flashes within your mind while you are reading. You may discover the secret in the first chapter or the last chapter. But you can only uncover the secret by *actively* searching for it. As you search, remember that *the secret already exists within your own mind.*

The first nine chapters will lead you to the secret. Each chapter in the book contains additional clues to the secret and is like pieces to a jigsaw puzzle. Use the pieces to put the puzzle together and figure the secret out. Chapters 10 and 11 will show you how to 'read' an unknown owner's personal property and handwriting just as did Sherlock Holmes. In Chapter 12, you will learn specific exercises to improve your natural abilities to use Holmes's method in everyday life.

Almost everyone is born with the same natural ability as Sherlock Holmes. In fact, we all use his method in our daily lives to read both people and inanimate objects. Some people, however, are better at it than others. This book will show you how to develop Holmes's method to your fullest potential. But for the tips in the book to work, you must make an effort and practice them each day.

Chapter 12 is perhaps the most important chapter in the book. It will train you to improve your abilities to their fullest potential. Read the entire book to discover the secret mentioned earlier. Practice the exercises in Chapter 12 to improve your skills. Then go out into the world and apply the Holmes method.

When you go out into the world, you will find that the Holmesian method is different from cold reading. Why? The answer is because it does not rely on manipulating a person to get clues to his or her background. It is different from astrology. Why? The answer is because it does not rely on stars in the sky to help you understand human behavior. It is different from fortune telling or psychic reading. Why? The answer is because it does not rely on a so-called supernatural ability to read people.

The Sherlock Holmes' Method is a practical way to evaluate strangers. It relies on asking questions and using principles. It does not rely on mystical tricks but *natural* abilities most people already possess. Teachers, doctors, lawyers, reporters, interviewers, supervisors, cab drivers, waiters, bartenders, politicians, detectives — anyone dealing with the public on a daily basis uses the Holmesian method. Most of them, however, do not even realize they are using it.

Once you realize and use the questions and principles in this book, your ability to evaluate strangers will improve. You will uncover hidden personality traits, motives and background information about the strangers you meet. You will gain new insight into people — *once you learn what to look for.* This book will teach you how and where to look.

You will learn how Holmes applied these practical questions and principles to easily and quickly see through strangers. You will find the questions and principles in this book simple to understand and easy to use. Whether you are a novice with little experience or an expert with lots of it, you will find useful tips in the book that you can apply in your everyday encounters with strangers you meet.

But no matter what your experience level, as you read, remember that to find the secret you must actively search for it. In *The Adventure of Black Peter,* Sherlock Holmes said, "...as long as the criminal remains upon two legs so must there be some

14

indentation, some abrasion, some trifling displacement which can be detected by the scientific searcher."

What Holmes meant is people must leave trace evidence about themselves that reveals who they are. Humans are *thinking* beings. We strive to express ourselves, to release what is inside of us. It is in our nature to leave clues about who we are to others — whether we want to or not. Once you understand this, your search for the secret will not be in vain.

But during your search, you will only find the secret once you also understand how everything is connected. In *A Study in Scarlet,* Sherlock Holmes said: "...all life is a great chain, the nature of which becomes known whenever we are shown a single link of it." Holmes believed people always leak clues about themselves to others in their everyday activities. He believed the clues are 'links' that reveal who the people are.

Sherlock Holmes recognized that everything pertaining to a person — no matter how seemingly insignificant — could tell you something about that person. A stranger's clothes, a person's behavior, an individual's hands — all tell a story. Everything about the person links together like a chain. It all reveals his or her personal history, background and prior activities — but only if you *know what to look for.*

Pay attention to trifles!

Keep this clue constantly in mind during your search and you will recognize the secret the moment you come upon it in any of the upcoming chapters. Then you will unlock the secret's full power and instantly size up any stranger you meet — just like Sherlock Holmes.

Chapter 1

Read A Stranger Like a Book
With This Sherlockian Tip

"...I may arrive at my facts most directly by questioning you."
Sherlock Holmes, The Adventure of the Noble Bachelor

Many writers, when describing how to think like Sherlock Holmes, have focused on how Holmes arrived at his amazing conclusions. The mental process behind his conclusions is important. What these writers failed to emphasize equally, however, is the *questioning* method Holmes used to reach the conclusions. Holmes famously explained to Doctor Watson that he had asked himself a *question* upon instantly sizing up Watson when he first met him.

Questions are a powerful tool for sizing up strangers because they focus your attention and stimulate your perceptions. Asking the right questions can direct your awareness towards an important fact. Questions can help you to concentrate on specific details. They can steer you towards relevant information. They can assist you in not jumping to seemingly obvious but wrong conclusions about strangers.

Asking yourself or a stranger questions teaches you to avoid making random assumptions when evaluating people. They aid you in making an educated guess about the stranger. They require you have specific data upon which you will form the basis for your conclusions. They guide your thinking so you can reach accurate impressions about the person. And last, asking basic questions makes it easier to solve problems.

How Asking Questions Helped Sherlock Holmes

Sherlock Holmes developed the habit of asking himself questions whenever he met a person. When a client appeared at 221B Baker Street, Holmes often sized him or her up in a few seconds. He would then question the client to obtain facts about the problem the client presented to him. Often Holmes would ask the client seemingly mundane questions. The questions later proved critical in helping him to solve the case.

Asking questions is the starting point from which Holmes began his investigations. They came from his personal system. A system that he had no problem in revealing to others who showed an interest in learning his methods. In *The Reigate Puzzle*, Holmes stated: "...it has always been my habit to hide none of my methods, either from my friend Watson or from anyone who might take an intelligent interest in them." It is with this Holmes assertion in mind that you will learn his personal system of asking questions.

The Four Basic Questions

The Sherlock Holmes personal system is a simplified version of the scientific method. The scientific method gathers facts and evidence, forms a preliminary hypothesis, tests the hypothesis and states a conclusion. In his personal system, Holmes used four basic questions to size up a stranger. Each question is similar to the steps in the scientific method.

Sherlock Holmes also used his personal system during his investigations. For example, in *The Boscombe Valley Mystery*, Holmes had asked himself several questions while examining a crime scene. Detective Lestrade laughed when Holmes described a murderer after his examination. Holmes simply replied to Lestrade's cynicism by saying: "You work your own method, and I will work mine."

In *The Adventure of Wisteria Lodge,* Holmes unraveled a mystery regarding his client Scott Eccles by asking questions. As he tracked down leads in the case, Holmes stated to Watson: "...we all have our systems. It was my system which enabled me to find John Warner." These two cases clearly show that the Holmes system relied on asking questions.

Asking questions is the framework upon which Holmes built his personal system. The four basic questions provided him with an accurate and systematic way to study people and investigate crime. You can apply the Holmesian method by asking the same four basic questions. Each question will help you to stay focused on what to look for with strangers. The four questions have a specific purpose and it is important for you to know the reasons for asking each one.

Ask The First Question to Observe

The first question Sherlock Holmes asked himself is: *"What do I observe?"* The purpose of this question is to gather details, facts and evidence. When looking at a stranger for the first time always ask yourself this question. The answers you get will give you clues to the stranger's personality and background.

Holmes clearly asked himself a question like this whenever he met a stranger for the first time. He did not, however, always ask the question directly. Whenever Holmes would say aloud "I observe" or "I perceive," he had already asked himself the first basic question.

In *The Adventure of the Speckled Band*, Holmes already asked himself the first basic question. He then said to Helen Stoner: "...I observe you are shivering." In *The Adventure of the Cardboard Box*, Holmes already asked himself the first basic question. He then said to Susan Cushing, after noticing a portrait of her sister: "...I observe that she was unmarried at the time."

19

In *The Adventure of the Priory School,* Holmes already asked himself the first basic question. He then asked Watson what "Do you observe" while examining a cyclist's tire tracks. In *The Hound of the Baskervilles,* Holmes already asked himself the first basic question. He then said to Watson: "You have been at your club all day, I perceive.' All these examples show how Holmes would ask, "What do I observe?" either directly or indirectly when seeking to size up a stranger or solve a problem.

Ask The Second Question to Make Inferences

The second question Sherlock Holmes asked himself is *"What can I deduce?"* The purpose of this question is to help you draw an inference about a stranger that you have observed. An inference, as defined in this book, is an assumption used to deduce a person's appearance. You will base your inference on the specific details and relevant facts about the stranger that you noticed. In asking this question, you are seeking to interpret correctly and understand the details and facts you find.

For example, smelling a perfume scent in the air is a fact. Assuming a woman's presence from the perfume scent is an inference. Sherlock Holmes often based his inferences on the trifles he observed and the questions he asked himself. Making inferences about strangers help you to form a hypothesis. A hypothesis, as defined in this book, is an educated guess or theory used to explain a problem or understand a person. Holmes always relied on specific data to create a hypothesis.

In *A Scandal in Bohemia,* Sherlock Holmes asked Watson: "What do you deduce from it?" after handing him an unsigned note. Holmes then examined the note and made several inferences from it before the writer arrived. In *The Five Orange Pips,* Holmes examined a postmark on a letter. He asked Watson: "What do you deduce from that?" Holmes then scrutinized the postmark and made several inferences from it about the writer.

20

When you size up a stranger, the "What can I deduce?" question is open-ended. It allows you to analyze vast amounts of facts, details and evidence. Sherlock Holmes unconsciously asked himself "What can I deduce?" when he met Doctor Watson for the first time. Holmes explained it this way:

> "...I knew you came from Afghanistan. From long habit the train of thoughts ran so swiftly through my mind, that I arrived at the conclusion without being conscious of intermediate steps...The train of reasoning ran, 'Here is a gentleman of a medical type, but with the air of a military man. Clearly an army doctor, then. He has just come from the tropics, for his face is dark, and that is not the natural tint of his skin, for his wrists are fair. He has undergone hardship and sickness, as his haggard face says clearly. His left arm has been injured. He holds it in a stiff and unnatural manner...'"

Sherlock Holmes automatically picked up details (dark and haggard face, fair wrists, injured left arm) that Doctor Watson unwittingly placed before him. He used the evidence he gathered to infer things about Doctor Watson that were spot on. He knew the details implied certain facts about Doctor Watson. Holmes asked himself questions in order to reach the fact that Watson had just come from Afghanistan. Holmes then asked himself the third basic question.

Ask The Third Question to Test a Hypothesis

Once you have formed a hypothesis, you must then test it. To test a hypothesis, Holmes asked himself the third question: *"How can I verify it?"* The purpose of this question is to help you make sure your facts are correct. Never size up a stranger without checking to see if your estimations are accurate.

Always follow up after asking yourself questions and deducing facts about a stranger by verifying your hypothesis. This is similar to the scientific method scientists use to test a theory to ensure that it is valid. There are several ways for you to verify your assessments regarding strangers you meet.

First, you can check out your hypothesis by simply making a statement and have the stranger confirm it. Sherlock Holmes did this on numerous occasions when he met strangers for the first time. For example, in The "Gloria Scott" case, Sherlock Holmes made several deductions about Victor Trevor father's appearance. The senior Mr. Trevor confirmed the deductions when he said: "Well, that's true enough" "Right again" and "Quite true" to Holmes's inferences.

Second, you can simply ask the stranger if the hypothesis you reached is true. Strike up a casual conversation with the stranger and casually draw out the information you seek. For example, in A Study in Scarlet, Doctor Watson verified one of Holmes deductions when he casually asked a stranger what his trade is. The stranger answered, "A sergeant, sir, Royal Marine Light infantry."

Third, you can check with another source such as a website, a directory or a witness to see if your hypothesis is accurate. For example, in The Hound of the Baskervilles, Doctor Watson checked one of Sherlock Holmes's deductions. He looked up a medical directory to determine James Mortimer's age and profession. Watson's inquiry ultimately supported Holmes's inferences regarding the country doctor.

Finally, you can simply test the stranger and see what they say or do. Make a prediction about their behavior and wait to see if the stranger acts accordingly. For example, in The Adventure of the Blue Carbuncle case, Holmes put an advertisement in several evening papers. He sought to test his theory that the man who left behind his hat at 221B Baker Street had nothing to do with the stealing a valuable stone. When the man, Mr. Henry Baker, saw the advertisement and came to get the goose and his hat, he confirmed Holmes's hypothesis.

Ask The Fourth Question to Reach a Conclusion

The fourth question Sherlock Holmes asked himself is *"What do I conclude?"* The purpose of this question is to help you reach an accurate conclusion about what you see. As with the last step in the scientific method, you can either accept or reject what you find depending on the facts and evidence. When you accept the results, you know you asked the questions correctly. When you reject the results, then you must go back to the drawing board.

Usually when you must reject the results it is because you did not weight every available possibility. You might have obtained wrong data or did not have enough information. Sometimes you may interpret the evidence incorrectly or think illogically. These faulty ways of thinking will cause you to reach flawed conclusions. If this happens, start from question one and repeat the questions until you get it right. Once you get it right, you can state your conclusion just as Sherlock Holmes did in many of his cases.

In *A Study in Scarlet*, Sherlock Holmes reached a conclusion about a culprit. He stated: "All these considerations led me to the irresistible conclusion that Jefferson Hope was to be found among the jarveys of the Metropolis." In *The Case of the Noble Bachelor*, after cross-questioning a client, he stated: "I had formed my conclusion as to the case before our client came into the room." In *A Case of Identity,* he reached a conclusion when he noticed a typewritten signature. He stated: "The point about the signature is suggestive — in fact, we may call it conclusive."

Once you state your conclusion, it is not the end but the beginning to sizing up strangers. When you start asking yourself the four basic questions, you will naturally begin asking even more questions. Those additional questions, will in turn lead to further questions. Each extra question you ask will help you to evaluate the stranger more accurately.

23

Ask Additional Questions to Learn Information

In many Holmes' cases you will find him asking the questions *What, Why, When, Where, Who* and *How.* These questions helped him obtain additional information. For example, in *The Adventure of the Priory School,* Sherlock Holmes asked the questions 'What,' 'When,' 'How,' and 'Why' when he said to Dr. Huxtable:

> "...kindly tell me what has happened, when it happened, how it happened and....what Dr. Huxtable....has to do with the matter, and why he comes three days after the an event — the state of your chin gives the date — to ask my humble services."

In *A Study In Scarlet,* after young Stamford introduced him to Doctor Watson, Holmes quickly glanced at Watson. He instantly recognized that Watson recently came from Afghanistan. Holmes *unconsciously* asked himself a 'Where' question. He then answered it when he said to himself:

> "...Where in the tropics could an English army doctor have seen much hardship and got his arm wounded? Clearly in Afghanistan."

In *The Naval Treaty,* Holmes formed several theories. He needed to test the theories further after investigating a missing State document. Holmes then asked an important 'Who' question regarding the crime:

> "Who is it who profits by it?"

Sherlock Holmes asked himself or a client the above additional questions to get a clear understanding of the facts and evidence. He considered asking questions so important in his detective work that often he would ask a client several questions. He would then immediately solve the case!

For example, in *The Naval Treaty,* Holmes asked 41 questions before he solved the case. In *The Adventure of the Noble Bachelor,* Holmes asked 31 questions before he solved the case. In *The Valley of Fear,* Holmes solved the case by asking himself just *one* question! The questions Holmes asked that solved the cases came directly from his personal method.

The Sherlock Holmes Method

Critics claim that the Sherlock Holmes Method is too hard for the average person to learn. They allege that you have to be a genius like Holmes to do what he did. The truth is, to successfully size up strangers you must *believe* that you can do it. Your *mental attitude* will determine your success or failure. If you believe it is too hard, then it will be too hard. *Think positive* that you can do what Holmes did and you will improve.

You will improve because the Holmes method is not as hard as many people think. Developing a mindset that you *can* and *will* use his method successfully is the first step to doing it. Do not allow negative thoughts such as "this is not realistic" or "this is not practical" to creep into your thinking. These are the same negative thoughts Watson had when he first met Holmes. Do not let negative thinking like Watson's enter your mind.

The Holmesian method only seems hard because Arthur Conan Doyle did not reveal everything Holmes did in the stories until the end. Conan Doyle *intentionally* does not let you see everything Holmes sees. Doyle left subtle clues that only Holmes knew. If you were present and could see what Holmes saw, the solutions would be simple and obvious to you. Sherlock Holmes meant this when he said that once he explained his method, people considered him a very ordinary individual.

We all have made Holmesian styled deductions at various times in our lives. The difference with Sherlock Holmes is that he does it *consistently.* But even at his best, Holmes did not have a one hundred percent success rate. Watson wrote more about his 'hits' than his 'misses.' To increase your chances of success, you must understand how the Holmesian method works.

The Sherlock Holmes Method comes in two parts. The first part is asking questions. The second part is using principles. Both parts together help you to evaluate strangers and study people. You start-off with basic questions, then ask additional questions as needed. Asking follow up questions such as What, Why, When, Where, Who and How, will get you the information necessary to size up strangers accurately.

In the upcoming chapters, you will find eight principles that will enable you to put the four basic questions to practical use. In each chapter, you will learn about a principle that will enhance your ability to size up a stranger. The principles will enable you to get answers to both the basic and follow-up questions.

Sherlock Holmes used these same principles, either singly or in various combinations, with the four basic questions. He used them together to perform an accurate and systematic examination of each stranger that came his way. That all the questions and principles united should fail to enable you to size up any stranger you meet just as Sherlock Holmes did is almost inconceivable.

Go to Pages 281 to 286 if you want to practice
the question exercises now.

Chapter 2

Use This Holmesian Ability to Instantly Scan Strangers

"...You appeared to read a good deal upon her which was quite invisible to me."

"Not invisible but unnoticed, Watson. You did not know where to look, and so you missed all that was important..."
Sherlock Holmes, A Case of Identity

Doctor Joseph Bell, Conan Doyle's inspiration for Sherlock Holmes, lectured at the *University of Edinburgh* medical school during the late 19th century. Dr. Bell taught his students that they could obtain an accurate medical diagnosis from a patient by paying close attention to the patient's symptoms. Dr. Joseph Bell described it this way:

> "In teaching the treatment of disease and accident...all careful teachers have first to show the student how to recognize accurately the case. The recognition depends in great measure on the accurate and rapid appreciation of small points in which the diseased differs from the healthy state. In fact, the student must be taught to observe. To interest him in this kind of work we teachers find it useful to show the student how much a trained use of the observation can discover in ordinary matters such as the previous history, nationality and occupation of a patient."[2]

---

[2] *Teller of Tales: The Life of Sir Arthur Conan Doyle* (2000) by Daniel Stashower, Page 28.

Dr. Bell sought to keep his students interested in his lectures. To do this, he would pick a stranger at random. He would point out the stranger's occupation and past activities. He relied on minute observations of the stranger's appearance. Once during a lecture, Dr. Bell sized up a patient he just met. He stated the patient previously served in the army. He noted the patient recently received a discharged after being stationed at Barbados. Professor Bell then explained to his students:

> "...you see, gentlemen...the man was a respectful man but did not remove his hat. They do not in the army, but he would have learned civilian ways had he been long discharged. He has an air of authority and he is obviously Scottish. As to Barbados, his complaint is Elephantiasis, which is West Indian and not British."[3]

Dr. Bell would often astonish his students because the demonstrations seemed so simple that anyone could do it.

As you can see, the natural ability which Conan Doyle gave his fictional character Sherlock Holmes comes from a real person — Dr. Joseph Bell. The skills Dr. Bell used to size up his students came from reality, not from fiction. You can learn them. One skill Dr. Bell taught is *observation.*[4] Most people have good natural eyesight from birth. We all have the ability, unless we have vision problems, to see what is in front of us.

---

[3] Conan Doyle describes this lecture in his autobiography, *Memories and Adventures*, Page 330.

[4] In a famous demonstration, Dr. Joseph bell illustrated how most people do not pay attention to the things around them. He asked his students to watch while he stuck his middle finger in a bowl of sticky liquid. He then put his finger in his mouth. Dr. Bell then instructed his students to stick their fingers in the bowl and put their fingers in their mouths. After they followed his instructions, he told them that he had switched his middle finger with his index finger and had not stuck the liquid substance in his mouth. He taught them this lesson to show the benefits to being observant. – From *Observe Carefully, Deduce Shrewdly: Dr. Joseph Bell,* August 18, 2009, *The Forensic Examiner*, Dr. Katherine Ramsland.

In *The Adventure of the Blue Carbuncle,* Watson claimed he could see nothing after examining an old battered hat. Sherlock Holmes replied: "On the contrary, Watson, you can see everything."

In *The Adventure of the Speckled Band*, after examining a room, Watson said: "You speak of danger. You have evidently seen more in these rooms than was visible to me." Holmes replied: "No...I imagine that you saw all that I did."

In *A Scandal in Bohemia*, Watson said to Holmes: "...I believe that my eyes are as good as yours." Holmes replied: "Quite so. You see, but you do not observe."

Watson could see just as well as Holmes. Watson simply did not use his observational skills to his fullest potential. Like Watson, most people who met Holmes thought he had super human observational powers. Holmes, however, considered his eyesight ordinary. He saw no more than the average person.

In *The Adventure of the Blanched Soldier*, Mr. Dodd said to Holmes: "You see everything." Holmes replied: "I see no more than you, but I have trained myself to notice what I see." This chapter will teach you how to develop your own natural observational ability to its' fullest potential. You will learn to notice what you see just as Sherlock Holmes did.

How To Look When Observing A Stranger

How did Holmes develop his almost superhuman observational skill? While a young man in college, Sherlock had already formed his observational skill into a system. Even then, he understood that you must learn *how* to look at people before knowing where to look and what to look for with them. Therefore, the first step in learning how to observe another person is to start with yourself.

Observe Yourself First

In *The Greek Interpreter,* Holmes said to Watson: "...all things should be seen exactly as they are, and to underestimate one's self is as much a departure from the truth as to exaggerate one's own powers." Holmes then told Watson clearly that his older brother Mycroft Holmes had superior observational skill than himself. Holmes could do this because he knew his own perception limitations.

Just as Sherlock Holmes did, accept the fact that you cannot see everything about people — just look for the important things. Develop the habit of using your five senses — seeing, hearing, smelling, tasting and touching — as the basis of your observations. Stay aware that your own experiences, thoughts, beliefs, expectations and ways of viewing the world can influence what you see. Guard against allowing your personal views to unduly affect what you observe with people.

In addition, do not let your feelings warp what you see. Know your limitations and do not allow emotions such as fear, anger, joy, envy, jealously or sadness cloud what you see with people. Recognize that you have natural biases. Constantly correct yourself while you are observing people so that you do not distort what you see. Look at people as they are and do not let feelings or anything else distract your attention.

When Sherlock Holmes looked at strangers, he viewed them impersonally. In *The Sign of Four,* when Watson commented on a client's attractiveness, Holmes replied: "Is she? I did not observe...it is of the first importance to not allow your judgment to be biased by personal qualities. A client is to me a mere unit, a factor in a problem." Holmes did not let a client's appearance or behavior influence what he observed. He did this because he observed strangers for a reason.

Observe With A Purpose

Sherlock Holmes never observed strangers randomly. Whenever he first looked at people, he always observed them with a *purpose.* He had a goal in mind, a specific reason for every observation he made. His goal? He strived to learn as much about strangers in the first few seconds as he could.

In *A Study in Scarlet,* Sherlock Holmes stated on meeting a fellow-mortal, he would: "...distinguish the history of the man, and the trade or profession to which he belongs." Holmes then used this information when necessary to solve his cases. In *The Adventure of the Three Garridebs*, Holmes stated: "...these little digressions of mine sometimes prove in the end to have some bearing on the matter."

Always have a goal in mind when you observe strangers. You will know how to look once you have a *goal* when you look. Your goal will direct your attention. It will help you stay focused and alert. It will make you more *conscious* and *aware* of what you see. When you observe a person with a *purpose* you are more likely to *see* what you are looking at.

For example, a sales person will not look at a customer the same way that a detective will look at a suspect. The sales person will look for signs from the customer that will help him make a sale. The detective will look for clues from the suspect to determine whether the suspect is guilty or innocent.

Likewise, a young man seeking to date a woman will not look at her the same way a doctor looks at her before he physically examines her. The young man will look for non-verbal cues from the girl that will enable him to get her name and phone number so he can date her. The doctor will look for physical health symptoms that reveal a medical condition she may have so he can cure her.

31

Each person will have a different reason for observing a stranger according to his or her own profession, motives, interests and goals. As Holmes stated to Dr. Watson in *The Adventure of the Copper Beeches*: "...I must look at everything with reference to my own special subject." Just as Sherlock Holmes did, always know *why* you are observing strangers when you look at them.

Glance — Do Not Stare At People

Once you have observed yourself and know *why* you are looking at people, the next step is to actually watch them. Never stare at a stranger. The person will become uncomfortable and uneasy because they do not know you. Sherlock Holmes once said: "...there's nothing to be learned by staring." He also told Watson while they waited for a suspect to arrive at 221B Baker Street: "Don't frighten him by looking at him too hard."

Whenever you meet a stranger for the first time, glance at him or her for a second. Look them up and down quickly. Let your eyes scan from their head to their feet or from their feet to their head. Do this fast but casually. It is socially acceptable to look at people this way as long as it lasts for a second or less.

In *A Case of Identity*, Watson describes how Holmes observed a stranger upon meeting her for the first time:

> "...He looked her over in the minute and yet abstracted fashion which was peculiar to him..."

In *The Adventure of the Speckled Band*, Watson describes how Sherlock Holmes observed a stranger upon meeting her for the first time:

> "...Sherlock Holmes ran her over with one of his quick, all-comprehensive glances..."

In *The Adventure of the Solitary Cyclist,* Watson describes how Sherlock Holmes observed a stranger upon meeting her for the first time:

"...His keen eyes darted over her..."

In *The Adventure of the Copper Beeches,* Watson describes how Sherlock Holmes observed a stranger upon meeting her for the first time:

"...He looked her over in his searching fashion..."

All of the above examples show how Sherlock Holmes, on meeting a person for the first time, quickly looked them over. In *The Gloria Scott* case, Holmes's quick eye enabled him to obtain data from a man's elbow. He did this even though the man's elbow became visible only for a second. In *The Adventure of the Norwood Builder* case, Holmes's quick eye enabled him to figure out Mr. McFarlane's occupation. He did this even though he saw only the slightest information.

But Sherlock Holmes did not only glance at strangers face to face, he also observed them from a distance. The *Study in Scarlet* case illustrates Holmes's long-range observational ability. From their window, Holmes and Watson watched a man walk slowly down the other side of a street. Holmes then observed the man as a retired sergeant of marines. In *The Greek Interpreter,* Holmes and his older brother Mycroft, looking down from a window, took turns sizing up two strangers in the street below. They could tell, even from a long distance, that one man looked like a soldier and the other looked like a widower.

In *The Resident Patient,* Sherlock Holmes and Watson returned from a three-hour stroll. Holmes, from a distance, observed several items in a horse-drawn carriage waiting in front of 221B Baker Street. He then deduced the occupant to be a general practicing doctor. In *The Final Problem,* Watson describes how Holmes's "...quick glancing eyes and his sharp scrutiny of every face that passed us..." showed him alert as they strolled down a street.

These examples prove Sherlock Holmes looked swiftly at a stranger's slightest movements. Holmes stayed observant even at long distances. Like Holmes, you can develop a quick eye by practicing watching people from long distances such as a window or car. Observe them as they walk towards you in the street. Look at them quickly. Do this whenever you see a stranger in public.

Observe Strangers In A Offhand Manner

When Holmes glanced at a stranger, he did it in a nonchalant and casual manner. As he looked them over, he made it appear as though he had little interest in the person. He did not draw attention to his actions. You can often observe strangers while they are talking, reading a book, listening to music or doing some other activity that has their attention. You can use that time to quickly look them over without making them aware you are watching them.

For example, in *The Red-Headed League*, Holmes had observed Watson studying a client without success while the client read a newspaper article. Holmes glanced at the client. He quickly stated several things about him that caused the client to look up in surprise from the newspaper. The client never knew Holmes had observed him until Holmes made it known to him.

In *The Adventure of the Cardboard Box*, Holmes observed a woman's profile as she looked in another direction. When she turned around to glance at him, he quickly changed his expression back demurely. Watson had also looked at her but could see nothing that had aroused Holmes excitement. Yet Holmes, with a quick look at the woman, had already obtained the data he needed to solve the case.

In *The Adventure of the Blanched Soldier*, Holmes sat with his back to a window in his sitting room at 221B Baker Street. He then had a client sit in the opposite chair so that the light from the window shined down on him. The client's delay in starting the interview gave Holmes extra time to observe him. Holmes used the extra seconds to size up the client, without him realizing what Holmes had done.

Just as Sherlock Holmes did, when you observe a stranger, do it in a non-conspicuous way. Make yourself as unobtrusive and unnoticed as possible. Pick a location like a park bench or a café to watch the stranger. You can read a newspaper, book or wear headphones to blend into your surroundings. Make yourself appear uninterested and a natural part of the environment. Then pick out a stranger and focus your attention. You can watch a stranger on the subway, bus, in a store or as you go about your daily activities. The important thing is to not appear as if you are stalking or staring at the person.

Stay Alert — Even With People You Know

Sherlock Holmes also stayed alert and aware even when he knew the person. On many occasions, Holmes sized up Dr. Watson as if he had met him for the first time. He observed Watson at different times and noticed different things about him. For example, in *A Scandal In Bohemia,* he noticed Watson gained weight. In *The Stock-Broker's Clerk,* he noticed Watson had recently been sick. In *The Crooked Man,* he noticed Watson's medical practice kept him busy.

Often people get used to seeing family members, friends, co-workers and neighbors. They do not notice subtle changes in their appearance, personality, behavior and moods. Sherlock Holmes constantly observed everyone. He rarely became complacent with people he knew. It is why he told Watson: "...I have the advantage of knowing your habits..." after Watson expressed surprise at how Holmes knew his medical practice kept him busy.

You will not be surprised at what the people you know say or do if you stay alert to them. Often people will act 'normal' even when they are going through serious problems in their lives. Keep alert for events in people's lives such as divorce, illness or injury, job or home loss, a loved one's death, financial troubles, bad relationships and so forth that may cause them to change. Notice subtle changes in their behavior. Such as a person who normally dresses neat, suddenly dressing sloppy or a person who is normally outgoing, suddenly keeping to himself.

Never take anyone for granted, no matter how close you are to him or her. The people who take others for granted, and who do not remain alert, are usually shocked when individuals who they thought they knew do something unexpected like kill someone or commit suicide. Sherlock Holmes would have noticed subtle changes in a friend or stranger because he always kept his mental radar on when observing people — even when he knew the person.

Observe Your Surroundings

Sherlock Holmes also kept his mental radar on when he observed his surroundings. His eyes constantly moved back and forth to observe relevant details in the areas he investigated. In *The Adventure of the Speckled Band*, Dr. Watson described how he entered a room and his "...eyes travelled round and round and up and down, taking in every detail of the apartment...."

In *The Adventure of the Cardboard Box,* Sherlock Holmes walked into a room and observed photographs.[5] He saw that

---

[5] Although Sherlock Holmes did not realize it, he had applied a technique that Author Robert Akeret would discuss over 75 years later in his book *Photo Analysis: How To Interpret The Hidden Psychological Meaning of Personal and Public Photographs.*

Susan Cushing had two sisters. He noticed from a photograph that one sister had not yet married.

In *The Disappearance of Lady Frances Carfax*, Dr. Watson described Sherlock Holmes as having an *"ever-active attention."* Most people know someone who has a very active attention.

My mentor and friend, retired Brooklyn Branch President Thomas Stanziale Sr. (from Local 300, National Postal Mail Handlers Union), had an ever-active attention like Holmes. Tom and I worked at the U. S. Postal Service as mail handlers. We were also union stewards.

As we sat in the post office cafeteria, I often watched Tom as he observed other employees. His eyes constantly moved around, darting from right to left. Even as he engaged people in conversation, he watched his surroundings, always staying alert and aware of everyone around him. In fact, Tom reminded me of both Sherlock Holmes and Dr. Joseph Bell from the many times I watched him size up strangers through his ever-active attention.

Be Skeptical and Suspicious

In addition to having an ever-active attention, Sherlock Holmes kept a skeptical and suspicious attitude when meeting strangers. He did not believe everything he saw with them. In *The Hound of the Baskervilles,* Holmes once observed: "...My eyes have been trained to examine faces and not their trimmings. It is the first quality of a criminal investigator that he can see through a disguise."[6]

Sherlock Holmes instinctively recognized that you cannot judge a book by its' cover. As a result, Holmes always looked

---

[6] Yet, in *A Study In Scarlet,* it seems Holmes did not follow his own advice. A young man, disguised as a little old lady, tricked Holmes into giving him a ring that Holmes believed would lead him to a prime suspect. The 'old woman' then gave Holmes the slip when Holmes tried to follow 'her'.

beneath a stranger's surface appearance. He once told Percy Phelps, a client who had requested his services in *The Naval Treaty* case, that his fiancée's brother Joseph Harrison's "...character is a rather deeper and more dangerous one than one might judge from his appearance..."

In *The Adventure of the Norwood Builder,* Holmes hit a wall regarding obtaining evidence that would exonerate his client. Watson suggested to Holmes: "Surely...the man's appearance would go far with any jury." Holmes replied: "That is a dangerous argument, my dear Watson. You remember that terrible murderer, Bert Stevens, who wanted us to get him off in '87? Was there ever a more mild-mannered, Sunday-school young man?"

Holmes did not let appearances fool him. He did not accept people at face value. He looked for proof to confirm what he saw. If he did not find it, then he remained skeptical and suspicious until he obtained the evidence he needed. Holmes could do this because he also knew *where* to look.

Where To Look When Observing A Stranger

In *A Case of Identity,* Watson attempted to study a stranger using the method he learned from Holmes. Watson believed that Holmes read things about a woman that were invisible to him. Holmes replied that the things he read Watson had not noticed. Why? The answer is because Watson did not know where to look and so he missed everything important.

Although it would seem obvious that the average person can describe a stranger's appearance after meeting them, many people cannot do it accurately. Most people will miss what is important about a stranger once you put them to the test. Sherlock Holmes meant this when he said in *The Red-Headed League* case that "...a commonplace face is the most difficult to identify." If you are to master the Sherlock Holmes Method, you must first learn the more elementary art of obtaining a stranger's description.

How to Identify Strangers

Holmes often challenged Watson to describe strangers after first meeting them. In *The Case of Identity*, Holmes asked Watson: "...What did you gather from that woman's appearance? Describe it." In addition, Holmes noted Dr. Watson's ability at describing a person's general appearance by stating: "...you have hit upon the method, and you have a quick eye for color."

Sherlock Holmes also sought descriptions from clients regarding the people they spoke about. He did it with Miss Mary Sutherland, the typist from *A Case of Identity*. After she explained to him about a mysterious suitor, Holmes stated: "...I should like an accurate description of him."

Like Holmes and Watson, whenever you meet a person for the first time, pay close attention to everything about them. For a few seconds, practice making a mental list of their appearance. Observe the whole person for a good description. One important lesson the police academy teaches new recruits in training is how to identify potential suspects.[7]

In the police academy, recruits learn to notice an individual's appearance. Once they notice it, they must then describe it. Like a police officer, look at the following physical indicators to get a stranger's accurate description:

---

[7] Sizing up strangers is not the same as prejudging them. Sizing up a stranger by a physical appearance focuses on *identifying* the individual. Your evaluation is based on a *description* of the person. Prejudging a stranger by a physical appearance focuses on *stereotyping* the individual. Your evaluation relies on factors such as their race, gender, religion, sexual orientation, handicap, ethnicity, age or housing status.

1. **Height, Weight and Age:** How tall is the stranger? How old does he or she look? How much does the person weight? In *A Study in Scarlet*, Sherlock Holmes deduced a man's height from the length of his stride and an inscription on a wall.[8] He deduced another man's age from his jumping over a puddle. In *A Scandal in Bohemia*, Sherlock Holmes deduced that Watson had gained weight since the last time he saw him.

2. **Race and Gender:** Is the stranger African American? Caucasian? Asian? Latino? Caribbean? European? Middle-Eastern? Mixed Race? A man or woman? Gay? Transgender? Bi-sexual? In *The Adventure of the Creeping Man*, Holmes deduced a man as being a Slavonic of European origin by his name.

3. **Body Type:** Is the stranger muscular? Thin? Heavyset? Stocky? Shapely? In *The Greek Interpreter*, both Holmes and his brother Mycroft deduced a stranger as being in the artillery through observing his muscular body type.

4. **Posture:** How is the stranger standing or sitting? Erect? Stooped? Slumped? Stiff? Loose? In *A Study in Scarlet*, Holmes deduced a man's occupation from his "...military carriage..." and "...the way in which he held his head and swung his cane..."

5. **Complexion:** How is the stranger's skin tone? Rough? Smooth? Tanned? Dark? Freckled? Fair? Pale? Sallow? Florid? Pockmarked? Does the stranger have a skin disorder? Rash? Did the stranger have cosmetic surgery? In *The Adventure of the Solitary Cyclist*, Holmes deduced that a woman came from the countryside from her complexion.

---

[8] In *The Adventure of the Three Students*, Holmes used his own height to deduce that the tallest student was the one who stole the college test papers.

6. **Head:** What is the shape of the stranger's head? Long? Short? Broad? Narrow? Large? Medium? Small? Square? Round? Inclined forward, backward or sideways? In *The Adventure of the Blue Carbuncle,* Holmes deduced a man's intelligence from his head size.[9]

7. **Hair:** How does the stranger style his or her hair? Is it cut short? Long? Conservative? Radical? What color is the hair? Black? Brown? Auburn? Blonde? Red? Grey? White? Is the color natural or did the stranger dye it? What is the hair texture? Thick? Thin? Kinky? Wavy? Curled? Straight? Braided? Parted in the front or back? A ponytail? Is the hair receding? Is the stranger bald? Does the stranger have a weave, wig or toupee? In *The Adventure of Wisteria Lodge,* Holmes deduced from Mr. Scott Eccles's un-brushed hair that he had not come immediately to consult him.

8. **Mustache or Beard:** Is the stranger's mustache or beard short? Medium? Long? Colored? Does it have pointed or dull ends? Does it turn up or down? Is it straight? Is it thick or thin? Is it trimmed? Does the stranger have sideburns? Is the stranger clean-shaven? In *The Adventure of the Blanched Soldier,* Sherlock Holmes deduced a stranger's prior background from his having a short beard among other details. In *The Boscombe Valley Mystery,* Holmes deduced the window in Watson's bedroom being on the right hand side from observing the left side of Watson's half-shaven face. In *The Hound of the Baskervilles* Holmes deduced a man, who he observed in a cab, had a false beard because he reasoned that: "a clever man upon so delicate an errand has no use for a beard save to conceal his features."

---

[9] Holmes was wrong with this deduction because he based it on a belief that "a man with such a large head must have something in it." Phrenology is the 'science' of judging a person's character and traits by their facial structure. The scientific community has since falsified Phrenology as a science.

9. **Forehead:** Is the stranger's forehead broad? Narrow? High? Low? Receding? Vertical? Is the forehead protruding or bulging? In *The Adventure of the Golden Pince-Nez,* Sherlock Holmes deduced a woman had a puckered forehead from analyzing her eyeglasses.

10. **Eyebrows:** Are the stranger's eyebrows thin? Bushy? Penciled? Natural? Arched? Horizontal? Slanting up or down? Do they meet? Does the stranger have eyebrows? Did the stranger shorten, trim or cut his or her eyebrows? In *The Adventure of the Devil's Foot,* Watson read from Holmes contracted eyebrows the uselessness in persuading him against taking the case.

11. **Eyes:** What color are the stranger's eyes? Are they blue? Black? Brown? Grey? Green? Clear? Bloodshot? Jaundiced? Straight? Oblique? Cross-eyed? Squinting? Narrow? Close-set? Widely separated? Piercing? Dull? Fixed? Mobile? Are the stranger's eyelashes short or long? Natural or fake? Is the stranger blind or missing an eye? Is the stranger wearing an eye patch? A fake eye? Is the stranger wearing contact lenses? Eyeglasses? If so, what type of glasses is the stranger wearing? Designer frames? Prescription frames and lenses? Bi-focal? Casual? In *The Adventure of Wisteria Lodge,* Holmes read in a man's dark, deep-set, brooding eyes that the man knew about Holmes motive in speaking to him.

12. **Ears:** What is the shape of the stranger's ears? Small? Medium? Large? Close to the head or projecting? Oval? Round? Rectangular? Is the ear cauliflower or pierced? Hairy or not hairy? What is the shape of the ear lobe? Descending? Square? Medium? Gulfed? Is the person missing an ear? Does the person wear a hearing aid? Earrings? Blue-tooth device? In *The Gloria Scott* case, Holmes deduced Victor Trevor's father to be a boxer from observing his flat, thick ears.

13. **Cheeks:** Are the stranger's cheeks full? Fleshy? Sunken? In *The Adventure of the Lion's Mane,* Sherlock Holmes deduced a man lay dying by observing his "...glazed sunken eyes and dreadful livid cheeks."

14. **Nose:** Is the stranger's nose long? Large? Medium? Short? Thin? Turned up or down? Horizontal? Turned to the left or right? Are the nostrils large? Small? High? Low? Flared? Pierced? In *The Adventure of the Second Stain,* Holmes tells Watson how he became suspicious of a woman's motive at Margate because she had no powder on her nose.

15. **Mouth:** Is the stranger's mouth turned up or down at the corners? Does the stranger keep his or her mouth open or closed? Is he smiling? Does she distort her mouth with speech or laughter? Is her tongue pierced? In *The Adventure of the Illustrious Client,* Watson described how he noticed Baron Adelbert Gruner murderer's mouth. He saw the Baron's thin-lipped mouth as Nature's danger signal to any potential victims.

16. **Lips:** Is the stranger's lips thick? Thin? Puffy? Overhanging? Pendant? Compressed? Are they protruding? Retracted over teeth? Are they a pale color? Bright? Unusual? Bruised? Cut? Swollen? Is the stranger wearing lipstick? If so, what color? In *The Adventure of the Three Gables,* Holmes observed a man's big lips and sized him up as a prizefighter.[10]

17. **Teeth:** Are the stranger's teeth yellow? White? Dull? Stained? Firm? Loose? Decayed? Filled (color of filling)?

---

[10] Some Sherlockians believe that Arthur Conan Doyle wrote this story but someone else changed it. They believe the racism displayed in describing African American Steve Dixie's smell and big lips is not Doyle's writing style. See Kyle Freeman's introduction to *The Complete Sherlock Holmes, Volume II* (Barnes & Noble Classics).

Do they have braces? Are any teeth broken or chipped? Missing? Capped? Are the teeth receding or projecting? Are there any false teeth? Is there a gap between any teeth? Do the teeth have any cosmetic surgery such as tattoos? In *The Adventure of the Copper Beeches,* Sherlock Holmes stated he could tell a weaver by his tooth.

18. **Chin:**   Is the stranger's chin small? Large? Square? Curved? Pointed? Flat? Dimpled? Do they have a double chin? Is it jutting or protruding? Is it vertical or normal? Is it receding?   In *The Adventure of the Priory School,* Holmes deduced from Dr. Huxtable's unshaved chin that the doctor waited three days to consult him.

19. **Jaw:** Is the stranger's jaw long? Short? Wide? Narrow? Thin? Fleshy? Is it delicate or heavy? In *The Hound of the Baskervilles* Holmes deduced from a family portrait of an ancestor's jaw that Sir Henry was a Baskerville. In *The Boscombe Valley Mystery,* Sherlock Holmes deduced Watson's bedroom window on the right side of his room by observing the left side of Watson's jaw.

20. **Neck:**   Is the stranger's neck short? Long? Straight? Curved? Thin? Fat? Prominent? Medium? Can you see the Adam's apple? In *The Adventure of the Six Napoleons,* Sherlock Holmes deduced someone committed a murder from a message boy's rounded shoulders and outstretched neck as the message boy watched a house during a police investigation.

21. **Shoulder:**   What type of shoulders does the stranger have? Are they small? Heavy? Narrow? Broad? Square? Round? Muscular? Is one higher or lower? Stooped? In *The Final Problem,* Sherlock Holmes deduced Professor Moriarty studied a lot from observing Moriarty's rounded shoulders.

22. **Waist:** Is the stranger's waist small? Medium? Large? Extra Large? What is the stranger's waist size?

23. **Stomach:** Is the stranger's stomach flat? Bulging? Flabby? Trim? Muscular? Does the stranger have any scars or stretch marks? Does the stranger have a baby bump? Is the stranger hiding the bump or bulge with clothing? Is the stranger showing off his or her stomach?

24. **Hands:** Are the stranger's hands long? Short? Broad? Narrow? Thin? Fleshy? Bony? Soft? Rough? Colorful? Smooth? Hairy? Square? Tapered? In *The Adventure of the Solitary Cyclist,* Holmes deduced Violet Smith was a musician by observing her hand and fingers.

25. **Fingers:** Is the stranger's fingers short? Long? Slim? Thick? Tapered? Square? Nicotine stained? Is the stranger missing fingers? Are the nails painted? In *The Hound of the Baskervilles,* Holmes deduced Dr. James Mortimer made his own cigarettes by the nicotine stains on his fingertips.

26. **Feet.** What is the stranger's shoe size? Are their feet small? Medium? Large? Are their toenails painted? Do they have crow's feet? Corns? Do they have ingrown toenails? Are they missing any toes? Are they missing a foot? Are they wearing a cast? Bandage? A leg brace? What type of shoes is the stranger wearing? What color and style? Dress? Casual? Sports? Business? Orthopedic? Are the shoes expensive? Cheap? Designer? Are they sandals? Sneakers? Boots? High heels? Pumps? Are they new or old? Do they have scuffmarks? Stains? Do they have lifts to appear taller? How does the stranger tie the laces? In *The Naval Treaty*, Sherlock Holmes deduced a man as having financial trouble from looking at the man's resoled boots.

27. **Walk:** How is the stranger walking? Fast? Slow? Casual? Aggressive? Dopey? Is the stranger's stride long or short? Is the stranger using a cane or walker? Is the stranger limping or walking unnatural? In *A Case of Identity,* Sherlock Holmes deduced typist Mary Sutherland's involvement in a love affair by how she wavered back and forth across the street from 221B Baker Street.

28. **Distinctive Marks/Behavior:** Does the stranger have any marks such as scars? Birthmarks? Tattoos? Molds? Amputations? Does the stranger have any habitual mannerisms? Do they constantly blink their eyes? Tap their fingers or toes? Do they have any face or body piercings? Is the stranger knock-knee? Bo-legged? Lame or handicapped? In *The Boscombe Valley Mystery,* Holmes deduced a man as lame because the man put less weight on his right foot than his left foot as he limped.

29. **Speech:** How is the stranger's speech? Nasal? Tenor? Bass? Loud? Soft? Effeminate? Slow or fast speaking? Does the stranger have a speech impediment such as a lisp, stammer or stutter? Does the stranger speak with an accent? What part of the country or world is the stranger's accent? What language does the stranger speak? Does the stranger curse or use slang? Does the stranger use jargon related to a particular job, hobby or special interest? In *The Adventure of the Veiled Lodger,* Holmes deduced from the sound of her voice that a woman considered suicide.

Describe What You See

Noticing all the above details about a stranger means nothing, if you cannot describe the details to other people. You can practice listing basic facts (race, age, height, weight and gender) about the stranger's appearance in your mind. Then combine the basic facts together with other prominent features (big nose, tattoo on neck, scar on arm) into a mental list.

For example, observe a stranger walking towards you in the street. Then describe the person's appearance this way:

> "A Latino female, in her twenties, about 5'2," about 130 pounds, dark hair, shapely figure, wearing designer glasses, small rose tattoo on her neck, dark colored coat, white blouse, black pants, shoes and carrying a small designer handbag."

When you are in public and observing people, practice putting the details together and describing them in your head.

Pay Attention to the Clothing Strangers Wear

In *A Study In Scarlet*, Sherlock Holmes became frustrated with Constable John Rance for not observing a suspect's features and clothing. "His face — His dress — didn't you notice them?" Holmes stated impatiently after finding out that the man he had sought slipped through the constable's fingers. Holmes later told Watson that Constable Rance might have gained his sergeant's stripes that night had he paid close attention to the suspect.

In order to become proficient in the Sherlock Holmes' Method and gain your 'stripes,' you must pay close attention to a stranger's fashion. Clothing is one of the first things you see when you meet a stranger. Holmes understood that an individual's attire reveals a lot about him or her. The clothes strangers wear may reveal the following things about them:

1. Their attitude and mindset (serious, laidback, happy go lucky, etc.)
2. How powerful and wealthy they are.
3. How old they are (child, teenager, adult, middle age, elderly).

4. Whether they are male, female, straight, gay, bi-sexual or transgender.
5. How they make decisions, how they see and value themselves.
6. Their fashion sense and style; their hobbies and interests.
7. Their popularity and status (sociable, shy, etc.).
8. If they are single, married, divorced, separated or widowed.
9. Their religious, political, military or cultural associations.
10. Their health, education, business, professional and work background.

When you observe a strangers' clothing, ask yourself questions such as how is the stranger dressed? Conservative? Flashy? Neat? Slovenly? Sexy? Wealthy? Casual? Elegant? Professional? Cultural? Is the clothing a designer brand? What fabric is it? What is the style? Color? What is its' value? Is it for business? Recreation? Work? Is it for a party or other special event? Is it for a religious ceremony? Trendy? Sports?

Do the clothes match? Are the clothes high or low in quality? What image is the stranger projecting? Are the clothes new or worn? Is the clothing in or out of style? Is the stranger dressing appropriate for his or her age, weather or occasion? Do the clothes 'fit' the stranger? The questions you ask can help you discover revealing details about the stranger.

Focus On Specific Parts of A Stranger's Clothing

When Holmes observed a stranger's clothing, he always looked at specific areas where he could obtain data about the individual. Holmes once stated that when observing a woman, "My first glance is always at a woman's sleeve."

For example, In *A Case of Identity,* Holmes explained to Watson how he observed that Miss Mary Sutherland used a typewriter. He noticed her sleeves:

"...As you observe, this woman had plush upon her sleeves, which is a most useful material for showing traces. The double line a little above the wrist, where the typewriter presses against the table, was beautifully defined. The sewing-machine, of the hand type, leaves a similar mark, but only on the left arm, and on the side of it farthest from the thumb, instead of being right across the broadest part, as this was...."

When Holmes looked at a man, he determined that it was "...better first to take the knee of the trouser." For example, In *The Red-Headed League*, Holmes observed a young man's trouser knees to determine that a crime would soon occur. Holmes explained it to Watson this way:

"...I rang the bell, and as I hoped the assistant answered it...I hardly looked in his face. His knees were what I wished to see. You must yourself have remarked how worn, wrinkled and stained they were. They spoke of hours of burrowing..."

Just as Sherlock Holmes did, focus your attention on specific clothing areas. The clothing areas may give you relevant clues to the person's occupation, background and prior activities. The most important clothing areas on a stranger to look at first, in addition to the sleeves and trouser knees as Holmes suggests, is the stranger's pockets, outerwear, footwear and headwear.

One of the first clothing areas Sherlock Holmes looked at to obtain quick information is an individual's pocket. In *The Adventure of the Norwood Builder*, Holmes observed a bundle of legal papers protruding from a stranger's pocket to deduce the stranger as a solicitor.

In *The Adventure of the Blanched Soldier*, Mr. James Dodd entered into the sitting room at 221B Baker Street. Holmes then deduced Mr. Dodd had come from South Africa. How? He observed a handkerchief in Mr. Dodd's sleeve rather than his pocket. In *The Adventure of the Lion's Mane*, Holmes deduced that Harold Stackhurst planned to take a morning swim by observing his bulging pocket.

Sherlock Holmes also studied a stranger's outerwear such as a coat or jacket to gather data about him or her. In *The Crooked Man*, Holmes observed that Watson still smoked the Arcadia mixture from his bachelor days from the fluffy ash on Watson's coat. In *The Greek Interpreter*, Sherlock Holmes observed chalk marks over a stranger's waistcoat pocket to deduce the stranger as a billiard player.

In *The Hound of the Baskervilles*, Holmes observed a manuscript protruding one or two inches from Dr. James Mortimer's coat pocket. He then quickly deduced the manuscript's age. In *The Adventure of Wisteria Lodge*, Holmes observed a client's waistcoat buttoned unevenly. Holmes then deduced the client had rushed to seek his counsel.

Holmes often looked at an individual's footwear such as boots, shoes or slippers to gain insight into the person's past activities. In *The Crooked Man*, Holmes observed Watson's boots not being dirty. He then deduced Watson used a horse drawn carriage to travel because his medical practice kept him busy. In *The Five Orange Pips*, Holmes observed a distinctive clay and chalk mixture on a stranger's toecaps. He then deduced the stranger had come from London's southwest area.

In *The Stock-Broker's Clerk*, Holmes observed Watson had a summer cold because Watson stretched out his feet to a fire and scorched his new slippers. In *The Adventure of the Solitary Cyclist*, Holmes observed a woman as being a bicyclist from the bike pedal leaving a slight rough mark on the side of her shoe.

Sherlock Holmes also looked at a person's headwear such as hats to get clues to the stranger's background or trade. In *The Adventure of the Blue Carbuncle*, Holmes observed the hat a stranger left behind. He deduced from the hat that the stranger fell on hard times, drank too much, had marriage problems and did not exercise.

In *The Yellow Face,* Holmes observed writing on the lining of a stranger's hat to deduce the stranger's name. In *The Hound of the Baskervilles,* Holmes observed gloss on Watson's hat to deduce that Watson had been at the club all day. In *A Scandal in Bohemia,* Holmes observed a bulge on the right side of Watson's top hat to deduce that Watson started practicing medicine again.

Ask Yourself Questions About What You See

As you focus on a stranger's particular clothing area, ask yourself questions about what you see. In chapter one, you learned about the four basic questions and additional questions you need to ask yourself whenever you meet a stranger. Below are specific examples of additional questions you could ask:

Does this person have a tattoo? How many tattoos does the person have? Where are the tattoos located?
What kind of tattoo is it? A Symbol? Word? Image?
Do they have body markings or piercings? Where are they?
Do they have stains on their clothes? Where are they?
What kind of stains?
Do they have hair strands on their clothes?
What kind of hair strands? Man? Woman? Cat? Dog?
Where are the hair strands located? The leg? Arm? Chest?
Do they have dirt or mud on their shoes? Is it fresh or dry?
Do they have minor cuts, bruises or marks on their face, body, feet or hands?
What type of ring are they wearing? Engagement? Wedding? Graduation? Fraternity?
How many rings are on their fingers?
If no ring, do they have a ring mark?
Do they have pressure marks or indents on their nose?
Are they wearing makeup? If so, what parts of the face?

If not, why?
What is their skin tone? Do they have wrinkles?
Age spots? A tan? Dry skin? Skin rash? Pimples?
What kind of clothing are they wearing?
Designer? Causal? Formal? Business?
Do they have creases in their clothing?
If so, where are the creases? How many creases?
Is a bulge in their coat or pants pocket?
If so, what is it? A gun? Wallet? Smartphone? Keys?
Is it cash or coins?

Asking yourself questions about specific areas on a stranger's face, body, hands or feet will focus your attention on what you see. The questions you ask will make you more observant because you will scrutinize the stranger's appearance for the answers. Asking yourself questions regarding precise locations on a person's appearance will lead you to the next step, which is knowing what to look for.

What To Look For When Observing A Stranger

In chapter one, the first basic question required that you ask yourself: *"What do I observe?"* Asking yourself this question is important because it focuses your attention on the "data" you need to size up a stranger. In *The Adventure of the Copper Beeches,* Holmes said: "Data! Data! Data! I can't make bricks without clay." The exact facts about a person are the data you must look for. In order for you to obtain this data, you must do the following:

Concentrate Upon Details

Whenever Watson looked at a stranger, he always judged them by his first, general impression. In many cases Watson chronicled, he would often describe a stranger's appearance in a general way. For example, in *The Case of Identity*, Watson described a client who entered 221B Baker Street like this:

> "...she had a slate-colored broad-brimmed straw hat, with a feather of a brackish red. Her jacket was black, with black beads sewn upon it, and a fringe of little black jet ornaments. Her dress was brown rather darker than coffee color, with a little purple plush at the neck and sleeves. Her gloves were grayish and were worn through at the right forefinger. Her boots I didn't observe. She had small round, hanging gold earrings, and a general air of being fairly well-to-do in a vulgar, comfortable easy-going way."

After Watson gave his general impression of the woman, Holmes pointed out that Watson had missed the most important clues to her appearance. Watson missed the clues because he relied *totally* on a general, first impression. Holmes then advised Watson to:

> "...Never trust to general impressions, my boy, but concentrate yourself upon details."

Holmes then pointed out that Watson had missed the woman being a typist and that she had come in a hurry to see them. Watson did not notice the traces on her sleeve, the dints from her eyeglasses on both sides of her face, her half-buttoned boots nor the ink stain on her glove and finger.

What Holmes meant by not trusting a general impression is to always look for exact facts to size up a stranger accurately. What separated Holmes's observations from Watson's? Sherlock Holmes always paid attention to small but relevant *details!*

Watson believed that he could see just as well as Holmes but Holmes proved that Watson overlooked the small things. How? During the *Scandal in Bohemia* case, Holmes asked Watson to tell him how many steps led up to the hall to their room at 221B Baker Street.

Watson did not know although he saw the steps every day. Holmes then explained it this way: "...You have not observed. And yet you have seen...I know there are seventeen steps, because I have both seen and observed." Holmes knew the hall leading to their room had seventeen steps because not only did he see them, he paid attention to detail by counting the steps!

Small details are trifles that most people overlook. But as Holmes once told Watson in *The Boscombe Valley Mystery*: "You know my method. It is founded upon the observation of trifles." In several cases, Holmes proved that noticing small details about strangers could reveal significant information about their background and personal history.

For example, in the *Study in Scarlet* case, Holmes spotted a man walking slowly down the opposite side of the street. He noticed important details such as a blue anchor tattoo on the back of his hand. He noticed his regulation side-whiskers. He noticed the way the man swung his cane and his age. All these details revealed the man had been a retired marine sergeant.

In *The Gloria Scott* case, Victor Trevor's father challenged Sherlock Holmes to figure out something about him. Sherlock Holmes observed several small but relevant details. Holmes observed the melted lead in Trevor's father stick. Holmes observed his thick, flat ears. Holmes observed the callosities on his hand. Holmes observed the initials tattooed on his elbow. These small but relevant details revealed that Mr. Trevor feared a personal attack, boxed, worked as a digger and wished to forget about a past intimate acquaintance.

In *The Red-Headed League* case, Holmes observed significant details about red headed Jabez Wilson. Holmes observed Mr. Wilson's right hand being larger than his left. Holmes observed Mr. Wilson owning an arc-and-compass breastpin. Holmes observed his shiny right cuff and smooth elbow patch. Holmes observed his fish tattoo. Holmes observed a coin attached to his watch chain. The details revealed that Mr. Wilson did manual labor; held membership as a freemason, traveled to China and recently wrote a lot.

In *The Greek Interpreter* case, Holmes and his older brother Mycroft scrutinize two strangers in the street. They alternately noticed specific details about each stranger. They noticed one man's sun baked skin and ammunition boots. They noticed the other man holding a rattle and a children's picture book. Their observations revealed the men's occupations and martial status.

In all these examples, Sherlock Holmes's ability to figure out strangers' jobs and prior activities came from his spotting specific details. His ability to spot details came from his studying *science.* Holmes once stated that while a young man, he filled his spare time studying the different branches of science to become more efficient.

Just as Sherlock Holmes did, you can become more efficient once you know what to look for. You will know what to look for once you *reason* as you look. Using reason to pay attention to trifles is the practical way to size-up strangers. Holmes used his reasoning skill constantly. He did not rely solely on first impressions when he met people.

Check Your First Impressions

Holmes did not believe first impressions alone could help you read strangers accurately. Nevertheless, he sometimes relied on them when he sized up strangers. For example, in *A Study in Scarlet,* Holmes ended his analysis of a messenger with a general first impression. He told Watson that the individual who delivered a large blue envelope:

> "... was a man with some self-importance and a certain air of command. You must have observed the way he held his head and swung his cane. A steady, respectable, middle-aged man, too, on the face of him

all facts which led me to believe that he had been a sergeant."

The facts Holmes observed about the stranger resulted, in part, from his overall first impression as the stranger walked towards their Baker Street residence. Holmes had an accurate overall impression of the retired marine sergeant because he observed a group of actions and cluster of facts about him. The stranger's overall appearance and behavior allowed Holmes to use them in combination to arrive at his conclusions about the stranger. Whenever you meet people, first look for details, and then look at their appearance and behavior as a whole.

Sherlock Holmes meant this when he wrote in the *Book of Life* article from *A Study in Scarlet*: "...By a man's finger-nails, by his coat-sleeve, by his boots, by his trouser-knees, by the callosities of his forefinger and thumb, by his expression, by his shirt-cuffs — by each of these things a man's calling is plainly revealed. That all united should fail to enlighten the competent inquirer...is almost inconceivable."

People send messages by their body language, facial expressions, fashion and speech. The clothing they wear and their behavior reflects their personality and who they are. Watch for patterns and clusters in their behavior. Scan their appearance thoroughly but quickly to get a "feel" for them.

What is your first impression of the person? What does their grooming say about them? What does their physique and carriage say about them? What do their actions; their manner and dress say about them? What do their facial expressions; their complexion and their apparel say about them? What do their gait and tone of voice say about them? Does the person have any scars, physical deficiencies or unusual characteristics?

Look at the "total" person when you seek to get a first impression. Also, watch for specific tics or mannerisms about the stranger. For example, a person may habitually shake their leg while sitting or rub their chin while thinking. Then sum up both the general impression and specific tics with a short word or phrase that describes them in your mind. You can mentally sum up the person with such words as "executive" "friendly" "successful" "dangerous" "lady" or "gay."

Doing this is a form of categorizing or labeling. It helps you to make quick assessments of people. But as you are making these quick scans make sure to correct yourself. Check to see if the assessments are accurate.[11] If you always check your first impressions to make sure they are correct, it will become automatic. You will find yourself doing it without thinking and making few errors.

Look For Appearance and Behavioral Changes

One way to check your first impression with strangers is to watch their normal appearance and behavior. That way, you will notice small differences when they occur. Many individuals are people of habit. They follow certain behavioral patterns and personality trends. They do things a certain way all the time. They park their cars in the same parking space. They dress in a particular style. They eat at the same restaurants. They hang out with the same friends. They express themselves with specific hand gestures. They speak in a specific manner. Their appearance and behavior is consistent and follows a pattern or routine. Once you have noticed the stranger's normal appearance and behavior, stay alert for anything unusual, strange or out of the ordinary that varies from it.

For example, in *The Adventure of Wisteria Lodge*, Sherlock Holmes became suspicious regarding a meeting between two

---

[11] Sherlock Holmes did this in *The Adventure of the Solitary Cyclist*. He corrected himself after noticing Violet Smith's fingertips. He first thought her to be a typist. Then after double-checking his first impression, he correctly deduced her as a musician.

men.   Holmes said to Watson: "There is, on the face of it, something unusual about this strange and sudden friendship between the young Spaniard and Scott Eccles."   Holmes later figured out that the Spaniard sought Mr. Eccles' acquaintance to use him as an alibi.

In *The Valley of Fear,* Sherlock Holmes tried to figure out the reasons for Mr. Douglas' behavior before his death. He asked Mr. Douglas' wife: "Had you noticed anything unusual in his conduct?" In *The Adventure of the Noble Bachelor,* Holmes asked a groom did he observe any change in a bride's behavior before she suddenly disappeared after the wedding ceremony.

Just as Sherlock Holmes did, you must observe or learn the stranger's normal appearance and behavior. Then use it as a measuring stick to notice anything unusual that departs from it.

Watch For Micro Expressions

In addition to noticing a stranger's normal and abnormal behavior, another thing to closely watch for with strangers is their facial expressions.   Sherlock Holmes keenly watched people's faces to glean details about their inner thoughts, motives and emotions. He once stated: "...the features are given to man as the means by which he shall express his emotions." He then explained to Watson how he read his thoughts in *The Adventure of the Cardboard Box.*

Sherlock believed that you could read a person's inner thoughts by watching their facial expressions. As Holmes once stated: there is nothing new under the sun, it all has happened before.   Over a hundred years ago, he wrote about minutiae expressions. In the article entitled *The Book of Life* from *A Study in Scarlet,* Holmes stated he could: "...by a momentary expression, a twitch of a muscle or a glance of an eye, to fathom a man's inmost thoughts." Scientists today officially call these minutiae facial movements 'micro' expressions.[12]

Micro expressions are rapid facial movements that happen in less than a second. They occur for only an instant on a person's face. If you blink, you will miss them. You can spot brief emotional displays on a stranger's face by paying close attention to the eyes, mouth and observing any slight muscle movements around them. All people convey emotions (happiness, anger, sadness, disgust, surprise, fear and contempt) through their faces. The key is spotting the fleeting facial expressions as they occur.

For example, to spot a micro expression of joy, look at the lines around a stranger's eyes. To spot an anger micro expression you would look for eyebrows that slant downward, with tight lips and glaring eyes. To spot a sadness micro expression you would look for drooped eyes and corners of the lips turned down. To spot a fear micro expression you would look for raised eyebrows, wide eyes and slightly extended tense lips.

To spot a contempt micro expression you would look for the stranger's head to tilt to one side as their lips rise to look down on you. To spot a surprise micro expression you would look for the stranger's eyes to widen, eyebrows to rise and mouth to slightly open. And last, to spot a disgust micro expression, look for an upper raised lip and a nose wrinkle.

---

[12] In 1872, Charles Darwin wrote about micro-expressions in *The Expression of the Emotions in Man and Animals*. In 1966, Researchers A. Haggard and K. Isaacs discovered 'micro-momentary expressions' while examining films of couples in therapy. A few years later, Dr. Paul Ekman, building on their research, coined the term 'micro-expressions' while studying deception. Professor Ekman wrote about his findings in several books (some scientists such as Professor Lisa Barnett challenged his theory. She contends it is wrong. See the online article by Sharon Fischer in *Boston Magazine*. http://www. bostonmagazine.com/ news/article /2013/06/25/ emotions-facial-expressions-not-related/).

You can look right at a person and not spot these fleeting expressions. You will miss them, if you are not paying attention and do not know what to look for. This happened to Watson on at least two occasions.

First, in *The Valley of Fear*, Holmes and Inspector MacDonald questioned Mrs. Douglas after someone had slain her husband. Watson, standing with them, described how he could have sworn, "...that the faintest shadow of a smile flickered over the woman's lips...." when she heard someone took her husband's wedding ring.

Second, in *The Adventure of the Dying Detective*, Watson caught a glimpse of poisoner Culverton Smith's face in a mirror over a mantelpiece. He observed it set in a malicious smile after Smith believed he successfully poisoned Holmes. Then Watson observed that Calverton's devious smile instantly disappeared.

Although Watson did not know it at the time, he had just seen two micro expressions. He completely missed their significance, however, because he did not know what he was looking at.

Look For Eye Movements

Once you have studied a stranger's face and know how to spot micro expressions, the next thing to do is focus on the stranger's eye movements. In *The Adventure of the Cardboard Box*, Sherlock Holmes demonstrated to Watson his ability to track Watson's eye movements and break into Watson's train of thought. Watson had expressed surprise at Holmes's ability to do this by saying: "Do you mean to say that you read my train of thoughts from my features?"

Holmes replied: "Your features and especially your eyes." Holmes then described how he followed Watson's eye movements. He observed the eye movements from the point when Watson looked at a newly framed picture of British Military General Charles Gordon. Holmes further observed the eye movements to the point where Watson looked away from the unframed picture of Henry Ward Beecher. He then began a new train of thought. Holmes described it this way:

> "...After throwing down your paper, which was the action which drew my attention to you, you sat for a half a minute with a vacant expression. Then your eyes fixed themselves upon your newly framed picture of General Gordon, and I saw by the alteration in your face that a train of thought had been started. But it did not lead very far. Your eyes flashed across to the unframed portrait of Henry Ward Beecher which stands upon the top of your books. Then you glanced up at the wall, and of your meaning was obvious. You were thinking that if the portrait were framed it would just cover that bare space and correspond with Gordon's picture there."

"You have followed me wonderfully!" I exclaimed.

> "So far I could hardly have gone astray. But now your thoughts went back to Beecher, and you looked hard across as if you were studying the character in his features. Then your eye ceased to pucker, but you continue to look across, and your face was thoughtful. You were recalling the incidents of Beecher's career. I was well aware that you could not do this without thinking of the mission which he undertook on behalf of the North at the time of the Civil War, for I remember your expressing your passionate indignation at the way in which he was received by the more turbulent of our people. You felt so strongly about it that I knew you could not think of Beecher without thinking of that also. When a moment later I saw your eyes wander away from the picture, I suspected that your mind had now turned to the Civil War, and when I observed that your lips set, your eye sparkled, and your hands clenched I was positive that

61

you were indeed thinking of the gallantry which was shown by both sides in the desperate struggle. But the, again your face grew sadder, you shook your head. You were dwelling upon the sadness and horror and useless waste of life. Your hand stole towards your own old wound and a smile quivered on your lips, which showed me that the ridiculous side of this method of settling international questions had forced itself upon your mind. At this point I agreed with you that it was preposterous and was glad to find that all my deductions and been correct."

Scientists have shown from several studies[13] that you can track an individual's eye movements as Sherlock Holmes did. Observing a stranger's eye patterns can reveal what the stranger pays attention to. Watching a stranger's eye patterns also reveals what distracts him or her. Tracking the direction a stranger's eyes move can indicate the stranger's personality, interests, motives, stress level, nervousness, anxiety, guilt, anger or curiosity.

For example, in an article from *Time* magazine, entitled *"What Your Eyes Say About Who You Are,"* writer Annie Murphy Paul references a study published in the journal *Cognition.* She notes researcher Evan Risko tested participants' curiosity level. The participants were tested through questionnaires and eye-tracking equipment as they observed several pictures. The researchers found that the test subjects who scored high in curiosity looked at many more elements. They constantly

---

[13] Study #1: *"The Impact of Salient Advertisements on Reading and Attention on Web Pages."* Simola J, Kuisma J, Oörni A, Uusitalo L, Hyönä J. J Exp Psychol Appl. 2011 Jun; 17(2): 174-90.doi: 10.1037/a0024042. Study #2: *Eye Movements and Problem Solving: Guiding Attention Guides Thought.* Grant, Elizabeth R.; Spivey, Michael J. *Psychological Science*, Vol. 14(5), Sep 2003, 462-466. Doi: 10.1111/1467-9280.02454. Study #3: *University of Exeter. "Surgeons Perform Better with Eye Movement Training."* Science Daily, 6 December 2011. <www.sciencedaily.com /releases/ 2011/11/111130100222.htm>.

moved their eyes over different parts of the pictures. What did researcher Risko conclude? She found that eye movements could reveal an individual's personality through the way the person thinks and acts.

In the book *"Frogs into Princes: Neuro Linguistic Programming (NLP)"*, authors Richard Bandler and John Grinder found that a person looking up to the left may mean the person is thinking. A person looking up to the right may mean the person is remembering an experience. A person looking down to the left may mean the person is recalling smells, sounds or taste sensations. A person looking down to the right may mean the person has intense feelings or may be thinking aloud by talking to him or herself. A person looking up may mean he or she is carefully considering what you are saying. A person looking down may mean he or she is being submissive. According to the authors, the way an individual looks at people, places and things reveals much about their inner thoughts.

Several experts do not believe you can tell whether a person is honest or lying from the way they move their eyes.[14] They claim no link exists between eye movement and deception. They claim the NLP model did not intend eye movement to be a diagnostic tool. They claim no evidence exists to support the concept that eye movement can detect lies nor is it scientifically established. They claim many law enforcement instructors have no formal training. They claim the instructors have no official certification to teach NLP concepts. Although experts may disagree on whether eye movements can reveal a stranger's

---

[14] See Stan 'The Lie Guy' Walters' video clip at http:// www.youtube.com/ watch?v=i3XPjDL99xo. Also refer to Aldert Vrij, Shara Lochun, *"Neuro-Linguistic Programming and the Police: Worthwhile or Not?"* Journal of Police and Criminal Psychology, Vol. 12, No. 1, 1997, pp. 25 - 31. See also Gary I. Wilson, *"Perspective on Neuro-linguistic Programming (NLP),"* The Police Chief 77 (December 2010): 40–51, http://www. nxtbook.com /nxtbooks /naylor/ CPIM1210/#/40 (March 1, 2014).

thoughts or moods, they do concur that body language is one important way to read a stranger.

Study Body Language Signals

Body language is one of the first things you see when you meet a stranger. It is the non-verbal movements, both conscious and unconscious, human beings make with their bodies to communicate their thoughts, feelings, moods and motives to others. Holmes understood that an individual's body language reveals a lot about him or her.

In *The Reigate Puzzle*, Watson describes how Holmes led Alec Cunningham and his father to reveal their murderous natures. The father and son attacked him as he searched for a torn note in the son's dressing gown pocket. Holmes yelled for help. Inspector Forrester, Colonel Hayter and Dr. Watson dashed to his aid and pulled the murderers off him. Holmes then cried: "...look at their faces!"

"Never certainly have I seen a plainer confession of guilt upon human countenances." Dr. Watson wrote: "The older man seemed numbed and dazed, with a heavy sullen expression upon his strongly marked face. The son, on the other hand, had...the ferocity of a dangerous wild beast gleamed in his dark eyes and distorted his handsome features." In this one paragraph, Conan Doyle showed how body language could reveal a person's innermost emotions and motives.

If you are to master the Sherlock Holmes Method, you must learn the basics of reading a stranger's body language. It is easy, not hard to do, because you already do it naturally every day. The key is to look at the non-verbal movements that strangers make as a whole rather than interpret each behavior separately.

You must also recognize that each gesture's meaning or behavior can change according to the situation, individual and culture. Therefore, always stay alert to the context in which you observe the gesture or movement. Also, keep alert to your circumstances or environment.

All human beings have the same basic emotions, thoughts, attitudes and motives. It is natural for these qualities to express themselves universally in our behavior and actions. Look for these universal behaviors and expressions in the strangers you meet. But make allowances for the individual tics and personal gestures each stranger may exhibit.

Look for both positive and negative body language signals a person may send. Be aware of the individual's age and gender as well as the distance they keep from others. Notice how they sit, stand and walk, their head movements and whether they touch other people or allow other people to touch them.

You can spot a stranger's attitude, mood and feelings by closely watching their positive or negative body language signals. Whether they realize it or not, strangers constantly send positive or negative messages about themselves. The key is to read these non-verbal clues correctly. Understand their meaning so that you can accurately size up the stranger.

The two basic non-verbal signals are as follows:

1. <u>Positive Non-Verbal Signals.</u> Positive non-verbal indicators usually show the stranger is happy, friendly, interested, attentive, cooperative or confident. A stranger that sends a positive non-verbal signal will usually look directly at a person while speaking or listening. He or she may have an open posture with hands and feet leaning toward the person. You may notice the stranger eyes widen or his eye pupils becoming larger. The stranger may wink, smile or laugh at what you say. He or she may tilt their head in your direction, lean it forward or to one side or nod it to show they agree. The stranger may copy

your face, hand and leg movements to show they like and agree with you. They may stand in front of you with open palms or arms. They may greet you with a firm handshake or sit beside you with uncrossed legs. They may touch your arm, hand, shoulder or leg to show interest. All these gestures and actions send a positive message that the stranger is interested, attracted, paying attention or cooperative.

2. Negative Non-Verbal Signals. Negative non-verbal indicators usually show the stranger is nervous, aggressive, frustrated, insecure, uninterested, defensive or unhappy. Non-verbal signals a stranger sends will usually include rolling his or her eyes or their pupils contracting. They may often blink, stay tight-lipped or have a clenched jaw. They may fake a smile or laugh. You may notice their teeth grinding or them biting their nails or a pen. They may show disagreement by shaking their head sideways, looking away, keeping their head down, crossing their arms or legs, clenching their fists or pointing a finger. Often their head, body or feet will lean away or they will move away. They may tightly interlock their fingers, maintain an unfocused gaze, lock their ankles or refuse a handshake. They may also not allow you to touch them or keep their distance from you. All of these gestures and actions send a negative message that the stranger is uncooperative.

Keep in mind the above non-verbal signals are only the tip of the iceberg when it comes to body language gestures. The signals do not represent even a fraction of the information currently available on the subject. That should not stop you, however, from learning more about body language. It also should not stop you from learning how to recognize when a stranger is deceptive.

Recognize Deception Red Flags

Sherlock Holmes always stayed alert to the signs of deception whenever he met a stranger. How did Holmes know when a stranger lied to him? He simply applied the precepts he had advocated from *The Book of Life* magazine article he wrote. In the article, he stated: "Deceit...is an impossibility to one trained in observation and analysis." Holmes knew the behavioral 'tells' that strangers reveal as they are moving or not moving their bodies.

In order for you to master the Sherlock Holmes Method, learn to read physical red flags. A stranger may unintentionally reveal the following behavioral tells while interacting with you:

1. Constantly blinking eyes
2. Crossing arms or legs
3. Constant fidgeting
4. Looking to the right or looking down
5. Staring while talking
6. Keeping a stiff upper body
7. Looking away
8. Doing something else while speaking
9. Heavy sweating brow or hands
10. Touching face (rubbing eyes, touching hair, covering mouth, tugging ear, etc.)
11. Taking a deep breath before speaking
12. Breathing heavy, pale skin or turning red in the face
13. Heaving chest (heart pounding)
14. Leaning away
15. Faking a smile
16. Using a desk or purse as a barrier
17. Leg shaking, foot tapping or trembling hands
18. Dilated eye pupils
19. Avoiding physical contact
20. Coughing or clearing throat
21. Shrugging shoulders

22. Keeping a tight lip, lip twitching or trembling
23. Restricting body movements (keeping still, etc.)
24. Pointing feet toward door or leaning body toward exit
25. Hiding hands (in pocket, behind back, under a desk, etc.)

Keep in mind these physical deception signs are not written in stone nor or they complete. They are not proof the stranger is lying; only *indications* the stranger's behavior is suspicious. They are guides to give you an idea of what to look for.

Scientific studies have shown that no single gesture, expression or behavior establishes deceit.[15] You must consider other factors (that are revealed in Chapters 6 and 9) before you can determine whether a stranger is truthful or not.

Watch for the Obvious

In *The Hound of the Baskervilles,* Sherlock Holmes once said: "The world is full of obvious things which nobody by any chance ever observes." The ability to spot the obvious is an overlooked skill. Often the most visible clues are hiding in plain sight for anyone to see. Holmes continually admonished Dr. Watson to pay attention to what is right before his eyes. Holmes knew that the details that are reliable usually are the easiest to observe. He noticed the things that are easy to see because he took the time to look for them. He watched for obvious details because he knew them to be the most simple.

---

[15] David Matsumoto, Ph.D. and three of his peers, in an online article entitled *"Evaluating Truthfulness & Detecting Deception,"* cite 23 studies published in scientific journals. The researchers state "...no one indicator of lying exists. If so, research would have identified it by now." See the *FBI Law Enforcement Bulletin (June 2011)* at http://www.fbi.gov/stats-services/publications/law-enforcement-bulletin/june_2011/school_violence. A 2013 *Government Accountability Office* (GAO) study also found that "the human ability to accurately identify deceptive behavior based on behavioral indicators is the same as or slightly better than chance." You can view the report at http://www.gao.gov/products/GAO-14-159.

Many Holmesian styled observations seem so easy because they are simple and obvious. In *The Yellow Face*, Holmes deduced a stranger's name from the writing on the lining in the stranger's hat. Almost anyone could have made this simple observation. In *A Case of Identity*, Holmes deduced that since Mr. Windibank had a different last name than Mary Sutherland that he must be her stepfather. Average people do this elementary observation every day. In *The Naval Treaty*, Holmes deduced a man as not being a member of the family Holmes visited by observing monogrammed initials on the man's locket. Most people can make this common observation.

How many times have you noticed a stranger coming towards you with a shopping bag that has the name of a store on it? Is it a complex observation to deduce that the stranger had just come from shopping at the store? How many times have you noticed a stranger wearing a T-shirt with a slogan, symbol or picture on it? Is it a far-fetched inference to assume that the stranger wearing the T-shirt has an interest in the subject? How many times have you noticed a stranger wearing a chain or bracelet with a name on it? Is it too hard to assume that the name belongs to either the stranger or a loved one?

These are obvious observations that we perform every day in our normal lives. They are simple, everyday observations that we make without thinking. They are the same observations that Sherlock makes; the only difference is he does it *consistently*. One reason Holmes is so reliable with his observations is that the obvious things he sees do not fool him. As he tells Watson in *The Boscombe Valley Mystery*: "There is nothing more deceptive than an obvious fact."

Often the most obvious facts are the most misleading because they can have more than one interpretation. They can be ambiguous. They can have several possible causes. Obvious facts did not fool Holmes. As he stated in *The Adventure of Black*

Peter: "...one should always look for a possible alternative, and provide against it. It is the first rule of criminal investigation."

In *The Adventure of the Norwood Builder,* Sherlock Holmes cautioned Detective Lestrade that his theory regarding a murder seemed a "trifle too obvious." He tried to make Lestrade aware of other possible theories. As usual, Detective Lestrade ignored his suggestion. The result? Lestrade's case ended in failure.

Look for What Is Missing

The failure to look for what is *not* there can also lead you astray. A stranger with no tattoos, bruises, scratches or other identifying marks can still reveal things about his or herself. Just because you cannot spot any wrinkles, bulges or dirt on a stranger, does not mean there is nothing else to observe. You can still read the stranger's body language, speech, attitude or fashion style just by observing their appearance and behavior. Often what strangers conceal can tell you more about them than what they reveal.

Sherlock Holmes often looked for what is missing when he observed a stranger or problem. Holmes knew that the *absence* of evidence is often more revealing than the *presence* of evidence. In the *Silver Blaze* case, Holmes became suspicious when a dog did not bark at night as a person entered the barn. He noticed the dog was not barking as the missing key element.

In *The Adventure of the Bruce-Partington Plans,* Holmes became curious when he discovered the authorities did not find a train ticket on a dead man's body. Holmes knew from experience that no one could enter a London train without a ticket. Since Holmes always looked for what is missing, the lost ticket sent up a red flag in his mind.

In *The Valley of Fear,* Holmes noticed only one barbell in a room. He had expected to see *two* barbells because most people exercise with two weights. The missing barbell made him suspicious and led to his solving the mystery.

In *The Adventure of the Dancing Men,* Inspector Martin missed seeing a third bullet hole in the window edge. Holmes knew he would find it there and looked for it. How did he know? He recognized the importance of the servants smelling gunpowder upon leaving their room. The smell suggested someone briefly left open the window and door to the room.

The more attention you pay to missing information regarding the people you meet, the better you will become at evaluating strangers. Sherlock Holmes stated as much in *The Book of Life* article from *A Study in Scarlet* regarding sizing up strangers. He said: "...Puerile as such an exercise may seem, it sharpens the faculties of observation, and teaches one where to look and what to look for."

The tips in this chapter have shown you how to look, where to look and what to look for just as Holmes instructed. We can all learn to observe like Sherlock if we make an effort to study how he did it. In the next chapter, you will learn another principle Holmes used to size up strangers. The principle will bring you even closer to discovering the secret to his method.

Go to Pages 286 to 302 if you want to practice
The observational exercises now.

Chapter 3

Apply Sherlock's Sure-Fire Way
To Size-Up Strangers

"...Logic is rare. Therefore it is upon the logic...that you should dwell."
Sherlock Holmes, The Adventure of the Copper Beeches

What did Sherlock Holmes do once he discovered small but relevant details about a stranger? How did he use the facts he observed to figure out the stranger's occupation, background and prior activities? What practical principle did he employ to determine if what he found was accurate? Holmes used a time tested and reliable way to size up strangers — logical thinking.

In Chapter 2, you learned how to spot small but relevant details about strangers. This chapter will show you how to analyze those minor but important details to figure out what they mean. The key to examining minor details about strangers is to think logically. You must *reason* from what you see.

Logic is the study of valid reasoning. Reason is the process of critical thought. It is the ability to think accurately. It is the chief tool scientists' use when they employ the scientific method. It is the main way you use the rules of deduction that Holmes wrote about in his magazine article *The Book of Life.*

The term 'rules of deduction' is misleading, however, because these are actually rules of reason and logic. Sir Arthur Conan Doyle used the term 'deduction' to describe Holmes's action because it sounded more pleasing to the ear. It made for an easy read.

Keep in mind that Sherlock Holmes, although inspired by a real life person — Dr. Joseph Bell — is actually a fictional character. He expressed whatever his creator placed in his mouth. Do not nick pick or quibble over the deductive term. Instead, focus on the main point Doyle made in his stories. The main point is — *using reason will enable you to discover facts and trifling details about strangers.*

Neither Dr. Watson nor Sherlock Holmes ever revealed the specific rules of deduction contained in *The Book of Life* article. In *A Study in Scarlet*, Sherlock Holmes told Watson: "...those rules of deduction laid down in that article which aroused your scorn are invaluable to me in practical work."

But what are those rules of deduction that Holmes used? Are they as practical as he claims? Can anyone use them as he did? You can find the answers to these questions by closely analyzing how Sherlock Holmes himself used reason and logic whenever he met a stranger. Holmes left many clues to his method, to which if you pay close attention, you can discover. Let us see what we can learn by studying the Master.

The Sherlock Holmes Rules of Deduction

Chapter 1 taught you to ask yourself "What Can I Deduce?" whenever you meet a stranger. The Sherlock Holmes rules of deduction will enable you to get an answer to this second basic question. Holmes himself applied these logical rules. He claimed they were extremely practical in his consulting detective work.

In *A Study in Scarlet,* Sherlock Holmes told Dr. Watson: "I am simply applying to ordinary life a few of those precepts of observation and deduction which I advocated in that article." We do not have the actual magazine article Sherlock Holmes wrote. Therefore, we must study the case histories Watson chronicled. We can then glean clues to the deduction rules Holmes relied on to write the article.

The logical rules below come from the case histories. The book numbers them for easy reading and reference. Do not take the rankings literally. Each rule is equally important. Use them singly, simultaneously or in various combinations.

As you use them, they may overlap or become interchangeable. Use each rule as a general guide and on an individual basis. Whenever he sized up a stranger or solved a problem Sherlock Holmes used, in different combinations, the following logical rules:

Rule #1: Reason from the General to the Specific

The first rule we glean from the case histories is Holmes's ability to reason from the general to the specific. When you think step-by-step from a general fact to a specific fact, you are reasoning by deduction.[16] Deductive reasoning ensures that when you observe true details and the reasoning you use is valid, you must reach the correct conclusion.

When you use deductive reasoning to size up a stranger you must rely only on the evidence you find on the stranger. Deductive reasoning limits your analysis to what you find because it deals with general assumptions that cannot be false. Deductive reasoning uses these general assumptions to reach particular facts. The facts then lead to inevitable results.

Sherlock Holmes often relied on simple generalizations of people to make specific deductions. They came from his prior knowledge and experience. For example, if Holmes observed a man and believed him to be unmarried, his deductive reasoning, from a broad rule to the precise fact, would be as follows:

---

[16] Modern day logicians now define deduction as reasoning from one or more statements or facts to reach a definite or certain conclusion – *Wikipedia*.

General rule: All unmarried men are bachelors.
Specific fact: This individual is an unmarried man.
Conclusion: This man is a bachelor.

In *The Elementary Methods of Sherlock Holmes,* author Brad Keefauver explains logical deduction.[17] He used *The Sussex Vampire* mystery as an illustration:

"...In deduction, general facts are narrowed down to fit specific instances in a manner which, properly done, yields sure results. To more precisely, define this form of deduction, an example is best given in a syllogism, a form of argument consisting of three statements: a major premise, a minor premise and a conclusion. For instance:

Major premise: No women are vampires.
Minor premise: Dolores Ferguson is a woman.
Conclusion: Dolores Ferguson is not a vampire.

The major premise states a general fact. The minor premise states a more specific one. If both are true, then they will combine to form a true conclusion. And, as Holmes said in *Silver Blaze*, "One true inference invariably suggests others." From the above syllogism, Holmes could then move on to:

Major premise: All people who suck blood are removing poison.
Minor premise: Dolores Ferguson was sucking blood.
Conclusion: Dolores Ferguson was removing poison.

And the train of logic could continue further until one reached:

---

[17] *The Elementary Methods of Sherlock Holmes; Chapter 18: A Simple Process Called Deduction;* Quotes from Pages 128-129.

Major premise:	All insanely jealous boys wish their stepbrothers were dead
Minor premise:	Jack Ferguson was an insanely jealous boy
Conclusion:	Jack Ferguson wished his stepbrother was dead."

The above example shows how Holmes reasoned from several general premises (no women are vampires, people who suck blood remove poison, insanely jealous boys wish step brothers dead).

He reasoned to specific premises (Delores Ferguson is a woman, Dolores Ferguson was sucking blood, Jack Ferguson was an insanely jealous boy). He then reached conclusions (Dolores Ferguson is not a vampire, Dolores Ferguson was removing poison, Jack Ferguson wished his step-brother were dead). As a result, he solved *The Sussex Vampire* case.

Sherlock Holmes's ability to size up strangers came from his applying broad assumptions about people in general to the specific individuals he met. Holmes frequently used deduction in sizing up strangers. He also applied the next logical rule from the *Book of Life* magazine article.

Rule #2: Reason from the Specific to the General

The second rule, which Holmes probably described in *The Book of Life* magazine article, is his ability to reason from the specific to the general. When you reason this way, you are reasoning by induction.[18] Inductive reasoning examines specific instances from observations and reaches a likely but not definite general conclusion. It is simply educated guessing based on what is most probable.

---

[18] Modern day logicians now define induction as reasoning that uses statements or facts to reach a probable or likely conclusion – *Wikipedia.*

Sherlock Holmes often reasoned inductively when meeting a client in his sitting room at 221B Baker Street. In *The Adventure of the Speckled Band,* Holmes used inductive reasoning to size-up client Helen Stoner:

> "...You have come in by train this morning I see."

> "You know me, then?"

> "No, but I observe the second half of a return ticket in the palm of your left glove. You must have started early, and yet you had a good drive in a dog-cart, along heavy roads, before you reached the station."

> The lady gave a violent start and stared in bewilderment at my companion.

> "There is no mystery, my dear madam," said he, smiling. "The left arm of your jacket is spattered with mud in no less than seven places. The marks are perfectly fresh. There is no vehicle save a dog-cart which throws up mud in that way, and then only when you sit on the left-hand side of the driver."

> "Whatever your reasons may be, you are perfectly correct," said she.

Sherlock Holmes drew several specific inferences from his observations to make a general conclusion that she came by train in the morning. He observed the return ticket in her palm to infer she came by the train. He observed mud stains on her jacket to infer she came by a heavy road. His knowledge of dogcarts enabled him to infer that she sat on the driver's left side and that the mud splashed on her jacket. These specific logical inductions allowed Holmes to reach the general conclusion that she traveled in a dogcart.

Sherlock Holmes also reasoned inductively after examining specific evidence when he investigated a case. In *A Study in*

Scarlet, Holmes scrutinized specific details from a garden path, a large room and a body on the floor. He then gave Scotland Yard Detectives Lestrade and Gregson a suspect's general profile based on his inductive reasoning:

> "...there was a murder done, and the murderer was a man. He was more than six feet high, was in the prime of life, had small feet for his height, wore coarse, square-toed boots and smoked a Trichinopoly cigar. He came here with his victim in a four-wheeled cab, which was drawn by a horse with three old shoes and one new one on his off foreleg. In all probability the murderer had a florid face, and the fingernails of his right hand were remarkably long..."

Holmes reasoned from induction based on his analyzing the specific cab wheel impressions from the mud on the pathway and the horse's hoof marks. He reasoned inductively to determine the writing on the wall and the scratched plaster. He used inductive reasoning to infer the tobacco ash, the wedding ring and the blood on the floor. Holmes often called his inductive reasoning "the balance of probability." He used it to describe his thinking process to Watson.

When Holmes reasoned using the balance of probability, he more often than not correctly estimated the problem. In *The Sign of Four,* he correctly predicted facts about Watson's older brother and did not expect to be so accurate.

In *The Hound of the Baskervilles,* he correctly analyzed a letter addressed to Dr. Mortimer and deciphered the message. In *The Adventure of the Six Napoleons,* he correctly traced the lost black Borgias pearl to the last Napoleon bust. In these cases, Holmes used inductive reasoning as a tool to solve the mysteries.

Yet, although inductive reasoning is a powerful logical tool for sizing up strangers and solving problems it does have limitations. Holmes learned these limits in *The Yellow Face* case.

In this case, Holmes used inductive reasoning to reach a flawed conclusion based on the available evidence in front of him.

He later admitted to Watson his grave mistake when developments in the case proved him wrong in his conjecture. Holmes's mistake could happen to anyone who reasons by probability. Why? The answer is because the inductive process does not guarantee a valid conclusion like deduction.

For example, in *The Adventure of the Cardboard Box*, Holmes observed a young woman in a picture and believed her to be unmarried. His inductive reasoning, from specific facts to a general rule, went as follows:

Specific fact:	This woman does not wear a wedding ring.
Specific fact:	The woman's sister also does not wear a wedding ring.
General rule:	All women who do not wear wedding rings are unmarried.

The above inductive thinking proved true because the woman's sister confirmed that she married a few days after they took the picture. Let us say for argument's sake that Holmes then met several more women in his travels. Let us further suppose Sherlock Holmes believed them unmarried because they did not wear wedding rings. It would confirm Holmes's general rule that unmarried women do not wear wedding rings.

What if Sherlock Holmes then met a married woman who does not wear her wedding ring? What if she lost it? Or someone stole it? Or she pawned it? Or she no longer wears it because it is too tight? He would have to revise his reasoning to account for the new information. And that is the danger in inductive reasoning. When you think inductively, often you do not know all the information. Therefore, your interpretation or explanation relies on incomplete observations.

Some critics claim that Sherlock Holmes incorrectly used *"deduction"* when describing his logic when he really meant *"induction."* In reality, Sherlock Holmes used whichever principle worked. He rarely concerned himself with the terms or what the terms meant. Often he used both deduction and induction simultaneously. Sometimes he would explain his reasoning process to others and sometimes he did not. Holmes once said: "...I follow my own methods and tell as much or as little as I choose."

Other critics contend Holmes's claim that "I never guess. It is a shocking habit — destructive to the logical faculty" is false. These critics claim Holmes used educated guessing when he made his analyses in many of his cases. The critics point to stories such as *The Adventure of the Noble Bachelor*, in which Holmes uses the word "conjecture" during his reasoning. In *Silver Blaze*, Holmes used the word "surmise" while reasoning. In *The Adventure of the Red Circle*, Holmes called his reasoning "intelligent speculation."

These cases tend to support the critics arguments. Nevertheless, Holmes inductive skill achieved its' legendary status because he succeeded more times than he failed. He also used the next rule of deduction when applying his method.

Rule#3: Reason to the Simplest Explanation

The third logical rule Sherlock Holmes used and which we can find in the case histories is abduction.[19] Abduction is the process of reasoning to the simplest or best explanation from several different possibilities. Abduction is similar to induction in that they both rely on educated guessing. The major difference between the two is abduction seeks to *explain* a problem while induction *infers* a general rule or theory. Abduction also does not guarantee a conclusion like deduction.

---

[19] American philosopher Charles Sanders Piece (1839 – 1914) coined the term abduction.

It can, however, predict a future event or unobserved data, which deduction cannot do.

In *The Red-Headed League* case, Sherlock Holmes reasoned to the best explanation to size up a common British tradesman Mr. Jabez Wilson. Watson had also observed the stranger but could see nothing significant about his appearance. Holmes, on the other hand, noticed several details then reasoned to the simplest explanation based on the available facts he saw. Holmes explained it this way:

> "Beyond the obvious facts that he has at some time done manual labor, that he takes snuff, that he is a Freemason, that he has been in China, and that he has done a considerable amount of writing lately, I can deduce nothing else."

> "How, in the name of good fortune, did you know all that, Mr. Holmes?" He asked. "How did you know, for example, that I did manual labor? It's as true as gospel, for I began as a ship's carpenter."

> "Your hands, my dear sir. Your right hand is quite a size larger than your left. You have worked with it and the muscles are more developed."

> "Well, the snuff, then, and the Freemasonry?"

> "I won't insult your intelligence by telling you how I read that, especially as, rather against the strict rules of your order, you use an arc and compass breastpin."

> "Ah, of course, I forgot that. But the writing?"

> "What else can be indicated by that right cuff so very shiny for five inches, and the left one with the smooth patch near the elbow where you rest it upon the desk."

"Well, but China?"

"The fish which you have tattooed immediately above your wrist could only have been done in China. I have made a small study of tattoo marks, and have even contributed to the literature of the subject. That trick of staining the fishes' scales of a delicate pink is quite peculiar to China. When, in addition, I see a Chinese coin hanging from your watch-chain, the matter becomes even more simple."

The general assumptions Holmes used he learned from his previous knowledge, experience and training. He knew that manual laborers usually have one larger hand (because they use one hand more than the other as they work). He knew that Masonic Order members are likely to wear jewelry with the arc-and-compass symbol.

Sherlock Holmes knew that when a man writes with a long sleeve shirt cuff, it might get shiny from moving it back and forth, as he writes. He knew that tattoo artists from China create tattoos that are distinctive to their region. Sherlock Holmes connected these broad rules to the details he observed on the visitor's appearance to reach specific explanations about the stranger's background.

Sherlock Holmes always looked for the simplest, most natural explanation to a problem. If you are to master the Sherlock Holmes Method, you must follow his example. Ask yourself: What best explains the problem? What is the most plausible explanation? What is the simplest solution? Given the facts that I know, is this the best answer? The best explanation or solution is often the most simple.

In *The Adventure of the Blue Carbuncle*, Holmes sought to solve a mystery by locating a man who may have known about a missing jewel. Holmes told Watson: "To do this, we must try the simplest means first." Holmes then placed advertisements in all the evening newspapers.

In *The Adventure of the Copper Beeches,* Sherlock Holmes considered several possible explanations to a mystery that a client had brought to his attention before he settled on one explanation. Sherlock Holmes had said, "...I have devised seven separate explanations, each of which cover the facts as far as we know them. But which of these is correct can only be determined by the fresh information which we, shall no doubt find waiting for us."

Once Holmes had gathered more information regarding the problem, he excluded the least likely scenarios. He then decided on the most feasible explanation and acted upon it. When Holmes decided to exclude the least likely scenarios in his analysis, he applied the next logical rule to do it.

Rule#4: Reason by Elimination

There is no doubt Sherlock Holmes included this logical rule in *The Book of Life* magazine article. In fact, it is his most famous deductive rule. He relies on the process of elimination rule so extensively during investigations that he uses it several times in other cases.[20] In *The Sign of Four,* he states it this way:

> "When you have eliminated the impossible, whatever remains, however improbable, must be the truth."

When you use this rule, you are reasoning by exclusion and proving your point by showing all other possibilities are wrong. To do this, create a mental list in your mind about the possible or most likely facts or details. Then remove each fact or detail that does not match up to the explanation you have devised. The fact

---

[20] Holmes reasoned by elimination in *The Adventure of the Beryl Coronet, The Adventure of the Noble Bachelor, The Adventure of the Blanched Soldier* and *The Valley of Fear* to name a few cases.

or detail which remains will be the one, which best fits your reasoning.

For example, Holmes used the elimination rule in *The Hound of the Baskervilles*. Watson described it this way:

"...You have been at your club all day. I perceive?"

"My dear Holmes!"

"Am I right?"

"Certainly, but how —?"

He laughed at my bewildered expression.

"There is a delightful freshness about you, Watson...a gentleman goes forth on a showery and miry day. He returns immaculate in the evening with the gloss still on his hat and his boots. He has been a fixture therefore all day. He is not a man with intimate friends. Where, then, could he have been? Is it not obvious?"

It is obvious that Sherlock Holmes figured it out by narrowing down all the known places Watson could have gone. He eliminated the most unlikely places such as Watson's medical practice. Holmes's prior knowledge of Watson's daily routine also helped him because he knew Watson did not have many friends and normally went to the club. He observed Watson's clean appearance with the shine still on his hat and boots. He knew it rained so he figured Watson had stayed inside. Sherlock Holmes excluded all the improbable facts and the one that remained proved correct.

In *The Sign of Four*, Holmes also used the reasoning by elimination rule to deduce that Watson had just recently mailed a telegram from the Wigmore Street Post Office. Watson expressed surprise at Holmes knowing this because he had mailed the telegram on an impulse and told no one. Sherlock Holmes replied with a chuckle:

> "...I knew you had not written a letter, since I had sat opposite you all morning. I see in your open desk there that you have a sheet of stamps and a thick bundle of postcards. What could you go into the post office for, then, but to send a wire? Eliminate all other factors, and the one which remains, must be the truth."

In *The Adventure of the Solitary Cyclist,* Sherlock Holmes used the process of elimination. He determined that a stranger who had followed Ms. Violet Smith on her bicycle had ridden to another area. Watson writes how Ms. Smith describes what happened to her:

> "....I laid a trap for him. There is a sharp turning of the road, and I pedaled very quickly round this, and then I stopped and waited I expected him to shoot round and pass me before he could stop. But he never appeared. Then I went back and looked round the corner. I could see a mile of road but he was not on it. To make it the more extraordinary there was no side road at this point down which he could have gone."

> Holmes chuckled and rubbed his hands. "This case certainly presents some features of its own," said he. "How much time elapsed between your turning the corner and your discovery that the road was clear?"

> "Two or three minutes."

> Then he could not have retreated down the road, and you say that there are no side roads?"

> "None."

> Then he certainly took a footpath on one side or the other."

86

"It could not been on the side of the heath, or I should have seen him."

"So, by the process of exclusion, we arrive at the fact that he made his way toward Charlington Hall..."

Sherlock Holmes reasoned that the stranger did not retreat down the road so he excluded that possibility. He reasoned no side roads existed so he eliminated another possible explanation. He reasoned the stranger did not take a footpath on the side of the heath so he tossed out that possibility. One by one, Holmes ruled out each possible explanation on where the stranger rode to until he reached the conclusion the stranger traveled to Charlington Hall.

Some critics call the reason by elimination rule the 'Sherlock Holmes Fallacy.' They claim unless you can know all possibilities, you cannot reach an accurate conclusion regarding a problem. They claim you have to know every possible explanation and disprove them all except one. They argue this is hard to do because no one knows everything. These critics also state Arthur Conan Doyle used the elimination rule in his personal life. They claim it led him to believe in spiritualism and fall for a fairy hoax.[21]

It is true that using the process of elimination may lead to wrong conclusions. It is also true that using the rule can cause you to reason incorrectly from the lack of evidence. You can minimize making errors in reasoning with this rule, however, if you do the following:

---

[21] In 1917, two young girls produced five photographs that showed fairies existed. Arthur Conan Doyle, writing an article for the *Strand Magazine*, used the photographs as evidence for psychic phenomena. Several decades later, scientists, led by skeptic James Randi, examined the photographs and concluded they were fakes. One of the young girls later admitted to faking the photographs. The whole episode is now called the *Cottingley Fairy Hoax* – *Wikipedia.*

(1) <u>Recognize it has limitations</u>. Keep your mind open to other possibilities. Do this even after you have eliminated the impossible or improbable ones. Consider any new previously unobserved or unknown possibility. Then revise your hypothesis. Sherlock Holmes always kept an open mind.

(2) <u>Always self-correct yourself</u>. Recognize that you are human and cannot know every possible outcome. Stay alert to any biases, assumptions, prejudices, beliefs or expectations you may have that might hinder you from keeping an open mind. Holmes always self-corrected himself and revised his theories when proven wrong.

(3) <u>Use it with the eight principles</u>. Use the elimination rule in combination with the eight principles to increase your probably of being correct. You can use the rule solely by itself but if you do so, you must remain aware of the pitfalls. Sherlock Holmes used all ten-deduction rules in various combinations with the eight principles whenever the situation called for it.

You can also increase the probably of being correct with the reason by elimination rule. How? Use it specifically with the next logical rule.

Rule#5: Reason by Synthesis

Sherlock Holmes, in all probability, wrote about the ability to reason by synthetic thinking in the *Book of Life* magazine article. It is an important skill, although he only mentions it one time in the Canon. In *The Adventure of the Copper Beeches,* Holmes admonishes Watson for embellishing their adventures to the public. He states Watson neglected to focus on the deduction and 'logical synthesis' faculties that he used to solve the cases.

Indeed, Sherlock Holmes wrote about logical synthesis because he often used it as he sought solutions to problems he faced. [22] Synthetic reasoning is the opposite of analytical reasoning. Analytical reasoning breaks down a problem into various parts to solve it. Synthetic reasoning gathers different parts together to form a new whole, which becomes greater than the sum of its parts.

Synthetic thinking creates a new idea, pattern or fact from a mixture of different things. For example, if you take two wheels, two pedals, a chain, a frame, a seat and a handlebar, you can then create a bicycle. The different parts alone do not serve a function but together they form a bicycle that can take you from point A to point B. When you think synthetically, you are thinking creatively. You are combining what you already know with new knowledge you learn to see original patterns or ideas.

In *The Elementary Methods of Sherlock Holmes,* author Brad Keefauver discusses how Holmes used logical synthesis.[23] He puts forth the hypothesis that Sherlock Holmes created stories in his own mind to fit the facts he gathered. Mr. Keefauver explained it this way:

> "...as fuel for his deductions, Sherlock Holmes took the data he had gathered and spun stories with it. Never straying from the solid contact points of the hard facts he had gathered, Sherlock Holmes would conjure up as many possible series of events as he could to cover those facts."

---

[22] Sherlock Holmes is famous for his logical thinking skills but he also had creative abilities, which he inherited from being a descendant of French artist Vernet. He created a test for bloodstains (*A Study in Scarlet*); he published several pioneering monographs on scientific topics (mud stains, tattoos, etc.); he played the violin *(The Norwood Builder)* and he composed music (*The Red-Headed League*).

[23] *The Elementary Methods of Sherlock Holmes; Chapter 17: The Strangest Form of Art in the Blood: Logical Synthesis;* Quotes from Page 119, Paragraph 3; Page 123, Paragraph 5.

Mr. Keefauver then described how Holmes used his creatively to gain several viewpoints regarding a problem. Holmes then used the process of elimination to narrow down the most likely solution:

> "Even as Holmes spun his great imaginary collection of stories surrounding the circumstances of each case, the process of elimination had to be constantly at work, that form of deduction being the logical part of logical synthesis. Having created each tale, Holmes had to test it carefully for flaws, making sure that he dismissed no story without solid evidence against it, yet at the same time looking very closely for the evidence. Synthesis created the raw materials; deduction would then refine them, whittling away until all that remained was the one story with the diamond-hard core of truth to it."

Using creativity and excluding unnecessary points to find truth sounds good in theory. But how do you make it work in the real world? How do you apply logical synthesis in a practical way to discover the truth about strangers? Easy. You simply observe everything about a stranger — body language, speech, clothing, facial expressions and other trivial details (such as tattoos, stains, scratches and bulges). Next, you put all the things you see synthetically together. You then apply 'logic' to the 'synthesis' to gain new insight about the stranger. The logic part comes from using, either singly or in various combinations, the other nine deduction rules.

In *A Study in Scarlet,* Sherlock Holmes states, "there are fifty who can reason synthetically to one who can reason analytically." Most people reason synthetically because it is the natural way to think. They observe others then make educated guesses about them based on combining various factors they see. The ability to draw new meaning after combining various facts and details is the key to synthetic thinking. But you will still need to use the next logical rule to succeed at it.

90

Rule#6: Reason Backwards

Sherlock Holmes, without any doubt, included the reasoning backwards rule in *The Book of Life* article. We know this because Holmes used the rule in several cases throughout the Canon. The first case where Holmes describes the reasoning backwards rule is in *A Study in Scarlet.* In this case, Holmes explains his thinking process to Dr. Watson:

> "In solving a problem of this sort, the grand thing is to be able to reason backward. That is a very useful accomplishment, and a very easy one, but people do not practice it much. In the everyday affairs of life it is more useful to reason forward, and so the other comes to be neglected...most people, if you describe a train of events to them, will tell you what the result would be. They can put those events together in their minds, and argue from them that something will come to pass...There are few people, however, who, if you told them a result, would be able to evolve from their own inner consciousness what the steps were which led up to that result. This power is what I mean when I talk of reasoning backward, or analytically...now this was a case in which you were given the result and had to find everything else for yourself. Now let me endeavor to show you the different steps in my reasoning..."

Sherlock Holmes then tells Watson how he figured out the evidence and caught the murder suspect Jefferson Hope. Sherlock Holmes understood most people naturally reason forward. When you reason forward you are reasoning from cause to effect. You already know the root problem and seek to predict an outcome. Forward reasoning requires you move step-by-step in a specific direction, with *one* cause in mind as you seek a definite result. Reasoning forward uses the scientific method to observe facts and details, create a theory and explain it, and then test the theory with a prediction to determine whether the theory is valid.

In *The Five Orange Pips,* Holmes explained to Watson the practical application of forward reasoning. He remarked:

> "The ideal reasoner...would, when he had once been shown a single fact in all its bearings, deduce from it not only all the chain of events which led up to it but also all the results which would follow from it. As Cuvier could correctly describe a whole animal by the contemplation of a single bone, so the observer who has thoroughly understood one link in a series of incidents should be able to accurately state all the other ones, both before and after."

In *The Red-Headed League,* Holmes used forward reasoning to predict when thieves would break-in at a bank vault and steal gold. He listened to his red-haired client's story then thought deeply about it. He figured a bank robbery as the only plausible *cause* for their behavior and then went to investigate the scene. He examined the houses, the pavement and the man who answered the door.

Holmes then sought out Scotland Yard Police Agent Peter Jones, Bank Director Merryweather and Dr. Watson. He needed them to assist him in testing his theory and catching the thieves. He predicted the day and time the thieves would attempt their break-in. He waited with the group in the dark vault. The *effect* came when the thieves arrived. Sherlock Holmes and the others then captured them. Watson described Sherlock Holmes using forward reasoning to see "...clearly not only what had happened but what was about to happen."

Although Holmes could reason forward, he preferred reasoning backward. Why? It enabled him to solve many more crimes. In *The Sign of Four,* Holmes explained to Watson why he disagreed with the way Watson presented one of his most famous cases: "Some facts should be suppressed, or at least, a just sense of proportion should be observed in treating them.

The only point in the case which deserved mention was the curious analytical reasoning from effects to causes, by which I succeeded in unraveling it."

Reasoning backwards is simply analytical thinking. When you reason backwards you are reasoning from what you know to what you do not know. You are looking at the result — the facts, the details and the trace evidence left on a person or at a crime scene to determine what caused it. In essence, you are reasoning from an effect to a cause.

Sherlock Holmes often took a problem apart to reason from effect to cause. He analyzed each piece in the problem to see how it fit as part of a whole. He used analytical thinking to understand each piece in the problem and its' connection to the other pieces. He would then draw a conclusion about the whole problem from his analysis.

When you analyze a problem by reasoning backwards, consider it may have many different causes, some of which you may not know about. Sometimes you need to make a decision based on what you know at the time and the limited information you have.

When this happens you must use the balance of probability to figure out the most likely cause from the many different causes you are considering. Your prior knowledge, common sense and experience will come into play here as you reject the unlikely causes and focus on the most probable one. Through trial and error, you can figure out which deduction rules apply. Use them as you test and confirm if the cause you chose is the correct one.

In *The Adventure of the Six Napoleons*, Sherlock Holmes reasoned backwards. He figured out the reason for the six busts mysterious destruction. He told Watson and Detective Lestrade: "Now you clearly see the sequence of events, though you see

93

them, of course, in the inverse order to the way in which they presented themselves to me." Holmes then explained to them how he traced the famous black pearl backwards from its original disappearance to its discovery in the last bust.

In *The Adventure of the Cardboard Box*, Sherlock Holmes used analytical thinking. He solved the mystery of two severed ears found in a box. He later stated to Watson: "The case...is one where...we have been compelled to reason backward from effects to causes." Holmes then explained to Watson how he determined the victims and killer's identities, discovered the essential facts of the case and gave Detective Lestrade the information he needed to capture and arrest the suspect.

In *The Disappearance of Lady Frances Carfax*, Sherlock Holmes mentally reconstructed the situation that led to him saving Lady Frances from certain death. He stated to Watson: "When you follow two separate chains of thought...you will find some point of intersection which should approximate to the truth. We will start now, not from the lady but from the coffin and argue backward." Holmes then explained to Watson how in a flash of insight he remembered a single clue he had dismissed before, which led him to rescue the Lady Frances just in time.

Dr. Thomas Young, in his online article entitled: *"Is Sherlock Holmes' "reasoning backwards" a reliable method for discovering truth?"*[24], states that backward reasoning, despite its' limitations, is useful in three situations:

(1) As a loosely defined, common sense, trial and error method during an investigation to develop leads.

(2) When only one plausible explanation for a problem exists.

---

[24] See *Heartland Forensic Pathology, LLC* website at http://www.heartlandforensic.com/writing/is-sherlock- holmes-reasoning-backwards-a-reliable-method-for-discovering-truth.

(3) As a plausible alternative explanation for physical evidence in circumstantial court cases.

Sherlock Holmes used reasoning backward in all three of these ways as well as with the next logical rule.

Rule #7: Reason from a Hypothesis

Throughout the Canon, you will find Holmes frequently instructing Watson regarding the correct way to form a hypothesis about a person or problem. You can rest assured then, that Holmes, more likely than not, included his method of hypothesis formation in *The Book of Life* article.

In Chapter 1, you learned that a hypothesis is an educated guess or provisional theory used to explain or understand a person's behavior or a problem's cause. In *The Adventure of the Sussex Vampire,* Holmes stated: "One forms provisional theories and waits for time or fuller knowledge to explode them."

Sherlock Holmes developed a practical system, which enabled him to reason from a hypothesis. Whether he sized up a stranger or solved a problem, he approached both using the same method. When he evaluated the stranger, he applied the method in seconds. When he examined the problem, it took him hours or days to figure it out. Either way, he used the following steps below, along with his rules of deduction, in forming a hypothesis and reasoning from it.

The first step Sherlock Holmes took is he approached the person or problem with a blank mind. He did not approach the stranger or problem with any preconceived notions, biases, impressions or opinions. He simply let the person, circumstance or occurrence reveal itself to him.

In *The Adventure of the Cardboard Box,* Holmes described his thinking to Watson this way: "We approached the case...with an absolutely blank mind, which is always an advantage. We had formed no theories. We were simply there to observe and to draw inferences from our observations."

In *A Study in Scarlet*, Holmes explained to Watson: "...I approached...with my mind entirely free from all impressions." And in *The Hound of the Baskervilles*, Holmes stated to Watson: "I will not bias your mind by suggesting theories or suspicions." These cases establish that Holmes deliberately kept a neutral mind whenever he sized up a stranger or investigated a case.

The second step Sherlock Holmes took is he gathered relevant facts and evidence. Sometimes he observed the facts from a stranger's appearance. Sometimes he obtained details from listening to a stranger's story. Other times he collected evidence from a crime scene. No matter how he did it, he always looked for 'data' before he formed a hypothesis.

In *A Study in Scarlet*, Holmes refused to form a hypothesis without facts. He told Watson: "No data yet. It is a capital mistake to theorize before you have all the evidence."

In *A Scandal in Bohemia*, Holmes would not create a theory until he had gathered specific details. He told Watson: "I have no data yet. It is a capital mistake to theorize before one has data. Insensibly one begins to twist facts to suit theories, instead of theories to suit facts."

In *The Adventure of Wisteria Lodge*, Holmes stated: "A further knowledge of facts is necessary before I would venture to give a final and definite opinion." Holmes always sought empirical evidence before he would form a hypothesis.

Once Sherlock Holmes obtained the relevant facts or evidence he needed, the third step he took is to form a hypothesis. Holmes always considered other possible theories before deciding on a specific one.

In *The Adventure of the Norwood Builder,* Holmes suggested to Detective Lestrade: "I don't mean to deny the evidence is in some ways very strongly in favor of your theory. I only wish to point out that there are other theories possible."

In *The Naval Treaty,* Holmes stated to Watson: "we are bound to take every possibility into account." And in *The Disappearance of Lady Frances Carfax,* Watson describes Holmes as a man who "...turned over in his mind every possible solution of the mystery."

After considering other possible theories, Holmes decided on a specific hypothesis by reasoning with his rules of deduction. For example, in *The Adventure of the Blanched Soldier,* Holmes used the reason by elimination rule. He narrowed down the possible theories regarding a young soldier's seclusion. He then reached the remaining theory that the soldier had a disease.

In *The Adventure of the Devil's Foot,* Sherlock Holmes used the reason by abduction rule. He settled for a natural explanation rather than a supernatural one regarding an alleged spiritual force driving three people mad with terror. Sherlock Holmes then reasoned to the best explanation. Holmes stated: "I fear that if the matter is beyond humanity it is certainly beyond me. Yet we must exhaust all natural explanations before we fall back upon such a theory as this."

After Holmes decided on a specific hypothesis, he then ensured it fit the facts he had developed. In *A Study in Scarlet,* Watson lay on a sofa. He thought in amazement how he could not figure out anything regarding a crime scene. Yet, Holmes "had already formed a theory which explained all the facts."

In *The Sign of Four*, Holmes explains to Watson his theory on how a buried treasure came to England. Watson says Holmes's theory is mere speculation. Holmes replied: "It is more than that. It is the only hypothesis which covers the facts." Holmes would gather facts and then weave a theory around the facts.

As Sherlock Holmes weaved his theory, he also looked for a common theme among any disconnected facts. In *The Hound of the Baskervilles,* Watson described Holmes' mind as "busy in endeavoring to frame some scheme into which all these strange and apparently disconnected episodes could be fitted."

In *The Adventure of the Golden Pince-Nez,* Watson stated: "I could not myself see the bearing of this incident, but I clearly perceived that Holmes was weaving it into the general scheme which he had formed in his brain."

In *The Adventure of Wisteria Lodge,* Holmes stated: "If the fresh facts which come to our knowledge all fit themselves into the scheme, then our hypothesis may gradually become a solution." Sherlock Holmes would look for a theme that tied all the facts together. He then combined it with a working hypothesis that explained everything regarding the case.

Sherlock Holmes then used the working hypothesis to see where it would lead him. In *Silver Blaze,* Holmes searched for a missing racehorse and theorized he would find it at Mapleton. He stated: "Let us take that as a working hypothesis and see what it leads us to." In *The Adventure of Wisteria Lodge,* Holmes stated: "We may take it as a hypothesis and see what consequences it would entail."

In *The Boscombe Valley Mystery,* Holmes stated: "I shall approach this case from the point of view that what this young man says is true, and we shall see whither that hypothesis will lead us." Holmes used the temporary or provisional hypothesis as a starting point in his investigation to give it direction.

Once Holmes found a theme that tied all the facts together with his hypothesis, he reviewed the facts he already had. In *The*

Five Orange Pips, Holmes stated: "...let us consider the situation and see what may be deduced from it." In *The Adventure of the Priory School,* Holmes stated: "Before we start to investigate...let us try to realize what we *do* know, so as to make the most of it, and to separate the essential from the accidental."

In *The Adventure of the Devil's Foot,* Holmes stated: "Now, let us calmly define our position...let us get a firm grip of the very little which we *do* know, so that when fresh facts arise we may be ready to fit them in their places."

If new facts came to Sherlock Holmes attention, which he had not considered or which did not cover the facts, he would reconsider his hypothesis. In *The Yellow Face,* when Watson called Holmes's theory all surmise regarding an unknown occupant in a house, Holmes replied: "But at least it covers the facts. When new facts come to our knowledge which cannot be covered by it, it will be time enough to reconsider our position."

In *The Adventure of Black Peter,* Detective Stanley Hopkins showed Sherlock Holmes a notebook that Holmes did not know existed. Holmes stated: "I confess that this notebook, which did not appear at the inquest, modifies any views which I may have formed. I had come to a theory of the crime in which I can find no place for this." After he reviewed any new facts, Holmes would take the fourth step.

The fourth step Holmes took after forming a hypothesis is he tested it. In *The Naval Treaty,* when Watson asked him whether he had a found a clue in a mysterious case, Holmes replied: "...we have several, but we can only test their value by further inquiry."

In *The Adventure of the Blanched Soldier,* Holmes tested his theory on why a young man stayed secluded at an outhouse in his father's mansion. Holmes stated: "It may well be that several explanations remain, in which case one tries test after test until one or other of them has a convincing amount of support."

Holmes also verified any facts he obtained even when others had already checked them. In *The Reigate Puzzle,* Inspector Forrester asked Holmes if he doubted the published report regarding a man dying from a gunshot wound. After inspecting the dead body, Holmes replied: "...it is as well to test everything." Once Holmes tested his hypothesis, which usually required him to make a prediction or conduct an experiment, he then proceeded to the fifth and final step.

The fifth step Sherlock Holmes took is he reached a conclusion. Sometimes he could reach the conclusion without doing a test. Clients or other professionals would consult him on a matter, give him the facts and evidence, and he would render an expert opinion.

Sherlock Holmes mentions how he did this in *A Study in Scarlet.* In that case, he states: "...Here in London we have lots of government detectives and lots of private ones. When these fellows are at fault, they come to me, and I manage to put them on the right scent. They lay all the evidence before me, and I am generally able, by the help of my knowledge of the history of crime, to set them straight."

In *The Adventure of the Noble Bachelor,* Holmes informed both Watson and a client that: "I had formed my conclusions as to the case before our client came into the room...My whole examination served to turn my conjecture into a certainty."

In *The Adventure of the Sussex Vampire,* Holmes informed both Watson and a client that he reached a conclusion regarding the problem: "...before we left Baker Street, and the rest has merely been observation and confirmation."

Other times Holmes went to the crime scene to confirm his theory. In *A Study in Scarlet,* Holmes told Watson that he normally solves cases without leaving his room. Then Holmes said: "Now and again a case turns up which is a little more complex. Then I have to bustle about and see things with my own eyes."

In *The Reigate Puzzle,* Holmes stated: "...I should like to have a quiet glance into the details of this case. There is something in it which fascinates me extremely...I will step around with the inspector and test the truth of one or two little fancies of mine."

In *The Adventure of the Bruce-Partington Plans*, Mycroft implored Holmes to go to the scene of a crime. Holmes then went to Aldgate Station and eventually found facts to support his working hypothesis. The observations and new facts that fit Holmes's theory verified he had the right solution. If at the fifth step Holmes found his conclusion wrong, he revised it and restated a new conclusion.

The five steps Holmes used to reason from a hypothesis are based on his own personal system. You do not need to know any technical or logical terms to use the Holmes method. The steps are not for use in a laboratory or as part of a double-blind study. They are for practical use in your everyday life. Use the steps informally in the street, at work or during your normal daily activities. To do this, you need the next logical rule.

Rule #8: Reason with Common Sense

It is self-evident that Sherlock Holmes used this rule. You can find it in the case histories. When you reason from common sense, you are reasoning based on your everyday worldly knowledge. You are combining basic logic with practical judgment to reach a conclusion.

Common sense reasoning deals with thinking in a natural and realistic way. It is thinking based on the obvious things in ordinary life and human experience. It is thinking based on common knowledge that most people possess (but rarely use).

101

You are using common sense reasoning when you ask questions such as: "Does this make sense?" "Is this practical?" "Is this natural?" "Is this reasonable?" "Is this credible?" "Is this plausible?" and "Is this realistic?"

The reason Sherlock Holmes considered his method so simple and obvious is that he based his thinking process on common sense. Often he seemed surprised when Watson, a client or a Scotland Yard rival like Lestrade did not grasp the significance of the common sense explanations he gave. He would respond with such comments as "Elementary," "Commonplace," "It is simplicity itself," "Is it not obvious?" or "...where is the mystery in all this?" after explaining how he arrived at his common sense reasoning.

In *The Adventure of the Blanched Soldier*, Sherlock Holmes used common sense reasoning to startle James M. Dodd upon first meeting him. Holmes said:

"What has been happening at Tuxbury Old Park?"

"Mr. Holmes—!"

"My dear sir, there is no mystery. Your letter came with that heading, and as you fixed this appointment in very pressing terms, it was clear that something sudden and important had occurred..."

It is evident Holmes used common sense reasoning to figure out Mr. Dodd's actions. He used it to determine the destination Mr. Dodd came from (Tuxbury Old Park) had something to do with the letter he received and Mr. Dodd's pressing issue.

Sherlock Holmes's common sense reasoning ran: "Here is a man who makes an urgent appointment. The letterhead he sent me to make the appointment comes from a specific area in London. He is at a loss on how to start the interview, for he remains silent while sitting in the chair. Clearly a sudden and important event occurred in connected to Tuxbury Old Park." Holmes then made the remark, which shocked Mr. Dodd.

As with the encounter with Mr. Dodd, Holmes used common sense reasoning extensively when scrutinizing a stranger or solving a problem. He would reason from what he saw, based on a natural understanding of how people behave, to reach accurate assessments. He would put two plus two together and connect the dots by providing a sensible explanation to the link in his chain of reasoning.

In *The Sign of Four,* Holmes gave Watson several common sense explanations regarding Watson's older brother from a watch he analyzed. For example, Holmes stated to Watson regarding his brother being careless:

> "Surely it is no great feat to assume that a man who treats a fifty-guinea watch so cavalierly must be a careless man. Neither it is a very far-fetched inference that a man who inherits one article of such value is pretty well provided for in other respects."

Sherlock Holmes's explanations about Watson's older brother came from an everyday understanding of human nature. Holmes considered it obvious that a man who is careless with a valuable item is also untidy in his personal habits. It is equally obvious with Holmes' reasoning that a person who inherits a valuable item usually receives financial support in other areas of his or her life. The reasons Holmes gives regarding Watson's brother make 'sense' because they are so obvious. Anyone reading the story naturally understands Holmes reasoning. They instinctively know it comes from everyday human experience.

The *Silver Blaze* case is another example how Holmes used common sense reasoning to solve a missing racehorse mystery. During an investigation into the horse's disappearance, Inspector Gregory asked Holmes:

"Is there any point to which you wish to draw my attention?"
"To the curious incident of the dog in the night-time."
"The dog did nothing in the night-time."
"That was the curious incident," remarked Sherlock Holmes.

Most people know from everyday experience that a dog will instinctively bark at strangers. Sherlock Holmes reasoned the dog did not bark at the person who entered the stable and took the horse away because the dog *knew* the person. Holmes based his reasoning regarding the dog not barking on everyday worldly knowledge most people have regarding a dog's nature. Dogs do not bark at people they know. They bark at people they do not know. He used simple common sense to reach that conclusion. He also used the next basic logical rule to size up a stranger.

Rule#9: Reason with If-Then Logic

When Holmes wrote *The Book of Life* article he included this basic logical rule because he used it many times in the Canon. When you use if-then logic, you are using conditional reasoning. Conditional reasoning relies on the logic that if 'A' is true then 'B' is also true. When applying if-then logic to observing strangers, 'A' is the detail you observe and 'B' is what the detail indicates.

For example, using the first basic question, you could ask yourself: "What do I observe?" This question is the 'A' or 'if' part of the rule because it is the detail, you see. The detail itself could be callouses you notice on the stranger's middle finger. You could then ask yourself the second basic question: "What can I deduce?" This question is the "B" or 'then' part of the rule because it is what the detail signifies or indicates. The callus located on the middle finger could tell you the person frequently writes with a pencil or pen. The if-then mental reasoning would go like this: "If this stranger has a callous on his middle finger, then he writes often with a pen or pencil."

When you ask yourself, "If A is true, then B is true. A is true. Therefore, B is true," you are using the same conditional reasoning that Sherlock Holmes used. You can apply the if-then deductive rule in a practical way.

For example, in a *Scandal in Bohemia*, Holmes used if-then logical thinking to deduce Watson got very wet lately and had *"a most clumsy and careless servant girl."* An astonished Watson asked Holmes how did he know this. Sherlock Holmes replied:

> "It is simplicity itself...My eyes tell me that on the inside of your left shoe, just where the firelight strikes it, the leather is scored by six almost parallel cuts. Obviously they have been caused by someone who has very carelessly scraped round the edges of the sole in order to remove crusted mud from it. Hence, you see, my double deduction that you have been out in vile weather, and that you have a particularly malignant boot-slitting specimen of the London slavery."

According *Wikipedia,*[25] Sherlock Holmes employed several connected principles:

- If leather on the side of a shoe is scored by several parallel cuts, it was caused by someone who scraped around the edges of the sole in order to remove crusted mud.
- If a London doctor's shoes are scraped to remove crusted mud, the person who so scraped them is the doctor's servant girl.
- If someone cuts a shoe while scraping it to remove encrusted mud, that person is clumsy and careless.
- If someone's shoes had encrusted mud on them, then they are likely to have been worn by him in the rain, when it is likely he became very wet.

> By applying such principles in an obvious way (using repeated applications of modus ponens), Holmes is able to infer from his observation, "the sides of

---

[25]See the section on Holmesian deduction at http://en. wikipedia.org/wiki/ Sherlock_Holmes.

Watson's shoes are scored by several parallel cuts," that:

"Watson's servant girl is clumsy and careless" and "Watson has been very wet lately and has been out in vile weather."

Sherlock Holmes also used if-then conditional reasoning in *The Naval Treaty*, when he deduced a thief came in a cab. He described his conditional reasoning to Watson in this way:

"....if Mr. Phelps is correct in stating that there is no hiding-place either in the room or the corridors, then the person must have come from the outside. If he came from outside on so wet a night, and yet left no trace of damp upon the linoleum, which was examined within a few minutes of his passing, then it is exceedingly probable that he came in a cab..."

Using if-then logic is one of the most practical ways to reason but also the easiest way to commit errors when you think. Several invalid forms of logic exist that are similar to conditional reasoning and which can lead you astray. To use the Sherlock Holmes rules of deduction to size up strangers, you must stay on guard against these errors in reasoning. Avoid them at all costs. You can do this once you learn and use the last logical rule.

Rule #10: Reason Clearly and Accurately

Throughout the case histories, you will find Holmes strived to use this rule. He sought to think rationally whenever he sized up a stranger or faced a complex problem.

In *The Adventure of the Priory School*, Holmes reasoned accurately that he would find a Palmer tire track on the moor. After he found the bicycle track he stated: "My reasoning seems to have been pretty sound, Watson."

106

In *The Sign of Four,* Holmes reasoned accurately regarding Major Sholto's reaction to several men he wronged escaping from prison. Holmes asked Watson: "Does the reasoning strike you as being faulty?" Watson replied no; he found the reasoning clear and concise.

In *The Valley of Fear,* Sherlock Holmes reasoned accurately when he analyzed a coded message informant Porlock sent to him. He relied on logic to figure out the secret code when he stated: "Let us consider the problem in the light of pure reason." After figuring out the cipher message, Holmes asked Watson: "What do you think of pure reason and its fruit?" From the many case histories, it is clear Holmes placed a high premium on critical thinking.

If you are to master the Sherlock Holmes Method, you must learn to think as he did. You have consciously to make yourself think rationally and check your reasoning to ensure it is correct. Sherlock Holmes constantly self-checked himself regarding his thinking processes.

In *The Adventure of the Priory School,* Sherlock Holmes realizes a mistake in his reasoning regarding a missing boy. Holmes said to Watson: "...It is impossible as I have stated it, and therefore I must have in some respect stated it wrong...can you suggest any fallacy?"

Watch Out for Errors In Thinking

Why did Holmes ask Watson for a suggestion to help find a flaw in his thinking? The answer is Holmes wanted to know if he committed any logical fallacies. A logical fallacy is an error in thinking. It is a logical mistake many people make when mentally processing their thoughts. Most people do not think critically although they have the potential to do so.

Many people think incorrectly because their thinking relies on flawed reasoning. Their thoughts are incorrect because their beliefs, emotions, biases, expectations and assumptions sway the way they think. They also rely on outside influences such as hearsay, gossip and rumors. These flawed ways of thinking lead them to reason fallaciously and come to wrong conclusions.

Sherlock Holmes avoided reaching wrong conclusions because he resisted using faulty reasoning. There are many logical fallacies. All of them are important to know and identify.

Although you should learn about all types of logical fallacies, this chapter will focus on the fallacies where you can reach incorrect judgments about strangers. The fallacies you should stay on guard against when sizing up strangers are as follows:

1. **Jumping to a Conclusion.** When you assume facts about a stranger without specific proof, you are reasoning with this fallacy. Sherlock Holmes always based his reasoning on what he actually observed. Usually this mistake in reasoning occurs when you judge too soon without getting all the facts. Resist the urge to make snap judgments by controlling your feelings. Refuse to speculate and wait until you have all the available facts or evidence. Observe as many facts or details as you can when sizing up a stranger before making a judgment.

2. **Stereotyping.** When you see a stranger and include him or her into a certain group because of the way they speak, look or dress you are using stereotypical thinking.[26] Stereotypes are negative because they focus on a person's race, religion, gender, ethnicity, sexual orientation or physical handicap rather than his or her personality,

---

[26] Several critics' claim Holmes used stereotypical thinking when it came to women, the lower Victorian classes and other minorities. They state he looked down on women, which is how Irene Adler out maneuvered him (*A Scandal in Bohemia*).

attitude or behavior. Thinking that all blacks are criminals, all Muslims are terrorists; all women are sluts and all whites are racists, based on the actions of a few, are stereotypical thinking. Resist the urge to label or lump a person into a specific category. Judge the person as an individual and based on facts just as Sherlock Holmes would do.

3. **Conjunction Fallacy.** When you size up a stranger based on several complex facts being more likely than one simple fact, you are using the conjunction fallacy.[27] In a *Scientific American* online article, writer Maria Konnikova describes how Sherlock Holmes stuck to logic, regardless of his impressions and avoided using the conjunction fallacy.[28] She states that Holmes, when sizing up a specific individual, simultaneously cast off and exploited the conjunction fallacy. He evaluated each "fact separately and objectively as part of a consistent whole." Holmes did not allow likely or common facts to influence his thinking.

4. **Guilt by Association.** When you assume a stranger is good or bad, guilty or innocent simply because of the people he associates with, you are committing the guilt by association fallacy. Judging people by the company they keep is a strong human urge that is hard to resist. It seems natural that 'birds of a feather flock together' and so people come to know individuals by who they socialize

---

[27] In 1983, psychologists Daniel Kahnerman and Amos Tversky conducted an experiment known as the 'Linda Problem' where they described a woman's personality and let students decide whether she was a bank teller or a bank teller and a feminist. Most of the students committed the conjunction fallacy when they chose her as more likely to be a bank teller and feminist.

[28] *Scientific American, Lessons from Sherlock Holmes: Why Most of Us Wouldn't Be Able to Tell That Watson Fought in Afghanistan* by Maria Konnikova, November 1, 2011. Ms. Konnikova is also the author of *Mastermind: How To Think Like Sherlock Holmes,* wherein she also discusses the conjunction fallacy in detail.

or hangout with. The key to avoiding this fallacy is simply judging a person based on his or her own actions and not solely by the people he or she associates with.

5. **Hasty Generalization.** When you reach general conclusions that rely on one or two limited facts, you are making the hasty generalization fallacy. This fallacy is so easy to make because its human nature to generalize about people. Sherlock Holmes always stayed on guard against making hasty generalizations. How? He always made sure he had specific data first. He did not allow any prejudice or bias to enter into his thinking because he did his homework before reaching a conclusion.

6. **Composition/Division.** When you assume because something is true about a specific part it is also true about the whole, you are committing the composition fallacy. For example, when you infer because a stranger exhibits one positive personality trait such as kindness, that the stranger's whole personality is positive or kind. A stranger can express kindness and still treat you cruelly. The opposite of this is the division fallacy, where you assume that because something is true about the whole it is also true about a specific part. For example, this fallacy occurs when you assume that because a baseball team is good that every player on the team is equally good.

7. **False Cause.** This fallacy is one of the most common reasoning mistakes people make when sizing up strangers. They judge a person based on the wrong cause. Often there are several possible causes for a stranger's appearance or behavior. Sometimes a common cause exists that explains it. Other times a cause may have a correlation with another event that makes it seem like it is related when in fact it is not. Sometimes the cause happens right before the effect and so it seems to have caused it. Sherlock Holmes always considered

various possibilities when evaluating causes. He separated relevant facts from unnecessary ones. He sought to interpret the facts accurately relying on the most probable cause.

8. **Face Value Fallacy.** When you judge a person by their appearance without considering other factors, you commit this fallacy. Many people assume physically attractive people have positive personalities. They assume rich people are successful in their personal lives. They assume intelligent people are smart in all subjects. They assume baby face people are innocent or trustworthy. The truth is you cannot always judge a book by its cover. Just because a person appears a certain way does not mean that is who they are. Sherlock Holmes never took people at face value.

Identifying logical fallacies is just one aspect of reasoning accurately. To reason accurately means to think critically. It means to use the rules of deduction singly or in various combinations. It means to separate opinion from fact. It means to rely on facts or the dependable evidence of facts. It means to think for your self and require proof. It means to remain skeptical. Sherlock Holmes applied this philosophy in everyday life when he said in *The Reigate Puzzle*: "I make a point of never having any prejudices and of following docilely wherever fact may lead me."

Control Your Feelings Like Sherlock Holmes

In addition to following the facts, you must also control your feelings to think accurately. Sherlock Holmes trained himself to control his feelings. He did not let emotions bias his mind. In *A Scandal in Bohemia*, Watson noted about Holmes:

"All emotions...were abhorrent to his cold, precise but admirably balanced mind...He never spoke of the softer passions, save with a gibe and a sneer. They were

111

admirable things for the observer — excellent for drawing the veil from men's motives and actions. But for the trained reasoner to admit such intrusions into his own delicate and finely adjusted temperament was to introduce a distracting factor which might throw a doubt upon all his mental results. Grit in a sensitive instrument, or a crack in one of his own high-power lenses, would not be more disturbing than a strong emotion in a nature such as his..."

In *The Sign of Four,* Watson described Holmes as being: "...an automation — a calculating machine." Indeed, Holmes possessed a scientific mind and used *reason* as his primary thinking tool. He once said, "Whatever is emotional is opposed to that true cold reason which *I place above all things.*" Train yourself to not depend solely on your feelings when making judgments about people. Watson let his feelings influence his thinking, which is why he often missed clues about people and romanticized the writing in his Holmesian chronicles.

Holmes often complained how when Watson wrote about his adventures; Watson romanticized his method rather than focusing on logic. Holmes stated to Watson: "Detection is, or ought to be, an exact science and should be treated in the same cold and unemotional manner." Holmes believed that feelings had little or no place in his logical method. He always sought to keep his emotions in check.

For example, Holmes would deliberately suppress his feelings when interviewing a client. He would focus on the facts and evidence when applying his rules of deduction. In *The Sign of Four,* Mary Morstan sobbed while she told the story about her missing father. Holmes ignored her tearful manner. He coldly requested the last date her father came home. Holmes did not allow a client's emotional state of mind to keep him from getting the facts.

He also would not allow Watson to embellish the facts when describing people or places to him. In *The Adventure of the Retired Colourman,* Holmes stopped Watson from giving a flowery description of a wall. He said: "Cut out the poetry, Watson...I note it was a high brick wall."

Keeping his feelings under control is why Sherlock Holmes often appeared cold and distant with people. It is why Holmes stated he would never marry because his emotions for his wife would bias his judgment. It is why *Holmes valued reason more than anything else.* And it is why Holmes used his rules of deduction, rather than his emotions, to size up strangers and investigate crime.

The Sherlock Holmes rules of deduction are basic concepts that the average person can use. In fact, you probably already apply the rules while using informal logic in your everyday life. You do not need to know technical terms to use these rational rules. You do not have to delve deeper into sophisticated logical formulas to reason properly. But, if you should want to learn more about reason and logic, then use the principle in the next chapter. It will aid you in finding any information you seek.

Go to Pages 302 to 312 if you want to practice
the logic and reason exercises now.

Chapter 4

Learn Holmes's Key
To Evaluating
Any Stranger You Meet

"...I have a lot of special knowledge, which I apply to the problem...."
Sherlock Holmes, A Study In Scarlet

I n *The Sign of Four,* Sherlock Holmes described to Watson how French Detective Francois Le Villard consulted him on a case involving a Will. Holmes suggested two parallel cases that enabled Detective Le Villard to solve the case.

According to Sherlock Holmes, Detective Le Villard possessed "...two out of the three qualities necessary for the ideal detective. He has the power of observation and that of deduction. He is only wanting in knowledge, and that may come in time." As Sherlock Holmes noted, before Francois Le Villard could become a proficient detective, he had to first acquire specialized knowledge.

Specialized knowledge, as defined in this book, is the detailed information you need to size up a stranger. It is the knowledge you gain from researching different subjects that will improve your ability to read people. It is the data you use to recognize subtle cues with the strangers you meet. The average person misses the cues because they do not have specific training to guide them. This chapter will reveal why you need specialized knowledge to size up strangers, what you can do to acquire it and how you can use it.

Study with a Specific Purpose

In *A Study In Scarlet,* after Dr. Watson had roomed with Holmes for several weeks at 221B Baker Street, he became curious as to what Holmes did for a living. Watson noticed that Holmes's zeal for studying bordered on fanatical. Watson thought to himself: "...no man would work so hard or attain such precise information unless he had some definite end in view."

Dr. Watson began to ponder over his conversations with Holmes and tried to figure out his occupation. He remembered Holmes told him once during a short conversation that he would acquire no knowledge that did not bear upon his object. Therefore, Watson reasoned, all the knowledge Sherlock Holmes obtained he used towards a goal.

Watson eventually learned that Sherlock Holmes amassed a lot of out-of-the-way knowledge because he used it in his work as a consulting detective. He learned that Holmes had a passion for definite and exact knowledge. Finally, he learned that Sherlock Holmes only cared about knowledge that had a direct bearing on his work.

In *The Five Orange Pips,* Holmes told Watson: "...a man should possess all knowledge which is likely to be useful to him in his work, and this I have endeavored in my case to do." As a result, Watson soon realized that: "Sherlock Holmes's smallest actions were all directed towards a definite and practical end."

Holmes studied subjects such as opium, poisons, geology, chemistry, anatomy, crime literature and British law. These subjects had a direct relevance to his detective consulting service. Holmes trained himself to read tire tracks, fingerprints, tattoos, handwriting, footprints, perfumes, mud stains, bloodstains and other obscure trace evidence.

He did this until he became a recognized expert in these areas. Holmes's expertise allowed him to publish at least ten scientific monographs throughout his career. Experts translated several monographs he wrote into other languages, with many becoming the final word in their fields. You do not have to write a technical monograph or become an expert in obscure things like Sherlock. You must, however, have a specific goal in mind if you want to learn his method. The goal you choose will determine what you study.

For example, if you choose to become a salesperson, you would study sales techniques to help you increase customer sales. You would study sales psychology: how to open up customers to make them receptive to your pitch. You would study what motivates customers to buy. You would study how to read a customer's non-verbal clues to tell when you can close the sale. Once you set a goal, you can then use the key that unlocks the special knowledge you need to achieve it.

The Key to Getting Specialized Knowledge

Watson first met Sherlock Holmes as he conducted a chemical experiment in a laboratory at a hospital. At the time, Holmes did not concern himself with anything that did not relate to fighting crime. It stunned Watson to discover he knew next to nothing about contemporary literature, philosophy or politics.

In fact, Holmes only read the criminal news and agony columns. In *A Study in Scarlet,* he once told Watson after finding out that the earth travelled around the sun: "...What the deuce is it to me? If we went around the moon it would not make a pennyworth of difference to me or to my work."

As time passed, however, Sherlock Holmes's beliefs about what information he needed and its importance to his work slowly evolved. He soon learned knowledge does not end after you gain expertise on a specific subject. As a result, Holmes began seeking knowledge from different sources and not just the obscure areas that held his interest.

Sherlock Holmes became knowledgeable in politics (*A Scandal in Bohemia*). He learned about events in America (*The Valley of Fear*). He sprinkled his conversations with indirect mentions from the bible (*The Golden Pince-Nez*). He discussed Shakespeare (*The Empty House*). He spoke about Art (*The Three Gables*). He listened to Music (*The Cardboard Box*). He talked in Latin (*The Abbey Grange*). Sherlock Holmes did all this until he finally reached the conclusion that "All knowledge becomes useful to the detective."

The key to Holmes evolving and getting knowledge is that he *kept an open mind and desired to learn new things.* In fact, Holmes made it a point to always take on only unusual or bizarre cases. He believed these cases had the most fascinating features about them. This desire to investigate only the most peculiar cases is what kept his mind open.

It is what allowed him to grow in knowledge regarding his particular interest. *The Adventure of the Red Circle,* best expresses Holmes's evolution from only having an interest in a narrow range of subjects to learning about a wide area of interests. In that case he told Watson: "Education never ends...It is a series of lessons with the greatest for the last."

The Information You Need To Size-Up Strangers

Like Sherlock Holmes, your education should never end but continue as a series of lessons. In fact, your education in his method should begin with the 'Canon.' The Canon is all the original Sherlock Holmes stories and novels that Sir Arthur Conan Doyle wrote throughout his lifetime. If you have not already done so, read the 56 short stories and 4 novels. Read and study these stories like Christians study the Bible. Read them repeatedly so you can learn something new each time.

The series of lessons you will learn start with the Canon but your education will not end with it. After you read the Canon, branch out into reading related Sherlock Holmes articles and stories other authors have written for deeper insight. But always remember that the Canon is the foundation upon which you must build your knowledge in the Holmes method.

Sherlock Holmes built his special knowledge through reading. In *The Valley of Fear,* he once told Scotland Yard Inspector Alex MacDonald that: "...the most practical thing that you ever did in your life would be to shut yourself up for three months and read twelve hours a day at the annals of crime." Although Holmes had referred to reading crime history, he could just as easily have talked about reading any subject where you need special knowledge.

Once you decide on the specific information you need, whether its body language, psychology, logic and so forth, you must take time and read up on the subject. Holmes himself read extensively on topics that interested him. For example, in *The Adventure of the Lion's Mane,* he spoke about himself as being an omnivorous reader.

After you have established a goal, kept an open mind and read all the original Sherlock Holmes stories, you need specific information that will enable you to size up strangers. For example, understanding a person's body language — the facial expressions they make, the gestures they use, how they sit, stand and walk — is information you can research to make you better at sizing up a stranger.

Learning about psychology — understanding the human mind, how it works, the motives, the conscious and unconscious processes — is information you can study to make you better at evaluating people. Chapter 2 gave you a brief body language and psychology overview to start you in the right direction. You must now do additional research to learn detailed information about these subjects.

Specialized Knowledge is Easily Available and Acquired

You can research subjects by consulting reliable sources that will help you obtain the information necessary to size up a stranger. When Sherlock Holmes needed information, he consulted reliable sources such as encyclopedias and almanacs. In *The Five Orange Pips,* Holmes used the *American Encyclopedia* to look up information on the Ku Klux Klan. Researching the encyclopedia enabled him to pursue John Openshaw's killers.

In *The Valley of Fear,* Holmes used *Whitaker's Almanac* to decipher a coded message sent to him by an undercover operative. In Holmes' time, encyclopedias and almanacs were the main informational sources available to anyone who needed knowledge on specific subjects. In modern times, you have access to more informational sources than Holmes ever could have imagined.

Specialized knowledge is easily available and acquired in modern times if you are willing to put in the effort to find it. The information you need to size up strangers is available from a wide variety of reliable sources. You can obtain the information you need to become proficient in the Sherlock Holmes Method from five major sources. The five major informational sources are as follows:

1. **The Internet.** No matter what subject you are interested in learning about, you can find it on the Internet. Looking for information on reading body language? Fashion? Micro-expressions? Logic? Tattoos? The Internet is the go to source for these subjects and any other topic you need to know.

As you search the Internet for informational sources, however, keep in mind not all the sources are reliable. Only go to websites and blogs that are reputable. You can use search engines such as *Google, Bing* or *Internet Explorer* to look for specific topics. You can go to websites such as *YouTube* to watch videos on the information you seek. You can search social media websites such as *Facebook* that allow you to interact with other people who may have the information you need. The Internet did not exist in Sherlock Holmes's time. He used his own personal reference and filing system to collect and record information. Today, the Internet allows you easy access to specialized knowledge that Holmes never dreamed of finding.

2. **The Public Library.** This great institution is still relevant in the 21st Century. It has remade itself to reflect the modern times we currently live. Walk into almost any library and you will find computers that give you free access to the Internet. You can find specialized knowledge in the many books on its shelves. Librarians remain available to assist you in your search. Many libraries now loan e-books in addition to the paper bound books that line their shelves. You can also research specialized knowledge at private and corporate libraries that allow public access. These libraries cater to technical and business fields and have a wealth of specialized knowledge you can use if you know what you want.

3. **Books.** Many people still read hard cover and paperback books. You can find specialized books on most topics at *Barnes & Noble* and other retail bookstores. You can also buy books and articles on the information you need on the Internet through such online sellers as *Amazon.* E-books are rising in popularity because they are easy to use and simple to read. You can also search for hard-to-

find or out of print books online or at specialty bookstores in your local area.

4. **Colleges or Universities.** These higher learning institutions teach subjects such as psychology, science, philosophy and other topics that give you insight into human nature. You can find specialized knowledge and get the learning you need in your field of interest through attending college courses.

5. **Specialized Training/Courses.** You can seek a job or career that will train you in the special area you set as a goal. For example, you could get specialized training from law enforcement agencies such as the New York City Police Department, FBI or CIA. You can take specialized training courses from accredited teachers at night schools and technical training academies. These classes are usually devoted to special knowledge on out of the way subjects. You can also get online training from schools or experts on the Internet. These experts conduct in person training upon request. Expert trainers such as *Eyes for Lies (www.eyesforlies.com)* teach deception detection skills. Institutions such as *The Learning Center (www.learningcenter.com)* teach courses on many topics.

In addition to knowing where to get specialized knowledge, Sherlock Holmes also took advantage of the technology of his time. He often used modern 19th century technology when investigating a crime scene or sizing up total strangers. In *The Five Orange Pips,* he used a telegraph. In *A Case of Identity*, he used a typewriter.

In The *Shoscombe Old Place,* he used a microscope. In *The Adventure of the Missing Three-Quarter,* he used a telegram. In *The Mazarin Stone,* he used a gramophone. In *The Lions Mane,* he used an enlarged photograph. In *The Retired Colourman,* he used a telephone. Sherlock Holmes used these aids to solve crimes.

Just as Sherlock Holmes did, you can use modern technology to obtain the special knowledge you need to size up strangers. Modern devices such as your desktop or laptop computer can search the Internet for the information. Portable hand-held electronic devices such as tablets, smart phones and smart watches can help you obtain precise information while you are on the move.

You can discuss any questions you have with other like-minded Sherlockians on social media websites such as *Facebook*. You can use *Twitter* to follow specific individuals for information that interests you. All of the above are reliable sources to search for and obtain the exact knowledge you need. Once you have obtained the specialized knowledge, the next step is to use it.

How to Use Specialized Knowledge

You need two kinds of knowledge to size up a stranger. One is general and the other is specialized. General knowledge relies on experience, everyday living and common sense. You learn it from the school of hard knocks — the streets, the battlefield, the playing field; in other words, actual 'do or die' real life situations.

Specialized knowledge, on the other hand, relies on education, research and training. You learn it from the school of study — the classroom, the laboratory, the training facility; in other words, stimulated teaching environments. Each type of knowledge is crucial to the other and is most effective when used *together.*

Most people already possess general knowledge that they learn from personal experience and everyday living. Many people take their general knowledge for granted because they obtain it with little or no effort or cost. Their general knowledge is often inaccurate because it relies on their feelings, biases, assumptions, beliefs, experiences and expectations. They often waste general knowledge because they rarely *use* it or if they do use it, they use it improperly.

When an individual seeks specialized knowledge, however, they usually do so with a specific goal in mind. The individual will seek specific information he or she needs to use towards fulfilling a definite purpose. The person who seeks specialized knowledge usually does not take it for granted because he or she pays for it or puts much effort into getting it. Their specialized knowledge is often accurate because it relies on facts and evidence. They do not waste specialized knowledge because they use it *often* and correctly.

Specialized knowledge is important because it helps you to *recognize* details. It allows you to *know* what you are looking at. It assists you in making *sense* of the facts you find. It enables you to draw *meaning* from what you discover. It lets you fill in the *blanks* when information is missing. Sherlock Holmes used specialized knowledge to size up strangers in these ways:

Holmes Applied Specialized Knowledge to the Strangers He Met and Problems He Faced. In *The Boscombe Valley Mystery,* Sherlock Holmes stated his special knowledge of tobacco ashes enabled him to pinpoint accurately the specific cigar type he found at the crime scene. It also enabled him to deduce that the culprit smoked an Indian cigar with a cigar holder. In *The Hound of the Baskervilles,* Holmes's special knowledge of newspaper type enabled him to tell which newspaper the words in a sentence came from. In *A Case of Identity,* Holmes's special knowledge of typewriter keys enabled him to reveal the real suspect behind four letters written to a young woman who sought his counsel.

After you learn or get training in a subject, use the special knowledge you obtain. Apply it in your everyday life with the people you know, the strangers you meet or the job you work. For example, a *Transportation Security Administration (TSA)* agent may get specialized training in reading micro-expressions. He will use the *Micro Expression Training Tool (METT)* software program from recognized expert Doctor Paul Ekman. The TSA agent will then apply what he learned from the program to the real world. He will watch travelers' micro-expressions as the travelers enter the airport and check their bags. He will then pick out travelers for further questioning based on his special knowledge and training.

Once you apply your special knowledge and prior training to a problem or person, you will find it becomes easier to figure out the problem or decipher the person's behavior. The reason for this is that you will have prepared yourself through research and study. The more you research and study a specific subject, the better you will become. The more you use the special knowledge you obtain, the easier you can draw upon that knowledge when you need it. In *The Adventure of the Three Garridebs,* Holmes stated to a client: "In my profession all sorts of odd knowledge comes useful."

Holmes Used Specialized Knowledge to Recognize Things Others Missed. In *The Red-Headed League,* Holmes and Watson saw and heard the same facts. Yet, Holmes came away with far more information than Watson and predicted the case outcome. In *The Adventure of The Noble Bachelor,* Watson heard what Holmes heard regarding a problem presented to them. Yet, Sherlock Holmes solved the problem before the client even entered the room. What was the main difference between Holmes and Watson?

Holmes possessed specialized knowledge!

In *A Study in Scarlet,* Holmes explained to Watson how he spotted relevant facts from a garden path: "...No doubt to you it appeared to be a mere trampled line of slush, but to my trained eyes every mark upon its surface had a meaning." So, it is with spotting specific details about a stranger. Without prior knowledge, you will miss subtle meanings in the person's appearance. Without prior training, you will skip slight messages in the person's behavior. In both cases, you are likely to overlook small but important details.

For example, a stranger's tattoos may look like elaborate, fancy designs to the average person. To the trained eye, however, every 'tat' has a meaning. A detective, who has prior knowledge and training on recognizing prison tattoos, can tell at a glance the stranger's criminal status. The detective can tell whether the stranger is a gang member. He can tell if the stranger is part of a criminal organization such as the Russian Mafia, the Tong, the Arian Nation or the Crips and the Blood street gangs.

The trained detective can tell just by looking at a prison tattoo if the stranger went to prison. He can tell how long he stayed in prison. He can tell his status in the criminal world. He can tell how many murders the stranger committed. He can even tell the city or country the stranger comes from. All this from knowing the meanings of the particular tattoos the stranger wears on his face and body.

In the movie *Eastern Promises (2007)*, actor Viggo Mortensen plays an uncover agent who infiltrates the Russian Mafia. He wore several tattoos on his body, which depicted his status in the Russian criminal world. The crucifix on his chest revealed him as a thief. The three church domes on his back showed he served three terms in prison. He earned a star on his shoulder that showed him as a man of dignity, honor and who lived by the Russian criminal code. He also earned a star on his kneecap, which designated him as a high-ranking captain. It symbolized that he would never kneel down before anyone.

As the world's first consulting detective, Sherlock Holmes used his special knowledge of tattoos to size up the strangers he met. In *A Study in Scarlet,* Holmes read a stranger's blue anchor hand tattoo to determine the stranger was a marine.

In *The Red-Headed League,* Holmes read a stranger's fish tattoo on his wrist to determine the stranger had traveled to China. In *The "Gloria Scott,"* Holmes read blurred tattoo initials on a stranger's elbow to determine that the stranger wished to forget about a particular person.

Every mark has a meaning to the trained specialist!

A person, who has special knowledge on a specific subject such as body language, will spot subtle physical signs faster than the average person. An individual who has special training on a subject such as psychology will recognize mental red flags faster than someone who never had any training. The special knowledge and training you acquire will give you greater insight into people. You will have better perception because you will *know* what you are looking at.

Holmes Used Specialized Knowledge to Separate Important Facts from Non-essential Facts. Specialized knowledge helps you to make sense of what you see. It helps you draw significance from details you discover about strangers. The reason having prior knowledge and training is critical is because not every detail you notice is important or relevant.

You must learn to distinguish between important and relevant details and unimportant and insignificant ones. Some details about strangers are ambiguous. If you cannot tell the difference between minor details that are relevant and those that are not, you will reach the wrong conclusions. Train yourself to gather as many *relevant* details about strangers as you can when you first meet them. A relevant detail is a fact that you can use to size up a stranger.

In *The Red-Headed League,* Watson observed several incidental facts about Mr. Wilson such as his worn, faded and drab-colored clothes. Watson missed the vital facts regarding Mr. Wilson's appearance. Why? The reason is Watson focused on his baggy gray trousers, black frock coat, frayed top hat and faded brown overcoat. What were the vital facts? Mr. Wilson's shiny right cuff, smooth elbow patch, fish tattoo, muscular right hand and arc-and-compass breastpin.

In *A Case of Identity,* Watson observed several incidental facts about Miss Mary Sutherland such as her colorful clothing. Watson missed the vital facts regarding Miss Sutherland's appearance. Why? The reason is Watson focused on her red-feathered straw hat, black jacket, brown dress and gray gloves. What were the vital facts? Miss Sutherland's plush sleeve, marks on her nose, half button boots and violet ink on her finger. Both times Watson failed to spot the relevant facts because he focused on things he could not use to evaluate the person.

Many times when Sherlock Holmes investigated a case or sized up a stranger, he used his special knowledge to determine the most important fact, the main clue or the key issue. In *The Valley of Fear* case, the most important fact was the missing barbell. In the *Silver Blaze* case, the main clue was the silent dog. In the *Lady Frances Carfax* case, the key issue was the oversized coffin. Holmes's specialized knowledge enabled him to find the vital facts in these cases, and as a result, he solved them.

In *The Reigate Puzzle,* Holmes once said, "It is of the highest importance in the act of detection to be able to recognize, out of a number of facts, which are incidental and which are vital." In *The Naval Treaty,* Holmes stated: "The principal difficulty...lay in the fact of there being too much evidence. What was vital was overlaid and hidden by what was irrelevant. Of all the facts which were presented to us we had to pick just those which we deemed to be essential."

In *The Crooked Man*, Holmes said: *"...*Having gathered these facts, Watson, I smoked several pipes over them, trying to separate those which were crucial from others which were merely incidental." Holmes then explained how he used his special knowledge of tracing footprints to determine the presence in the room of the individual and creature he brought with him.

You can separate important facts from unimportant facts by first asking yourself does the fact help you evaluate the stranger. You can also ask yourself what do you know about the stranger. Then measure each fact in your mind and consider other possibilities. Then balance each fact against the other and decide which facts are vital. Last, place the vital facts in order in your mind. All this may seem complicated but if you do it every time you meet someone it will become second nature to you.

Holmes Used Specialized Knowledge to Understand Human Behavior. In many of his cases, Holmes used his knowledge of everyday psychology to understand both his clients and potential suspects. For example, in *The Adventure of the Dying Detective,* he knew suspected killer Culverton Smith would admit to murder when he requested for Watson to bring Mr. Smith to him. Holmes then set a trap for Mr. Smith and lured him into it with Watson's unsuspecting aide. Holmes would later tell Watson: "Knowing his vindictive nature, I was perfectly certain that he would come to look upon his handiwork."

In other cases, Holmes shows a deep understanding of human nature when he uses reverse psychology to obtain information he seeks. In *The Adventure of the Missing Three-Quarter,* miser Lord Mount-James adamantly refuses to pay any costs in finding his missing nephew. Holmes convinces the miser to cover the costs in the search. He tells the miser that kidnappers might use his nephew to gain access to his wealth. The miser immediately offers his financial assistance.

As they travel up the road after leaving the miser, Watson expresses his doubts that kidnappers took the nephew to get at his wealthy uncle. Holmes replies: "I confess, my dear Watson, that that does not appeal to me as a very probable explanation. It struck me, however, as being the one which was most likely to interest that exceedingly unpleasant old person."

Sherlock Holmes further demonstrates his psychological knowledge in *A Scandal in Bohemia.* In this case, Holmes gets Irene Adler to unknowingly reveal her secret hiding place. He tells Watson: "When a woman thinks that her house is on fire, her instinct is at once to rush to the thing which she values most...A married woman grabs at her baby; an unmarried one reaches for her jewel box."

It is clear from the many case histories Watson chronicled that Sherlock Holmes had specialized knowledge of 'type psychology' and used it to size up strangers. In *A Study in Scarlet,* Holmes thought to himself upon meeting Watson for the first time: "Here is a gentleman of a medical type, but with the air of a military man. Clearly an army doctor...."

In *The Greek Interpreter,* Sherlock and Mycroft Holmes engage in sizing up strangers through types. Mycroft states: "To anyone who wishes to study mankind, this is the spot...Look at the magnificent types!" In *The Illustrious Client,* Holmes states: "Women of the De Merville type do not act like that." These examples show how Holmes may have learned typology from his life experiences and adapted it to the practical 'system' he had already formed.

Just as Sherlock Holmes did, learn about the various typology theories (personality types, body types, etc.). Then adapt them into your own personal system. Rather than rely on a specific typology theory to help you label people, use whatever works for you. The fact is human nature is both simple and complex. It is simple in that every human being is alike and predictable. It is complex in that every human being is also unique and unpredictable. You can label or categorize people, but keep an open mind. Remain flexible with your evaluations and classifications.

Sherlock Holmes also excelled in what we now know as criminal profiling.[29] His specialized knowledge in this field is evident when he profiles a criminal from the trace evidence left at a crime scene. In *The Boscombe Valley Mystery*, Holmes tells detective Lestrade that the murderer:

> "Is a tall man, left-handed, limps with the right leg, wears thick-soled shooting-boots and a gray cloak, smokes Indian cigars, uses a cigar-holder, and carries a blunt pen-knife in his pocket."

Holmes had already developed criminal profiling as part of his investigative system. He did it over fifty years before the *Federal Bureau of Investigation* (FBI) implemented criminal profiling at its' Behavioral Analysis Unit. It took another fifty years before it became popular on TV shows such as *Criminal Minds (2005)* and *Profiler (2011)*. For example, in the *Criminal Minds* episode 'Tabula Rasa', Special Agent Hotch uses the Sherlock Holmes Method to profile a lawyer.[30]

In addition to knowing about criminal psychology, Holmes also used his knowledge of 19th century English caste society to classify the strangers he met. In London, each class had a specific social status, which enabled Holmes to size them easily up.[31] The upper class included kings, queens, princes, lords and

---

[29] Modern day criminal profiling is under fire. See http://www.skepdic.com/refuge/funk58.html.

[30] You can view the video clip on YouTube (http:// www.youtube.com/ watch?v=LPNvATtE3vA.

[31] Some critics believe Holmes could not size-up strangers easily today because much has changed since the 19th Century. These critics say the Holmes's method is not practical in modern times. They say in Holmes's day England had a caste society where its people had rigid lifestyles easily defined

ladies that had titles and privilege because they came from a royal bloodline or owned land. The middle class included shopkeepers, British tradesmen and merchants who relied on the English economy. The lower class included physical laborers, servants, country folk and small farmers who did manual labor and other minimal duties.

In *The Adventure of the Abbey Grange,* Holmes demonstrates his knowledge of Victorian class distinctions. He explains to Captain Jack Crocker how he knew where Lady Brackenstall and the captain met. He said: "Only once had this lady been brought into contact with sailors, and that was on her voyage, and it was someone of her own class of life."

In *The Adventure of the Second Stain,* Holmes explains to Watson his suspicion regarding Lady Hilda Trelawney Hope based on her position in London society: "What was the fair lady's game? What did she really want? Think of her appearance, Watson — her manner, her suppressed excitement, her restlessness, her tenacity in asking questions. Remember that she comes of a caste who do not lightly show emotion."

Sherlock Holmes combined his specialized knowledge of criminal, everyday psychology, personality, body types, and the 19th century Victorian class system to create his method. In order for you to become proficient in the Sherlock Holmes Method, you must also obtain similar specialized knowledge to understand human behavior.

---

by their station in life. They say most men who wore tattoos were in the military, sailors or from the lower part of society. They claim most women worked in professions such as music teachers, seamstresses, nannies and so forth. The critics argue Holmes would have a hard time sizing up strangers today because both men and women wear tattoos. They say we live in a society with many different cultures. They say women and minorities are no longer bound to specific professions or traditions. To these critics the author says the *questions* and *principles* Holmes used have not changed. They remain just as practical now as they did in his time. Therefore, Holmes would still deduce strangers in modern times like he did in Victorian times.

Holmes Used Specialized Knowledge to Solve Similar Problems by Comparing Them To Past Cases or Individuals. Whenever Sherlock Holmes encountered a stranger or came upon a new case, he looked for similarities with past people and crimes he already knew. Once he found similar elements or details, he used them to understand the current case or stranger.

For example, in *A Study in Scarlet,* Holmes used his prior knowledge of previous crimes to compare a current crime scene where a possible murder occurred. As he examined the body, he stated to Detectives Gregson and Lestrade that the current murder reminded him of a similar case in 1834. He suggested Detective Gregson read up on it because: "...There is nothing new under the sun. It has all been done before."

In *The Red-Headed League,* Holmes stated: "As a rule, when I have heard some slight indication of the course of events, I am able to guide myself by...thousands of other similar cases." In *The Adventure of the Noble Bachelor,* Holmes had already formed his conclusions to a case before the client entered the room. When Watson exclaimed in shock that he heard everything Holmes had heard, he replied: "Without, however, the knowledge of preexisting cases which serves me so well."

In *The Adventure of the Engineer's Thumb,* crooks needed to fix their counterfeit coin printing press. Holmes deduced, from previously knowing about an ad placed in a newspaper, that the criminals sought a missing hydraulic engineer. Holmes kept the newspaper clipping in a commonplace book on his shelf. He knew to make the connection between the engineer with the missing thumb and the first engineer who disappeared a year ago. The similarity in the engineer's story is what made Holmes realize the connection that the criminals needed the new engineer to service the machine again.

In Chapter 2, you learned how to observe relevant details about a stranger. Specialized knowledge will help you to use those details to identify similarities and differences. It will help you to recognize connections in the people you meet. When you meet a stranger, ask yourself: What do I already know that can help me understand this person? What characteristics, traits or gestures does this individual have in common with others that I have met in the past? As you see the similarities, the differences will leap out at you. As he investigated a case or sized up a stranger, this often happened to Sherlock Holmes.

Holmes Used Specialized Knowledge To Think of More Possibilities. In Chapter 3, you learned about reason by elimination (Rule 4) and how it may not account for all possibilities regarding a stranger or problem. Special knowledge or training can help you minimize errors in using this rule because it can increase your awareness of other possibilities.

The training and knowledge you get by studying a specific subject can open your mind to other possibilities you may not have considered before. You can also use special knowledge and training to self-correct yourself by asking questions. The questions you ask will help you minimize any faulty reasoning from insufficient evidence. Reasoning from incomplete data is the reasoning by elimination rule's Achilles heel.

When Sherlock Holmes encountered a problem, he would turn over the matter in his mind for days on end. He did it until he considered all possible outcomes. In *The Man with the Twisted Lip,* Watson described him in this way:

> "Sherlock Holmes was a man...who, when he had an unsolved problem upon his mind, would go for days, and even for a week, without rest, turning it over, rearranging his facts, looking at it from every point of view until he had either fathomed it or convinced himself that his data were insufficient."

In *The Naval Treaty,* Holmes had stated during an investigation that: "...we are bound to take every possibility into account." He then said he had seven possible clues to the problem, which values he could ascertain only by testing them. In *The Adventure of the Norwood Builder,* Holmes told Detective Lestrade that he could give him half a dozen theories. Holmes said each theory would fit the facts in the case but that he only wanted to point out other possible theories.

Holmes's ability to eliminate the impossible and come to the correct conclusion partly relies on the specialized knowledge he acquired throughout his long career as a consulting detective. He used the special knowledge he obtained to think over every possible solution to a puzzle until he found the answer. But sometimes, it was not enough. In those cases, Holmes relied on the next approach to reduce any mistakes in his logic.

Holmes Used Specialized Knowledge to Minimize Errors in Reasoning. You can use logic to reach clear and concise conclusions. You can just as easily reason improperly and reach invalid conclusions. Sherlock Holmes always corrected himself by checking his reasoning. Sometimes he checked his reasoning against his prior knowledge for any flaws in his thinking.

In *The Adventure of the Speckled Band,* Sherlock Holmes stated he had come to an erroneous conclusion because he had reasoned from insufficient data. He reconsidered his position when he realized a snake came through the ventilator. He then solved the mystery when he combined his knowledge about the snake with his knowledge that the doctor received a shipment of creatures from India.

Several times, Sherlock Holmes checked his logic by outlining his reasoning process to Watson. In *Silver Blaze,* Holmes tells Watson: "...nothing clears up a case so much as stating it to another person." Other times he checked his logic by testing his reasoning. In *The Man with the Twisted Lip,* Holmes mentioned to Watson: "I want to test a little theory of mine." He then went on to verify that a suspect the London police held in a cell was the man he searched for.

In *A Case of Identity,* Sherlock Holmes verified a theory that James Windibank wore a disguise to fool his stepdaughter. Holmes contacted Windibank's employer. Holmes then had the company send him Mr. Windibank's physical description. Once he saw the physical description, Holmes knew he had his man. These cases, establish that Holmes always checked his reasoning against his special knowledge.

Holmes Used Specialized Knowledge to Spot Patterns. In *The Adventure of the Creeping Man,* Holmes noticed a pattern in Professor Presbury's bizarre behavior that coincided with specific dates. He used his specialized knowledge in analyzing secret writings and codes[32] to decipher the rather elementary pattern before him. Holmes believed the professor's behavioral outbreaks were not mere coincidence. He formed a theory that "...every nine days the professor takes some strong drug which has a passing but highly poisonous effect." Holmes's theory proved correct. He noticed a dog's reaction to the professor and solved the mystery.

Just as Sherlock Holmes recognized a pattern in seemingly unrelated dates, so can you learn to recognize patterns in a stranger's behavior. You will find it easy, not hard to do, because you are by nature a pattern-seeking individual. Although most people do it on an unconscious level, you can learn to identify a pattern faster once you consciously make yourself aware of what you are doing.

The key to recognizing overall patterns is to look at each detail as part of a larger picture. For example, a chess master

---

[32] In *The Adventure of the Dancing Men,* Holmes states that he is familiar with all forms of secret writings and wrote a monograph on the subject in which he analyzed 160 separate ciphers.

looks at each past move an opponent makes on the chessboard as part of an overall pattern. He then determines the future moves the opponent will make so he can counter them.

Another way to recognize patterns is to change your perspective and the way you look at people. Step back and ask yourself is there anything you did not consider. For example, an expert poker player will watch closely how a dealer gives out the cards to each player. He will study how the player reacts to the hand he or she receives. If the expert poker player gets no clues from this strategy, he may take a mental step back to gain an advantage. He will consider the patterns in each opponent's playing style such as their body language or the way they hold the cards.

In *The Musgrave Ritual,* Sherlock Holmes used his special knowledge like an expert poker player. He recognized a pattern in seemingly unrelated information. He informed Watson that he sought to piece together events from the case into a common thread by which he could solve the mystery. He studied the Ritual and deduced from it relevant details that led him directly to the dead butler. This knowledge enabled him to see a pattern in the raw material. He then understood the Ritual's meaning and significance. He used both deductive and inductive reasoning to identify the Ritual's pattern and solve the mystery.

In the *Silver Blaze* mystery, Holmes expected a specific behavior pattern from a dog. When he discovered the dog did not bark it made him suspicious. Holmes always looked for patterns in things or people when he started an investigation. He would expect an event or behavior to occur. When it did not happen he would notice anything missing. His special knowledge enabled him to tell when something did not occur that should have.

He could see what others missed because he already started looking for it. He had already formed a theory that it should happen. Untrained people sometimes miss patterns because they cannot see where the seemingly unrelated data fits in the pattern. For example, an individual who has no body language training may focus on one specific gesture rather than a group of gestures when sizing up a stranger. He will therefore miss whether the person is truthful.

Yet, although Sherlock Holmes looked for patterns in the events and people he met, he did not become a slave to them. He recognized that it is human nature to see patterns in things or people *even when they do not exist.* He therefore always remained on guard against making connections between unrelated things and people.

How did Sherlock Holmes do this? He always asked himself the third basic question: "How Can I Verify It?" He relied on his critical thinking skills and always self-corrected himself. He did not blind himself to things that did not fit his theory and double-checked his logic. He always applied the special knowledge he obtained to the stranger or problem.

The important thing is that you *use* the special knowledge you acquire. In the next chapter, you will learn a principle that Holmes used to make his specialized knowledge extremely practical in everyday life.

Go to Pages 313 to 320 if you want to practice
the specialized knowledge exercises now.

Chapter 5

How To See Through Strangers
Like Sherlock Holmes

"...We all learn by experience."
Sherlock Holmes, The Adventure of Black Peter

In *The Adventure of Black Peter*, Sherlock Holmes taught the young ambitious Detective Stanley Hopkins a valuable lesson. Detective Hopkins insisted his investigation led him to catch the suspect in Peter Carey's death. Holmes suggested Detective Hopkins loss sight of an alternative explanation for the crime during his investigation. Thus, he held the wrong man.

Both detectives, the experienced teacher and his novice student, pursed their own lines of inquiry. Ultimately, Sherlock Holmes emerged the victor, when he lured the unsuspecting Patrick Cairns into the sitting room at 221B Baker Street and handcuffed him.

Detective Hopkins could only stand speechless with amazement at Holmes's dramatic conclusion to the case. Then he finally said, red-faced: "...It seems to me that I have been making a fool of myself from the beginning. I understand now, what I should have never have forgotten, that I am the pupil and you are the master." Detective Hopkins learned a valuable lesson that day — even more valuable than 'the never lose sight of the alternative' lesson Sherlock Holmes tried to teach him. What did Detective Hopkins learn?

Experience is the best teacher!

If you are to master the Sherlock Holmes Method of sizing up strangers, you must gain experience. When Holmes said anyone could acquire the science of observation and deduction by studying long and patiently, he meant you must develop those abilities through experience. It is easy, not hard to get experience, because you already possess the qualities you need to succeed. All you have to do to unlock your potential is apply the following five tips:

Tip# 1: Use Systematized Common Sense

In *The Adventure of the Blanched Soldier*, Sherlock Holmes refers to his method as "...systematized common sense." The Holmesian method of systematized common sense is nothing more than the scientific method made simple for everyday people to use in normal life. It is nothing more than a practical application of the four basic questions and eight principles. Holmes developed his own personal system, which used experience based on common sense as part of its' methodology to size up strangers. Holmes called it his 'simple art.' You can apply it just as he did and develop your own personal system.

In order to use the simple art that Sherlock Holmes described, however, you must use the common sense you already have and increase its' effectiveness. You begin turning common sense into a personal system when you start using it for practical purposes. You can do this by applying the four basic questions and eight principles in a specific manner with the practical goal of sizing up people.

In *A Study in Scarlet*, Holmes told Watson: "...The theories which I have expressed there, and which appear to you to be so chimerical, are really extremely practical." Whenever Holmes talked about his method as being practical, he meant to use common sense.

Common sense, as defined in this book, is the total everyday knowledge gained from using your five natural senses. It is good judgment learned from experiencing everyday natural events that happen to all human beings. We learn from these common experiences. They increase our practical knowledge of the world. The experiences we learn throughout our lives include but are not limited to growing up, making friends, attending school, getting a job, socializing, enjoying hobbies, traveling, dating, getting married, having children and growing old. Common sense allows you to learn from these life events in a practical way.

Common sense is natural thinking and realistic appraisals of things, events and people. It is the practical intelligence you gain from understanding people in general and using it with specific individuals. Using your common sense helps you to keep things simple. It allows you to understand the natural sequence and consequence of everyday life.

For example, a natural sequence is human beings are born, grow old and die. A natural consequence is if you touch fire, you will receive a burn or if you cut yourself with a knife, you will bleed. Therefore, common sense teaches you to accept the cycle of life and be careful with fire and knives.

In the cycle of life, people learn general truths and rules about human nature from their good and bad personal experiences. The more experiences you have, the more general statements and accurate assumptions you will learn and make about people. You can do this once you use common sense learned from personal experience. The next tip will show you how to use the common sense experience you acquire in a practical way.

Tip #2: Make The Method a Habit

In *The Gloria Scott* case, Victor Trevor spoke about the observation and inference skills Holmes used during their friendship in college. Holmes described Victor talking to his father about the habits Holmes had already formed into a system. Holmes had observed and deduced many things about his peers in college, which shocked and amazed them. Holmes developed over many years the techniques, in which he could accurately and systematically size up strangers he met. We are all born with this same natural ability. We just have to fine-tune it as did Holmes.

You can improve upon the natural ability you already have. Simply use the four basic questions and eight principles as a starting point. Make using them a habit to gain the experience you need. Experience is everyday knowledge you acquire consciously or unconsciously over time. It is a way to develop natural abilities through routine. It is constant repetition — doing the same thing repeatedly — until it becomes second nature to you.

In *The Adventure of the Creeping Man,* Watson describes Holmes as "...a man of habits, narrow and concentrated habits." You breath, walk and talk without thinking about it. You must do the same with the Sherlock Holmes Method. In *A Study in Scarlet*, Holmes spoke about being unaware of the steps he took to size up Watson. What Holmes meant is he developed the skill through long habit. Like Holmes, you must use the method without even thinking about it.

In *The Adventure of the Blanched Soldier*, Holmes describes how he used his method when interviewing clients. He habitually had clients sit with the light from a window shining on their faces. He did it so many times before that it became a natural part of him. It became so much a part of his general knowledge that he did it automatically — as if he was on autopilot or cruise control.

General knowledge is knowledge you learn from experience. Experience is going out into the real world to see what works and does not work for you. You cannot swim on dry land. You have to get wet to learn how to swim. You have to get in the water to feel how cold it is, how strong the current is and how it ebbs and flows. So, it is with the Sherlock Holmes Method. You must get experience with it to reach your full potential.

The way to do this is through habit. Repeatedly use the four basic questions and eight principles in your normal everyday life. Only by going out into the real world and using the four basic questions in real life situations with people can you find out what works for you.

Only by using the eight principles in day-to-day encounters with strangers can you become proficient in the Sherlock Holmes Method. You will stumble many times as you learn to size up strangers. You will often make the wrong assessments about people. The important thing is that you follow the next tip and do not give up.

Tip #3: Learn From Your Mistakes

Although Sherlock Holmes solved many cases successfully, he recognized that he did not succeed all the time. He admitted to one client that adversaries beat him four times.[33] In several other cases Holmes investigated, he made mistakes or did not find essential clues immediately.

In *The Yellow Face,* Holmes formed a theory regarding a wife's behavior, which he believed covered the facts. Yet, his conclusions were so off the mark that he told Watson when the case ended to whisper *'Norbury'* in his ear. Holmes did this so he would not become over confident or less attentive in a future case. In *The Adventure of the Priory School,* Holmes overlooked the importance of cow tracks on a path until he realized a horse made the fake cow tracks with cloven iron shoes.

In *The Stock-Broker's Clerk,* Sherlock Holmes admits he never thought of an important clue to a case that he sought to

---

[33] *The Five Orange Pips*, wherein Holmes stated: "I have been beaten four times — three times by men, and once by a woman."

solve. In *The Solitary Cyclist,* Holmes admitted he failed to grasp the significance of what Watson reported to him. Holmes missed seeing an unknown cyclist arrange his necktie in the shrubbery.

In *The Disappearance of Lady Frances Carfax,* Holmes admits he had a temporary slip. He did not notice the remark the undertaker's wife made regarding coffin measurements that hid another body. In *The Problem of Thor Bridge,* Holmes blamed himself for making a mistake. Why? He did not recognize sooner that a chip in the stonework suggested the true solution to the mystery he eventually solved.

Like Holmes, accept the fact that you will make mistakes. But it is learning from your mistakes that will make you good at seeing through people. Only through trial and error can you become proficient at sizing up strangers. The Sherlock Holmes Method is not foolproof. It has limitations because it relies on concrete evidence and facts. Unlike other unscientific methods, it does not rely on the spiritual, supernatural or magical.

Although astrology, fortune telling, cold reading and psychic reading do not rely on science, these ancient arts use the same principles as the Sherlock Holmes Method. *The key difference with the Holmes method is that it does not claim any supernatural or spiritual influences.* It requires no magical powers. It only requires natural abilities most people already possess. Unlike these fake sciences, the Holmes Method does not claim to know everything about a person.

Sherlock Holmes recognized and accepted his limitations. He did not claim to know more about a stranger than he actually knew. On many occasions, Holmes stated his limitations explicitly. For example, in *The Sign of Four,* Holmes told Watson: "...I never even knew you had a brother until you handed me the watch." Holmes said this after studying a watch that Watson gave him. He upset Watson after reaching accurate conclusions about Watson's older brother.

In *The Adventure of the Norwood Builder,* Sherlock Holmes informed John McFarlane upon meeting him that "I know nothing whatever about you." Holmes said this after observing details from McFarlane's appearance after McFarlane rushed into the room at 221B Baker Street.

In *The Red-Headed League* case, Holmes observed several obvious facts about a stout, fiery red hair client. Holmes then admitted he could deduce nothing more other than the few facts he gathered from glancing at the client.

In *The Gloria Scott* case, Victor Trevor's father challenged Holmes to deduce anything about him. Holmes replied: "...I fear there is not very much." Holmes then made several minor deductions, which caused the old man to faint.

Holmes never used manipulation to con strangers into thinking he knew things about them. He never used trickery to see through people. When he sized up strangers, he usually made only a few deductions. The facts and evidence before him put a limit on what he could observe and deduce.

If he saw limited evidence on a stranger, he could only make limited inferences about the stranger. Yet, Holmes would always justify his deductions by explaining the exact fact or detail upon which he based his conclusion. Then Holmes honed his method by constantly using the next tip.

Tip #4: Meet All Kinds of People

Holmes sharpened his skills and gained experience by meeting people from all walks-of-life. For example, before his adventures in *A Study in Scarlet,* he met a group of young streetwise kids he called 'The Baker Street Irregulars'. In *A Scandal in Bohemia,* he met a king. In *The Adventure of the Priory*

School, he met a nobleman. Last, in *The Adventure of the Bruce-Partington Plans*, he met a queen.

When Holmes needed hard to get information, he went undercover. In *The Adventure of Charles Augustus Milverton,* he obtained information from an unwitting house cleaner. In *The Adventure of the Blue Carbuncle*, he received it from a gambler. In *The Adventure of Wisteria Lodge*, he received it from a gardener. In *The Adventure of the Missing Three-Quarter*, he got it from a porter. In *The Adventure of the Abbey Grange*, he got it from a sailor.

In *Silver Blaze,* he received it from a stable boy. In *The Man with the Twisted Lip*, he received it from drug addicts. He also helped Miss Mary Sutherland, the typist from *A Case of Identity*. He helped the bicyclist Miss Violet Smith from *The Adventure of the Solitary Cyclist*. He helped the engineer Victor Hatherley from *The Engineer's Thumb.* Last, he helped the British tradesman Jabez Wilson from *The Red-Headed League.*

If you are to master Sherlock's Method, you must also meet people from every occupation. Get to know how people act and react from observing them in many different situations, contexts and circumstances. Meet people from different races, cultures, genders and backgrounds.

Study people of all ages, social status and financial levels. Learn from these experiences and you will understand why all people are alike. You will also understand what makes every person different. The more people you meet, the better you will become at sizing up strangers.

As you meet people, get to know them on an individual basis. If you are a bartender, salesperson, taxi driver, police officer, politician, teacher, postal letter carrier or have a job that deals with the public, you have an excellent opportunity to learn human nature and what makes people tick. While you are at work, practice studying the people around you.

How do people behave while they are in crowds? What do they say or do while in a bar or restaurant? How do they respond to a fight or car accident? Everyone in a crowd will reveal their personality when something unexpected happens or an emergency occurs.

How do people handle situations in their everyday lives? Go to different events and study people. How do people behave at graduations, award ceremonies, weddings, funerals, sports events, music concerts, political rallies and other large events? How do they act when they experience success, such as getting a job, winning at a sport or achieving their dreams?

How do people deal with failure or loss, such as bankruptcy, divorce, sickness, heartbreak, depression, death or other events that happen to everyone during the course of their lives? Only by getting experience can you answer these questions. Only by gaining experience, can you open up people and draw them out to obtain personal details that will help you size them up.

Sherlock Holmes used his experience in opening up people to get them to reveal information he needed. In *The Sign of Four*, Sherlock Holmes opened up the wife of a steam launch captain. He gave her mischievous little boy some coins and feigned disinterest in her husband. The unsuspecting woman not only described the boat Holmes searched for but also the wooden-legged suspect he sought.

Holmes later said to Watson: "...The main thing with the people of that sort...is never let them think that their information can be of the slightest importance to you. If you do, they will instantly shut up like an oyster. If you listen to them under protest, as it were, you are very likely to get what you want..."

Holmes also used his experience to draw people out to get information. In *The Adventure of the Blue Carbuncle,* Holmes used reverse psychology on a salesman by getting the salesman to bet him that the bird he searched for was country-bred. The salesman took the bait and Holmes left with the information he needed. Holmes later told Watson: "...I daresay that if I had put £100 down in front of him, that man would not have given me such complete information as was drawn from him by the idea that he was doing me on a wager."

In *The Adventure of the Illustrious Client,* Holmes explained to Watson how he liked to get up close and personal with a client. Holmes stated: "...I love to come to close grips with my man. I like to meet him eye to eye and read for myself the stuff that he is made of." Holmes could easily open up people and draw them out because he had years of experience in meeting and dealing with people from all lifestyles.

Tip #5: Watch The Experts

Watson often described how he attempted to follow Sherlock Holmes's methods in deducing strangers. For example, in *The Red-Headed League* case, Watson describes how: "...I took a good look at the man and endeavored, after the fashion of my companion, to read the indications which might be presented by his dress or appearance."

In *The Resident Patient* case, Watson describes how because he knew Holmes's methods he could follow Holmes's reasoning. He then followed Sherlock Holmes's thinking in deducing that a stranger waiting in a horse drawn carriage in front of 221B Baker Street practiced medicine.

In *A Case of Identity*, Watson again tried to decipher a stranger's appearance by applying Holmes's methods. Although Watson never gained the level of expertise Sherlock Holmes possessed, he did learn some of Holmes's method by studying him in action. And from Watson, we can all learn a valuable lesson: *watch the professionals.*

Expert lawyers, sales people, politicians, doctors, interviewers, psychologists and other professionals have a unique ability to size up strangers gained from experience. They have interacted with hundreds, if not, thousands of individuals over the course of their careers. This experience enables them to store vast amounts of 'people' knowledge.

You can gain experience by observing these experts in action. If you are a young trial lawyer just starting out on your first case, go to a courthouse to study veteran lawyers as they select juries. If you are a new trainee, learning how to sell cars or homes, watch how the veteran sales people approach prospective car or homebuyers. Study how they size them up to close the sale.

You can also watch 'natural' experts — people who possess the innate skill to size up strangers. These individuals never took any formal or technical training in evaluating strangers yet they do it instinctively in their daily lives. They did not need 'science' or 'education' to teach them what they learned from *experience.*

You know these people well. They are your parents, siblings, friends, relatives, neighbors, co-workers, teachers, cab drivers, doormen, waitresses, token booth clerks and thousands of other working people who deal with the public daily. Pick someone you know, who you can learn from just like Watson did with Holmes.

I learned from my friend and mentor Thomas Stanziale, Sr. I continually watched him as he used his natural skills to size up strangers and evaluate people. He had no college degree or formal training in psychology but he knew human nature. He had learnt how to deal with people from years of experience in watching and interacting with them. I personally observed him size up strangers upon first meeting them at work. Without even knowing it, Tom used the four basic questions and eight principles whenever he dealt with people.

Tom would always tell me to watch people's facial expressions, observe their body language, and listen closely to what they said or did not say, then reason from common sense to determine their motives and actions. I received my first real lessons in sizing up people from watching how Tom did it.

Tom opened up a new area of interest for me. I began reading books on body language and psychology to improve my people reading skills. Much like Watson with Holmes, I did not achieve the same level of skill or success as Tom but I did become better at sizing up strangers then when I first met him.

You can improve your ability to size up strangers just like I did by watching an expert in action. You can also apply the other four tips above. These tips will help you gain the experience necessary to apply the principles in the previous chapters. You can also use them with the principles in the upcoming chapters.

Getting experience is the key!

Once you have it, your ability to size up strangers will improve. How? Simply because you will have hit upon the method just like Watson. In *The Hound of the Baskervilles,* Watson thought to himself: "...I am certainly developing the wisdom of the serpent...I have not lived for years with Sherlock Holmes for nothing."

Go to Pages 320 to 323 if you want to practice the personal experience exercises now.

Chapter 6

Analyze A Stranger in Seconds With This Sherlockian Skill

*"...I listen to their story, they listen to my comments,
and then I pocket my fee."*

Sherlock Holmes, A Study in Scarlet

In October 2012, I returned to New York City from a cruise vacation to Cozumel Mexico. At the airport security checkpoint, a female passenger in front of me strolled pass without the *Transportation Security Administration* (TSA) agent stopping her.

As I entered the security checkpoint and approached the TSA agent, he stopped me. He asked me a series of casual questions such as: "How was your trip?" "Where did you go?" "Are you traveling alone?" Satisfied with what he heard, he waved me through to the next security checkpoint.

The TSA agent had used a listening technique learned from Israel airport security personnel at the *Ben-Gurion International Airport* in Tel Aviv.[34] The Israeli behavior detection officers use the listening technique to spot terrorists. Sherlock Holmes used the same listening technique whenever he sized up a stranger or investigated a case. In fact, one of Holmes's most-underrated skills was his ability to listen accurately to people. How did he do it? You will learn his listening technique in this chapter.

---

[34] *"TSA Could Adopt Israeli-Style Behavior-Detection Techniques"* by writer-reporter Frances Romero online at Time.com. See: http://newsfeed.time.com/2011/08/01/ tsa-could-adopt-israeli-style-behavior-detection-techniques/#ixzz2tIyTX6zF.

Chapter 2 focused on using your *eyes* to pay attention to the *physical* cues a stranger reveals through his or her facial expressions, behavior, dress and trifling details. This chapter will focus on using your *ears* to listen to the *verbal* cues strangers reveal by *what* they say, *how* they say it and the *way* they say it. You will find it easy, not hard to do, because you probably already do it in your daily conversations with people. This chapter will simply make you more aware of your actions. As a result, you will become better at sizing up strangers.

Why Sherlock Holmes Listened To Strangers

Many Sherlockian adventures began with a client coming to 221B Baker Street and telling Holmes about a problem he or she faced. He listened to the client's story and decided if he would take the case. He applied his listening skills whenever he interviewed a client, a witness, a rival or a suspect. To use the Sherlock Holmes Method successfully, you must understand why he placed such importance on listening to strangers.

Holmes Listened to Strangers to Communicate With Them. Holmes always sought to communicate personally with his clients. He would engage people in casual conversations and conduct interviews to establish rapport. When a client came to 221B Baker to seek help with a problem, Holmes allowed the client to tell the story in his or her own words. He listened to make sure he understood the client's meaning, intent and the problem's seriousness.

In *The Adventure of the Three Garridebs,* Sherlock Holmes went to see Nathan Garrideb and listen to him. Holmes stated: "I prefer to establish personal touch with those with whom I do business." In *The Adventure of the Abbey Grange,* Watson describes how Holmes listened to a stern, cold nurse. She eventually opened up and told him everything he needed to know about her late employer.

152

Sometimes the problem seemed trivial but as he heard more about it, the problem often took on a more sinister nature. In *The Sign of Four,* Holmes listened to Mary Morstan's problem with little interest until he examined a curious piece of paper she gave him. Holmes later realized it had more far-reaching consequences than he first thought. He said: "I begin to suspect that this matter may turn out to be much deeper and more subtle than I at first supposed. I must reconsider my ideas."

In *The Reigate Puzzle,* Holmes considered it a petty crime when he first listened to the story that criminals burglarized a country magistrate's home. He soon realized it had serious overtones when he heard someone committed murder. His only clue laid in a torn paper scrap with some handwriting on it. After examining the paper Holmes said: "These are much deeper waters than I had thought." Holmes therefore, listened closely to the things a stranger said to draw clues from what he heard to help him later solve a case.

Holmes Listened to Strangers to Understand Them. When a client came to Holmes to tell his or her story, Holmes always listened to make sure he understood them clearly. He knew when communicating with people that it is easy to misunderstand what they say. Sometimes a client would get so angry or afraid that he or she could not speak clearly. Other times a client came to 221B Baker Street in such an excited state that Holmes had to calm him or her down in order to find out what the client wanted him to do. As a result, Holmes always listened to make sure he had a clear understanding of what clients wanted.

In *The Five Orange Pips,* Holmes told a client: "Pray give us the essential facts from the commencement and I can afterwards question you as to those details which seem to me to be most important." In *The Adventure of the Speckled Band,* he said to a client: "...I beg that you lay before us everything that may help us in forming an opinion upon the matter." In *The Adventure of the Beryl Coronet,* he said to a distraught client: "Pray compose yourself, sir...and let me have a clear account of who you are and what it is that has befallen you." All the above cases establish that Sherlock Holmes listened to understand his clients before he took on their case.

Holmes Listened to Strangers to Learn From Them. Whenever Sherlock Holmes interviewed a client, witness or suspect, he always listened to learn what they knew about the problem. He would listen to how they told the story to glean the information he needed to solve the case. He would listen for details, facts and evidence to understand the problem. Often Holmes heard important clues in the story that Watson missed because Holmes listened more effectively than Watson.

In *The Red-Headed League,* Holmes listened to a client's story about a man paying him to copy out the *Encyclopedia Britannica.* He learned enough from what he heard to realize that a bank robbery would soon occur. In *The Musgrave Ritual,* Holmes listened to Reginald Musgrave's story about an ancestor's ritual, a missing butler and housemaid. He learned enough from what he heard to realize the ritual's significance and connection to the missing butler and maid.

In *The Greek Interpreter,* Holmes listened to an interpreter's story about how he translated in Greek to a prisoner. Holmes learned enough from what he heard to realize the matter involved a very dangerous gang. Holmes always listened to a stranger to learn anything, which could help him solve a case.

How To Listen Like Sherlock Holmes

Sherlock Holmes did not have any superhuman ability that most of us do not possess. He simply developed the natural skills we all have to a higher level. He trained himself to use his natural senses until they became finely tuned. One of the natural abilities Holmes developed through self-training is his ability to listen effectively.

Most people have not learned how to listen effectively. They believe they are better listeners than they actually are. The average person does not hear, however, the obvious sounds and subtle meanings in everyday conversations. To use the Sherlock Holmes Method correctly, you must learn not only how to hear but also how to listen. Below you will find tips for doing both.

Holmes Improved His Hearing. Holmes trained himself through years of practice to hear well. He took long walks in the London countryside and neighborhoods, not only to analyze the soil or to know the streets, but also to hear the sounds around him. In the countryside, he heard birds chirping, wind blowing, leaves rustling and bees buzzing. In the London streets, he heard horses galloping, carriages rumbling, people walking and dogs barking. He then cataloged in his mind every sound he heard. As a result, he acquired a highly developed sense of hearing. In *The Adventure of the Speckled Band*, Holmes's keen hearing enabled him to listen for a deadly snake. He then attacked the snake before it could enter a room to bite an unsuspecting woman.

Holmes often used his excellent ears, before he even observed a person, to distinguish who had arrived at 221B Baker Street to consult him. In *The Adventure of the Noble Bachelor,* Holmes could tell just from the sound of his footsteps on the stairs that Lord St. Simon had come for Holmes's expert advice. Holmes said to Watson: "...I hear his step now upon the stairs."

In *A Scandal In Bohemia,* Sherlock Holmes could tell just from the sound of horse's hoofs on the pavement below that a German client came to consult him. "A pair, by the sound" Holmes said as he glanced at the carriage and horses below his window. He then heard a slow, heavy step ascend the stairs and passageway and "...a loud, authoritative tap" at the door before the German prince entered. As Watson stated in *The Adventure of the Blanched Soldier*, Holmes possessed an "...abnormally acute set of senses..." in which accurate hearing was one.

Holmes Concentrated While Listening. Holmes listened to a client's narrative with his full attention. He focused on what he heard and what he needed to find out. He concentrated on the client's story, the problem the client presented and any interesting features or points in the narrative. In *The Resident Patient,* Watson described how Holmes listened to a client's "...long narrative with an intentness which showed me his interest was keenly aroused..."

In *A Case of Identity*, Watson says he expected to see Sherlock Holmes impatient with a client's narrative "...but, on the contrary, he had listened with the greatest concentration of attention." In *The Sign of Four,* Watson described how Holmes paid attention to a client's story. Holmes "...rubbed his hands and his eyes glistened. He leaned forward in his chair with an expression of extraordinary concentration on his clear-cut, hawk like features."

Holmes would sometimes *close his eyes* while listening. This helped him to *focus* and *concentrate* on what the person said without letting their physical appearance distract him. Holmes's action seems contrary to the modern day wisdom of constantly observing a person while they are speaking but it is not. In fact, it *increased* his ability to *hear* what a stranger said.

In *The Hound of the Baskervilles,* Holmes listened to Dr. Mortimer read from a manuscript. Watson describes how Holmes: "...leaned back in his chair, placed his finger-tips together, and closed his eyes." In *The Adventure of the Norwood Builder,* Sherlock Holmes listened to John McFarlane's account regarding a recent incident where Scotland Yard wanted him for murder. Watson describes how Holmes: "...listened with closed eyes and fingertips together."

In *The Adventure of the Copper Beeches,* Holmes quickly looked a female client over. Watson describes how he: "...composed himself, with his lids drooping and his finger-tips together, to listen to her story." When Holmes needed a stranger to know he was listening, Holmes followed the next tip.

Holmes Gave Feedback While Listening. Sherlock Holmes communicated with strangers by looking directly at them, nodding his head or making verbal affirmations. Holmes often gave feedback that he heard something interesting by a simple glance, by leaning forward or by taking notes. These actions let strangers know Holmes paid close attention to what they said.

In *The Adventure of the Retired Colourman,* Watson described how Holmes listened as he gave an account of his mission. Watson stated: "...His eyelids drooped over his eyes so lazily that he might almost have been asleep were it not that at any halt or questionable passage of my narrative they half lifted, and two gray eyes...transfixed me with their searching glance."

In *The Hound of the Baskervilles,* Watson described how Holmes showed interest after Dr. Mortimer stated he observed the footprints of a gigantic hound. Watson stated: "Holmes leaned forward in his excitement and his eyes had the hard, dry glitter which shot from them when he was keenly interested."

In *The Adventure of the Priory School,* Watson described how Holmes took notes as he listened to Thorneycroft Huxtable's account of the Duke of Holdernesse's missing son. Watson stated: "Sherlock Holmes had listened with the utmost intentness to the statement of the unhappy schoolmaster...He now drew out his notebook and jotted down one or two memoranda." Holmes did all these things to show strangers that he listened to them as they spoke. Sherlock Holmes also followed the next tip while listening to a stranger.

Holmes Only Interrupted a Stranger When Necessary. When a client arrived at 221B Baker Street to tell a story, Holmes often listened silently as the client spoke. He would allow the client to tell the whole story without interference. Holmes let the client finish the story then questioned him or her afterwards regarding the particular details. During the client's narrative, Holmes would only interrupt to seek clarification on a fact or detail he deemed important.

In *A Study in Scarlet,* Holmes interrupted Constable Rance's story to confirm that the constable stopped and walked back to the gate. Holmes wanted to know why he stopped and walked back. In *The Five Orange Pips,* Holmes interrupted John Openshaw's narrative to ask for the dates Openshaw's uncle received a letter and died. In *The Musgrave Ritual* case, Holmes interrupted Reginald Musgrave's narrative to comment about the importance of reviewing the Musgrave family ritual paper the butler had taken from the bureau.

Sometimes a client would get annoyed at Holmes's seemingly trivial interruption. But the interruption would often later prove important to the case. In *The Adventure of the Blanched Soldier,* Holmes interrupted client James Dodd's narrative to ask what newspaper Mr. Dodd had seen a man reading. This disruption annoyed Mr. Dodd but the detail later proved critical to Holmes understanding the mystery he faced.

In *The Adventure of the Creeping Man,* Holmes interrupted Trevor Bennett's narrative to ask the date he noticed Professor Presbury crawling on the hallway floor. This interjection irritated Mr. Bennett but the fact later helped Holmes solve the mystery. All these cases show Holmes rarely interrupted people while they spoke unless he needed to know a key fact or detail.

Holmes Controlled His Thoughts and Feelings. Once a client began speaking, Holmes stopped talking and let him or her speak. As he listened to the client's narrative, Holmes did not let his thoughts wander. He did not allow himself to get distracted. He focused on the story, the facts and the details not the person stating them. He did not say or do anything that caused the client to stop speaking. He avoided making assumptions while listening or having any bias towards the person. He heard exactly what the client said not what he wanted to hear. He did not react emotionally to what the client said but listened in an objective manner. Sherlock Holmes listened the same way when he dealt with certain detectives.

In *The Valley of Fear*, Watson describes Holmes listening to Detective White Mason with respect. He states: "...Holmes listened to him intently, with no sign of that impatience which the official exponent too often produced." In the same case, Watson tells how Holmes listened to a discussion between Detectives MacDonald and Mason. He states: "...Holmes sat intently observant during this long discussion, missing no word that was said, with his keen eyes darting to right and to left."

In *The Adventure of the Norwood Builder*, Watson describes how Sherlock Holmes controlled his excitement after hearing that Inspector Lestrade had found a thumb mark on a wall. Watson explained it this way: "Holmes was outwardly calm, but his whole body gave a wriggle of suppressed excitement." These cases establish that Holmes controlled his feelings and thoughts whenever he listened to people.

Holmes Knew His Listening Speed. You can listen faster than a stranger can talk. But do not use this extra time to think about what you are going to say. Use the extra time to think about everything the stranger has said. Relate what you hear to your own knowledge and experience. Sherlock Holmes could hear things that Watson missed because Holmes understood the difference in listening speed. He used this speed difference to draw upon the facts he needed to size up a stranger or understand a problem.

In *The Red-Headed League,* Watson expressed amazement how Sherlock Holmes could listen to a client's narrative and come away with far more information than he did. Watson described it in this way: "...I had heard what he heard, I had seen what he seen, and yet from his words it was evident that he saw clearly not only what had happened but what was about to happen, while to me the whole business was still confused and grotesque." Holmes could do it because he used the listening rate difference to think about important points and similar cases.

In *The Adventure of the Noble Bachelor,* after hearing a client's story, Watson stated: "...I have heard all that you have heard." To which Holmes replied: "Without, however, the knowledge of preexisting cases which serves me so well." What Holmes meant is he took advantage of the difference in how fast he could listen. Holmes drew from his previous knowledge of similar cases, *as he listened to the client's narrative,* to reach his conclusions regarding the current case. The ability to think about and evaluate what a stranger is saying *as they are speaking* is vital to effective listening. Holmes listened effectively because he also used the next tip.

Holmes Asked Questions While Listening. In Chapter 1, you learned about asking questions to obtain data about a stranger. You can also ask questions as you listen. For example, you can ask questions to let a stranger know you are listening. You can ask questions to show the stranger you understand what he or she has said. You can ask questions to clarify a fact or detail you heard. And last, you can ask questions to avoid misunderstanding what the stranger says. Holmes listened in all these ways when he sized up people or investigated a case.

In *The Adventure of the Cardboard Box,* Holmes listened as Miss Susan Cushing rambled on about various topics. Watson stated: "Holmes listened attentively to everything, throwing in a question from time to time." Holmes asked questions to open up

Miss Cushing. She then started talking about what he really wanted to know — information about her two sisters.

In *The Adventure of the Three Garridebs,* an American gentleman told Sherlock Holmes the story of his search for Garridebs. Holmes went to Nathan Garrideb to find out what he knew. Holmes stated to Mr. Garrideb when he met him: "There are a few questions I need to ask, for I have your very clear narrative in my pocket." Holmes then asked Mr. Garrideb several questions to get an understanding of the mystery.

In *The Valley of Fear,* Holmes asked Cecil Barker several questions to clarify his understanding regarding a candle lit on a table. The family discovered the wife's dead husband lying on the floor in a room with the candle. Holmes listened to Mr. Barker's explanation regarding help arriving. Holmes then said: "And yet when they arrived they found the candle was out and that the lamp had been lighted. That seems very remarkable." Holmes later determined Mr. Barker lied due to the candle staying lit only for a short time.

The listening technique that follows can help you tell when someone is lying just like Holmes did with Mr. Barker. TSA agents and Israeli behavior experts have also used it to spot deceptive behavior.[35] The tips below will show you how Holmes used the same listening technique to size up strangers.

---

[35] Critics claim that Israel's Behavioral Detection Program; the TSA's *Screening Passengers by Observation Techniques* (SPOT) program and the New York City Police Department's Stop and Frisk policy are nothing more than racial and ethnic profiling. Rather than looking for suspicious, deceptive, criminal or terrorist behavior as they claim, critics charge these strategies use strangers' race or ethnic background as the criteria to screen or stop them. In the case of Israel's Behavioral Detection Program, critics state it unfairly targets passengers of Arabic or Palestinian descent. In the case of the TSA's SPOT and NYPD's Stop and Frisk programs, critics state they unfairly target minorities under the pretext of stopping terrorist or criminal activity. Israel, the TSA and the NYPD all state that their programs prevent criminal and terrorist activity and are not race or ethnic based.

What Sherlock Holmes Listened For

Sherlock Holmes' conducted investigations using a little known listening technique as he interviewed clients, witnesses and suspects. The technique enabled him to detect deceptive verbal reactions. *He would ask questions then listen closely for above normal signs of stress, fear or deception in the person's oral responses.* TSA agents and Israeli behavioral experts use the same listening technique when they screen passengers at airport security checkpoints.

For example, at the Israel airport in Tel Avi, trained behavioral detection agents notice travelers' suspicious behavior. They then ask seemingly innocent questions and mentally scrutinize the traveler's verbal responses. Any reactions that are out of the ordinary; do not make sense or seem odd; will cause the traveler to get taken to the side and given a more thorough interview.

Likewise, a good lawyer, detective, politician or sales person will always ask a stranger easy questions to see the stranger's natural way of speaking. They will then ask key questions and closely observe the stranger's reactions. Is the person suddenly nervous? Defensive? Hostile? Evasive? Any sudden changes in speech, mood, attitude or body language are red flags for the trained observer to take notice.

The listening technique concentrates not so much on *what* the stranger says but the *way* he or she says it. The key to the technique is to listen not so much to the person's answers, but to *their verbal replies and physical reactions as they speak.* For you to use the listening technique successfully, you must apply it in combination with the other principles you learn in this book.

Sherlock Holmes used all the principles as he listened for several things while sizing up a stranger. What did Holmes listen for? He listened for the person's reaction. He listened for the way they spoke. He listened for relevant information in their narrative. He listened for any similarities or inconsistencies in their voices and stories. He listened for what strangers did not say. He listened for trivial things a stranger said. He listened for deception and tested it. And above all else, Sherlock Holmes applied reason to what he heard. Study the information below to learn how he did it.

Holmes Listened for a Reaction. In Chapter 2 you learned how to look, where to look and what to look for when you meet strangers. As you are observing strangers, ask them questions or make statements and listen closely to their responses. Sherlock Holmes did this after he formed a hypothesis. Often how people react will tell you a lot about them. You can draw out the reaction with a shocking question or statement. He would ask a shocking question or make an unexpected statement to scrutinize a witness or suspect's reaction.

In *A Case of Identity*, Holmes told a client's father that he found her mysterious suitor. The father "...gave a violent start and dropped his gloves." Although the father seemed glad to hear the news, his reaction revealed all Holmes needed to know.

In *Silver Blaze*, Holmes whispered in a trainer's ear. The trainer jerked suddenly and reacted angrily, denying what Holmes told him. The trainer's reaction, however, revealed the truth about what Holmes said.

In *The Crooked Man*, Holmes told Henry Wood that Mrs. Barclay would go on trial for murder. Mr. Wood jerked violently. He then revealed everything regarding a murder to Holmes so Mrs. Barclay could go free.

In *The Adventure of the Retired Colourman*, Sherlock Holmes asked Josiah Amberley "What have you done with the bodies?" Amberley reacted in shock, standing up with a scream and trying to poison himself.

In *The Hound of the Baskervilles,* Sherlock Holmes interviewed Mrs. Laura Lyon. He suggested she withheld information in connection with Sir Charles Baskerville's death. She defiantly denied it. Holmes then stated he possessed evidence that could implicate Mr. Stapleton and his wife. Mrs. Lyons sprang from her chair and cried in shock: "His wife!" She did not know Mr. Stapleton was a married man. After Holmes had proved it to her with a photograph and documents, she told Holmes everything he needed to know.

In the cases above, Sherlock Holmes asked unexpected, shocking and truthful questions or statements. These types of questions or statements will always get a reaction from a stranger. Asking similar questions or making similar statements and listening to a stranger's reaction are important in sizing them up. But you must also follow the next tip to increase your chances of succeeding.

Holmes Listened to Speech. As Holmes listened for a reaction, he also focused on the stranger's voice tone, pitch, vocabulary and word phrasing. He listened for any answers that stumbled or stuttered. He listened for vague or ambiguous answers. He listened for inconsistent, evasive, defensive, defiant, sarcastic, odd, nonsensical or illogical answers. He listened for stress in the person's voice. Holmes knew fear; anxiety, anger, happiness, sadness and excitement all express themselves through a stranger's emotional speech.

In *The Adventure of the Veiled Lodger,* Watson described how Holmes listened to an unhappy woman tell a sad story. He explained there was "...something in the woman's voice which arrested Holmes's attention." Holmes then told her not to consider suicide because her life had value to others. Holmes detected a change in her voice tone from her earlier narrative, which signaled to him her intentions. He did it because he *listened* to her speak. He heard a change in her pitch, tone and word emphasis when she said: "Yes. The case is closed."

In *The Adventure of The Norwood Builder,* Watson described how he detected a change in Sherlock Holmes's voice tone after Detective Lestrade found a thumbprint on a wall. Holmes's voice went from monotone to suppressed excitement. Watson described it this way: "Something in his voice caught my ear, and I turned to look at him. An extraordinary change had come over his face. It was writhing with inward merriment." Watson noticed the change in Holmes's pitch, tone and word emphasis when Holmes said: "It is final."

The ability to detect feelings in speech is a skill you naturally have and can develop further. The online article: *"Behavior Detection Officers could have a few Questions as you clear Security,"[36]* quotes Psychologist Paul Ekman. Mr. Ekman states: "...it's tougher to mask emotions when you're answering questions...speaking takes a lot of attention and effort that can't be devoted to how you appear." Asking questions, listening for reactions and analyzing speech, are powerful tools for sizing up strangers. But you also must use the next tip for the listening technique to work.

Holmes Listened for Relevant Information. Whenever Sherlock Holmes heard a client's story or a stranger's narrative, he listened for relevant information. Relevant information, as defined in this book, is any data you can use to size up a stranger. Holmes always listened for the key issue, the most-important point and the most-critical fact to start his investigation or size up a stranger.

In *A Study in Scarlet,* Sherlock Holmes asked Detective Gregson: "You did not ask for particulars on any point which appeared to you to be crucial? Is there no circumstance on

---

[36] See article written by Alison Grant, *The Plain Dealer* on August 5, 2011 on *Cleveland.com* website at http:// www.cleveland.com/ business/ index.ssf /2011/08/ behavior_detection_officers_co.html

which this whole case appears to hinge?" After Holmes had solved the murder, he would later explain to Detective Lestrade: "All this seems strange to you...because you failed at the beginning of the inquiry to grasp the importance of the single real clue which was presented to you."

In *The Adventure of Black Peter,* Holmes spoke to Detective Stanley Hopkins after solving a murder. Holmes told Detective Hopkins that he simply had "...the good fortune to get the right clue from the beginning. All *that I heard* pointed in the one direction. The amazing strength, the skill in the use of the harpoon, the rum and water, the sealskin tobacco-pouch with the coarse tobacco — all these pointed to a seaman, and one who had been a whaler."

Holmes picked up the vital clue because he knew what to listen for. Strangers reveal information about themselves whenever they speak. Most people miss vital clues because they hear but do not listen. After Watson first met Holmes, he tried to determine Holmes's profession when he compiled a list of all Holmes's strengths. What Watson failed to do is really *listen* to what Holmes said when Watson first met him.

In their first meeting, Holmes conducted an experiment that resulted in a new test for bloodstains. Holmes talked about how his new test would have convicted several criminals from the past. Holmes talked about the impact it would have on criminals in the present. People talk about what is important to them. For some people it is their kids. For other people it is their job. Others talk about their accomplishments, their skills, their money, their clothes, their cars, their religion and so forth. Sherlock Holmes talked about catching criminals.

Watson failed to draw a connection between what he heard Sherlock Holmes say about crime history and Holmes' line of work. Watson failed to listen for the key fact — criminality — and instead focused on Holmes's other strengths and weaknesses. Young Stamford had already told Watson that Holmes did not study medicine. If Watson had concentrated on the main issue, he would have reasoned that Holmes's line of work involved law enforcement. Unlike Watson, as he listened for key issues in a conversation, Holmes also listened for the next tip.

Holmes Listened for Similarities. Holmes would compare what he heard to a parallel fact, detail or case. He would listen for relationships between facts to weave a cogent theory around them. He considered each fact or detail he heard as part of a common thread from which he followed to its logical conclusion. Holmes described these threads as "loose ends" and "tangled skeins" that he had to unravel before he could get at the truth.

In *The Musgrave Ritual,* Holmes heard the story of a missing butler and maid. He then said: "...I listened to this extraordinary sequence of events, and endeavored to piece them together and to devise some common thread upon which they might all hang." Holmes always listened for comparisons in the things he heard. He would compare them to similar things he knew from his knowledge and experience.

In *The Adventure of the Noble Bachelor,* Holmes stated he had come to a fast conclusion about the case. He said: "I have notes of several similar cases...my whole examination served to turn my conjecture into a certainty. Circumstantial evidence is occasionally very convincing."

In *A Case of Identity,* Holmes listened to Mary Sutherland's narrative about her missing suitor. He then suggested to Watson: "...you will find parallel cases, if you consult my index, in Andover in '77, and there was something of the sort at The Hague last year. Old as is the idea, however, there were one or two details which were new to me."

Sherlock Holmes listened for common threads in conversations, discussions and narratives that a client, witness or suspect told him. Once he found a common theme amongst the facts he heard, he then pursued the various threads until he uncovered the solution. Yet, even as Holmes listened for related facts he also would listen for conflicting facts.

Holmes Listened for Inconsistencies. Many times people speak and do not realize they contradict themselves. They may say something unusual or make illogical statements that strain their credibility. An astute listener will note these contradictions and use them to mentally pick apart the stranger's story. In *The Reigate Puzzle,* Holmes did exactly that. He listened to Alec Cunningham's explanation regarding what happened to a murdered coachman. He realized the story had a hole in it. Holmes described it this way:

> "...If Alex Cunningham's narrative was correct, and if the assailant, after shooting William Kirwan, had *instantly* fled, then it obviously could not be he who tore the paper from the dead man's hand. But if it was not he, it must have been Alex Cunningham himself, for by the time that the old man had descended several servants were upon the scene..."

Alex Cunningham, in explaining away what happened as he rushed down the stairs, contradicted himself without realizing it. Holmes listening skills helped him notice the inconsistency and make the arrest.

In *The Problem of Thor Bridge,* Holmes believed Miss Durbar's story when she claimed no knowledge about the gun found in her closet. Everything he heard revealed to him that she did not commit the crime. He figured a suspect so cunning would not carelessly leave the very gun that would incriminate her in her own closet where someone would find it. Holmes reasoned someone placed the gun there to incriminate her.

Holmes, therefore, suggested to Watson her alleged action did not make sense. He said: "We must look for consistency. Where there is a want of it we must suspect deception." Holmes always became suspicious when a stranger's story contradicted itself. He also listened between the lines of conversation for a stranger's silence to get additional clues.

Holmes Listened for Unspoken Words and Feelings. When strangers talk what they leave out while speaking can tell more than what they actually say. An astute listener notices a stranger's unspoken feelings, worries and thoughts. He stays alert to strangers' unconscious urges, motives and impulses that they express during everyday conversations. Sherlock Holmes paid attention to unspoken messages in conversation. He listened for hints, clues and subtle signals in what a stranger *means* without really saying it. These silent indicators reveal themselves in the stranger's voice — the pauses, the rate, the volume, the pitch, the tone, the word choices and so forth.

In *The Adventure of the Veiled Lodger,* Holmes listened to what Eugenia Ronder did not say after telling him her sad story. She did not directly say that she planned to poison herself with Prussic acid. Holmes read it, however, in the way she spoke. He knew from listening accurately to her that she intended to take her own life. He convinced her not to do it only because he had truly listened to her *meaning* rather than her actual words.

In *A Scandal in Bohemia*, after completing the case to the King of Bohemia's satisfaction, Sherlock Holmes subtly insulted the King. The King had cried about Irene Adler: "What a woman — oh, what a woman! Did I not tell you how quick and resolute she was? Would she have not made an admirable queen? Is it not a pity that she is not on my level?" Holmes replied: "From what I have seen of the lady she seems indeed to be on a very different level to your Majesty." The insult passed right over the King's head because the King did not recognize its true meaning.

That is how it is with most people. They do not listen between the lines of conversation. They do not use their common sense while listening. They do not listen for double meaning in words that others use.[37] As a result, strangers often mislead them during conversations.

In *Revenge of the Sith (2008),* the evil Emperor Palpatine told the separatists hiding on the volcanic planet Mustafar that Darth Vader would soon arrive to "take care of you." Darth Vader then went to the planet and killed them all. The separatists did not realize the Emperor's words true meaning. Sherlock Holmes did not make that mistake. He knew what to listen for and used that knowledge, along with the next tip, to accurately size up strangers and solve problems.

Holmes Listened for the Trivial. In everyday conversations, people reveal themselves through the minor things they say. They may make slips of the tongue, where they mean to say one thing and accidently say something else.[38] They may mishear what a person says and think they heard the person say another thing. They may make slight false starts and pauses in conversations that most people miss. Holmes noticed these small expressions in conversation. He based his method on hearing the littlest things.

In *A Case of Identity,* Holmes told a client: "It has long been an axiom of mine that the little things are indefinitely the most important." He therefore, listened for trivial verbal expressions in his conversations with strangers. In *The Boscombe Valley*

---

[37] In *The Godfather (1973)* Don Vito Corleone made a famous double meaning statement when he said: "I'll make him an offer he can't refuse" regarding a movie director who refused to cast his godson in a coveted role. Vito Corleone then had the director's prize racehorse head placed in the director's bed to send him a message. The director understood the message and gave Vito's godson the part in the movie.

[38] Sigmund Freud discussed slips of the tongue; mishearing's and other frivolous verbal expressions in his book *The Psychopathology of Everyday Life.*

Mystery, Holmes listened to young McCarthy's account of a murder. Two minor points in young McCarthy's narrative impressed Holmes favorably. Holmes focused on the trifling words "Cooee" and "Rat." He then used *reason* to eliminate the impossible. He found the important little thing, which proved young McCarthy innocent and saved his life.

Sherlock Holmes later stated to Watson: "You know my method. It is founded on the observation of trifles." He used this method to observe and listen to seemingly insignificant things a stranger said. He would listen for those trifling verbal tics in conversations even as he used the next tip.

Holmes Listened for Deception. In Chapter 2, you learned some body language signs that may indicate a stranger is behaving suspiciously or deceptively. Once you combine your body language knowledge with your listening skills, you can increase your ability to accurately size up strangers. Sherlock Holmes often used his listening skills to determine the verbal signs of deception.

In *The Resident Patient,* Holmes knew Mr. Blessington lied to him about a burglary because Holmes recognized his deceptive speech as he listened to him. He could tell it in the following ways: Mr. Blessington's nervous and quavering voice as he fearfully threatened to shoot anyone who ascended the stairs to his room. Mr. Blessington becoming defensive when Holmes asked him did he know the two men who hunted him. Mr. Blessington changing the subject by showing Holmes his black box. Mr. Blessington becoming verbally evasive. Mr. Blessington claiming he told Holmes everything when he did not. Mr. Blessington's words not matching his actions. All these verbal clues helped Sherlock Holmes identify deceptive behavior.

In *The Adventure of the Three Garridebs,* Holmes knew lawyer John Garrideb lied to him because he heard red flags in his story, which made Holmes suspicious. Holmes knew it in several ways: Mr. Garrideb's voice tone changed from friendly to distrust. Mr. Garrideb defensively forced a laugh after Holmes commented on his clothes. Mr. Garrideb hastily changed the subject from his clothing to the issue why he came to see Holmes. Mr. Garrideb's natural voice changed from anger to calmness after Holmes explained the reason he became involved in the matter. Mr. Garrideb talked too much and gave too many specifics in his story about the search for three men with the name Garrideb. Mr. Garrideb said he had been in London a short time yet his clothes and accent revealed otherwise. All these oral hints allowed Sherlock Holmes to recognize deceptive behavior when he heard it.

Below is a list of deception indicators that Holmes listened for while strangers' spoke. Listen and use them along with the stranger's body language to arrive at the truth. Strangers may use the following deceptive verbal clues while speaking to you:

1. They repeat the question you ask.
2. They hesitate or pause a lot while speaking.
3. They talk too much or too little during conversation.
4. They become defensive when you discuss certain topics.
5. They verbally distance themselves from the subject.
6. They use qualifying speech: "To best of my knowledge."
7. They are too specific in explaining their story.
8. They blame someone else to draw attention away from themselves.
9. They cannot tell their story backwards.
10. They do not match their words and actions together.
11. They repeat your words back to you.
12. They do not use contractions such as "I did not do it"
13. They are verbally evasive to your questions.
14. They leave out pronouns ('I" "me") and speak in a monotone voice.
15. They mumble their words. They do not speak clearly.
16. They change the subject or become relieved when you change the subject.

17. They use humor or sarcasm to avoid the topic or subject.
18. They speak in a tense or high-pitched voice.
19. They avoid giving details about what they say.
20. They change their speech patterns (normally talks fast now talks slow).
21. They answer questions you do not ask.
22. They change their natural way of speaking when asked sensitive questions.
23. They use words that do not make sense or they use poor grammar.
24. They take too long to answer questions that should not take long to answer.
25. They have a ready-made answer for everything you say.
26. They try to convince you they are telling the truth by saying: "I swear to God" or "I swear on my child's life."

When Holmes had no suspicions about a stranger and just sought to obtain information, he would close his eyes and concentrate on what the stranger said. When Sherlock Holmes had suspicions about a stranger, he would keep his eyes open. Holmes would look directly at the stranger as he listened to him or her speak. Sometimes Holmes would use the next tip to determine their credibility.

Holmes Tested Strangers While Listening. When Holmes suspected a stranger's credibility, he would test it with a question or statement. Sometimes he did it to catch a stranger in a lie. Other times he did it to let strangers know, they could not fool or outsmart him. Either way, he used the same listening technique to expose their deceptive behavior.

In *The Adventure of the Three Garridebs,* Holmes allowed lawyer John Garrideb to tell him about his search for two more men named Garrideb. He did not let the lawyer know he did not believe him. Instead, after listening to the lawyer's narrative, Holmes asked him about advertising in the newspaper agony columns. The lawyer stated he already did that. Then Holmes

173

asked him about a dead mayor named Dr. Starr. When the lawyer claimed he knew him, Holmes immediately understood he caught Mr. Garrideb in two lies. How? Because Holmes always checked, the newspaper agony columns and he made up the name Dr. Starr.

In *The Adventure of the Abbey Grange,* Holmes put Captain Crocker to a test when he told him to flee. Holmes led Captain Crocker to believe that the authorities would blame Mary Fraser (Lady Brackenstall) for her husband's murder. Captain Crocker refused. Holmes then said to him: "I was only testing you. You ring true every time." In *The Adventure of the Three Students,* Holmes asked the servant Bannister to tell him about the missing exam papers. Bannister denied knowing anything. Holmes then called the suspected student Gilchrist in the room. Holmes implied Bannister told him about the missing exam papers. The student Gilchrist then admitted taking the examination papers.

In *The Adventure of the Blue Carbuncle,* Holmes made James Ryder aware that he knew everything about the theft of Countess of Morcar's blue gem. Once Mr. Ryder realized it, he spilled out everything to Holmes and confirmed what he knew. In *The Adventure of the Devil's Foot,* Holmes tested Dr. Leon Sterndale when he accused him regarding Mortimer Tregennis' murder. Dr. Sterndale called Holmes accusation a bluff. Holmes replied: "The bluff is upon your side...as a proof I will tell you some of the facts upon which my conclusions are based." After Holmes had explained, Dr. Sterndale admitted everything.

In *The Adventure of the Second Stain,* Holmes told Lady Hilda that he knew everything about a crucial State letter she took from her husband's red dispatch box. Once Lady Hilda understood Holmes knew all about it, she told Holmes everything else and why she took it. These cases establish Holmes always tested a client, witness or suspect when he needed to determine their credibility. After Sherlock Holmes heard a stranger and used the above listening tips, he put them all together with the final and most-important one.

Holmes Used Reason While Listening. In Chapter 3, you learned about Holmes's rules of deduction and how he applied logic to size up strangers. Just as Holmes used reason while he observed strangers, he also used it while he listened to them. In fact, Holmes spent more time listening to strangers than he did observing them. He would hear their narrative then reason from what he heard to reach a conclusion. Holmes was not timid in drawing inferences from what he heard.

In *The Adventure of the Abbey Grange,* Sherlock Holmes reasoned from what he heard when he discussed with Watson his suspicion regarding Lady Brackenstall's story. He said: "Surely there are details in her story which, if we looked at in cold blood, would excite our suspension." He reasoned that normal burglars do not act the way she claimed. He then reached the logical conclusion that Lady Brackenstall and her maid covered up for the real criminal. Holmes used his logic and listening skills to reason that the wineglasses played an important part in the crime.

In *The Valley of Fear,* Holmes used logic as he listened to Mrs. Douglas and Mr. Barker's story regarding finding her dead husband. He reasoned from what he heard and believed they did not tell the truth. He said: "The whole story told by Barker is a lie. But Barker's story is corroborated by Mrs. Douglas. Therefore she is lying also." Holmes reasoned that the candle in the room stayed lit for a short time, showing no long interview had occurred. He then reached the logical conclusion that the true murderer was in the room and the couple let him escape. These cases establish that Sherlock Holmes reasoned from what he heard many times during his investigations and when he sized up strangers.

You cannot go wrong if you use reason while you listen to a stranger. It is the most-important tool you have when seeking to understand what makes a stranger tick. Without using logic as you listen, you will fail miserably in evaluating people. On the other hand, using the correct logic as you listen will enable you to communicate with strangers successfully.

The ten tips above make up the technique Holmes used whenever he listened to a client, a witness, a rival or a suspect. Use the listening principle together with the four basic questions and the other principles. Once you do this, few strangers will speak without you hearing what they are *really* saying.

Go to Pages 323 to 327 if you want to practice
the listening exercises now.

Chapter 7

Easily Read a Stranger's Mind With This Holmes Technique

"How often is imagination the mother of truth?"
Sherlock Holmes, The Valley of Fear

In *The Musgrave Ritual,* Butler Richard Brunton discovered the meaning behind a mysterious old ritual, which the Musgrave descendants overlooked for centuries. The butler believed the ritual contained the location to a buried treasure that held valuable riches. A Musgrave ancestor left the ritual for his descendants but died before he could tell them the message's last part. The Butler Brunton used his *imagination* to figure out clues in the ritual and decipher its' meaning. Sherlock Holmes would later use his own imagination to figure out what the butler discovered and solve the Musgrave mystery.

In this chapter, you will learn the simple technique Sherlock Holmes used to read the butler's mind. You will learn what Holmesian imagination is, why it is effective in solving problems and how to use it to size up strangers. The Holmesian imagination technique relies on three simple steps that can also help you discover the secret hidden in this book.

The Musgrave ancestors overlooked the ritual because they considered it trivial. Many readers overlook the secret because Sir Arthur Conan Doyle left it hiding in plain sight. But just as Sherlock Holmes discovered the secret contained in the ritual, you can discover the secret contained in this book. The fifty-six short stories and four novels reveal The Sherlock Holmes Method (asking questions and using principles). The stories also contain clues that reveal the secret you are searching for.

177

The secret originates in your ability to think for yourself. It arises from your ability to analyze people accurately and to reach valid conclusions about them. The secret is simple but it is powerful! It is simple because you already possess this natural mental ability. It is powerful because it checks and balances your imagination to ensure that what you visualize is accurate.

But the secret works best when you discover it for yourself. That is why the book has not revealed it to you directly. At some point while reading this book, you will realize what it is subtlety hinting to you. The secret's meaning will dawn on you and leap from a page in the book into your head! Mark that moment! For in that moment your mind will open! Why? Simply because *a revelation that comes from your own mind is a far more powerful stimulant than one that is simply told to you!*

You can make your brain receptive to revelations by stimulating it with your imagination. Once you do this, you will understand the significance in using the Holmesian imagination technique to read a stranger's mind.

The Power of Holmesian Imagination

It is clear Holmes valued imagination and considered it important in his detective work. In *Silver Blaze*, he describes Inspector Gregory as "...an extremely competent officer. Were he but gifted with imagination he might raise to great heights in his profession."

In *The Adventure of the Norwood Builder*, he tells Inspector Lestrade that the clues, which seemingly incriminate a man, are too obvious. Holmes then says: "You do not add imagination to your other great qualities..." and gives Lestrade his reasons for believing the young man is innocent.

Sherlock Holmes valued imagination but he did not use it like most people do. The average person wrongly uses imagination to fantasize about people. They wildly dream about all kinds of unrealistic things. They base their thinking on fantasies, rumors, gossip, hearsay, wild guesses and misinformation with no basis in reality. Holmes based his imaginative thinking on a scientific foundation.

In *The Hound of the Baskervilles*, Dr. Mortimer claimed Holmes used guesswork in his thinking. Holmes replied he balances "...probabilities and chooses the most likely. It is the scientific use of the imagination."

Imagination, as defined in this book, is the ability to think creatively with a scientific basis. It is visualizing the person or problem you face in a realistic and practical manner.

In *The Problem of Thor Bridge*, Sherlock Holmes described his creative thinking as "...that mixture of imagination and reality which is the basis of my art." Holmes limited his creative thinking to the natural world. He combined imagination with reality when he sought to size up a stranger or solve a problem.

In *The Adventure of the Sussex Vampire*, Holmes considered the possibility of vampirism. He then stated: "...are we to give serious attention to such things? This agency stands flat-footed upon the ground, and there it must remain. The world is big enough for us. No ghosts need apply."

Sherlock Holmes did not rely on the supernatural.[39] He relied on *reason* to fine-tune his imagination. Whenever he did allow his mind to wander into the regions of conjecture, speculation and surmise, he always brought it back down to reality by passing it through his critical thinking. He always

---

[39]Sir Arthur Conan Doyle turned to the supernatural and became a strong advocate of spiritualism after his oldest son, brother and mother died. He believed in life after death and published several books on spiritualism such as *The New Revelation, The Vital Message* and his two-volume work *History of Spiritualism*.

possessed facts to support his educated guesses. He always used evidence as his foundation. He meant this when he said to Dr. Mortimer that his imaginative thinking always has "...some material basis on which to start our speculations."

Sherlock Holmes would obtain that material basis from the facts and evidence regarding the problem or individual. He would apply his creative and reasoning skills in a realistic and practical way. Sherlock Holmes then used a simple three-step imagination technique in which he would get into an individual's mind to understand how he or she thought.

Three Steps To Reading A Stranger's Mind

The first step Sherlock Holmes took to get inside an individual's head is he estimated the person's intelligence. The formal way to do this is through an Intelligence Quotient (IQ) test. This test asks a series of questions, which tests your knowledge on various subjects and facts. The testers then do calculations, which give them a numerical estimate of your intelligence.[40]

The IQ test, however, does not work in the real world. You cannot use scientific tests, double-blind studies or written exams in everyday life to determine a stranger's mental capacity. These things are useless in real world situations where you do not have a controlled environment such as a laboratory. Most scientific studies simply confirm what most people already know anyway and have learnt from trial and error.

Instead, use a practical and common sense method to gauge a stranger's intelligence. Use the principles you learned in the previous chapters. These practical principles depend upon your asking questions, observing, reasoning, knowing, experiencing

---

[40] According to *Wikipedia,* the average person's IQ is between 86 and 115. A person with an IQ from 70 to 85 is considered slow or stupid. A highly intelligent or genius IQ ranges from 116 to above 130.

and listening to the stranger. You have to use them on the spot in everyday encounters with people. Holmes often used them to size up a stranger's intelligence when he first met him or her.

In *The Sign of Four*, Sherlock Holmes gauged Jonathan Small's intelligence. He sized up Small as having "...a certain degree of low cunning, but I did not think him capable of anything in the nature of delicate finesse. That is usually the product of higher education."

In *The Musgrave Ritual*, Sherlock Holmes estimated Butler Richard Brunton's intelligence. He sized up Brunton as being "...a very clever man, and to have had a clearer insight than ten generations of his masters."

In *The Final Problem*, Homes judged Professor Moriarty's intelligence. He sized up Professor Moriarty as being his "intellectual equal." But Sherlock Holmes also said to Watson: "There are limits, you see, to our friend's intelligence. It would have been a coup-de-maître had he deduced what I would deduce and acted accordingly."

In *The Adventure of the Abbey Grange*, Holmes assessed Captain Crocker's intelligence. Sherlock Holmes had described to Watson how Captain Crocker covered up the way a woman's husband died. Holmes sized up Crocker as being "...remarkably quick-witted, for this whole ingenious story is of his concoction."

In *The Adventure of the Mazarin Stone*, Sherlock Holmes calculated prizefighter Sam Merton's intelligence. He sized up Merton as having a "slow intellect."

In *The Adventure of the Creeping Man*, Sherlock Holmes measured Professor Presbury's intelligence. He sized up Presbury as having "...a particularly clear and logical brain from the little I saw of him." Sherlock Holmes had gone to meet the professor to ascertain the cause of his strange behavior.

In *The Adventure of the Three Gables,* Sherlock Holmes evaluated Isadora Klein's intelligence. He sized up Klein's intelligence as above average. But then she began playing games with him. When she did this, he stated: "I have underrated your intelligence." Sherlock Holmes' threaten to tell the police and eventually forced her to reveal what she knew about the assault on his client.

In *The Adventure of the Retired Colourman,* Sherlock Holmes appraised miser Josiah Amberley's intelligence. Holmes sized up Amberley's intelligence when he gave Inspector Mackinnon insight into Amberley's mentality. He described it by saying, "...Amberley excelled at chess — one mark...of a scheming mind."

All the above examples establish how Sherlock Holmes sized up strangers' by their intelligence when he first met or heard about them. Remember, the Sherlock Holmes Method to estimating intelligence does not use any scientific tests or studies. It is a practical way to size up strangers based on your subjective evaluations, which could be right or wrong. Therefore, use caution when you apply it. Do not offend people by telling them how you rate their intelligence.

How To Estimate a Stranger's Intelligence

The reason it is important for you to rate a person's intelligence is so that you can understand how the person *thinks.* Keep it simple. Ask yourself is the stranger's intelligence above average; average, or below average. A person with above-average intelligence can range from being extremely bright to a genius. A person with average intelligence has the normal mental capacity you would expect to find in the typical stranger you meet. A person with below-average intelligence can range from being slow to idiotic.

In addition, keep in mind that people have different kinds of 'intelligence.' Some people are 'book smart' but not 'street smart.' Others are 'experts' in particular fields but 'dummies' in other areas of their lives. Some people are 'slow' and take longer to learn and understand things. Some people quickly grasp the significance of issues, problems and events they face. Some people think analytically while others think creatively. To gauge a person's intelligence, ask yourself: How knowledgeable is the person? Are they creative and practical? Do they learn fast? Are they resourceful? How much experience do they have?

Another practical way to estimate a stranger's intelligence is to listen as the person speaks. You can tell a lot about people from the words they use. Their vocabulary tells you how smart they are. Do they use big words or do they speak plainly? Do they speak clearly? Use slang? Curse? Is their conversation positive or negative? Do they speak realistically or idealistically? Their vocabulary reveals how educated they are and the way they communicate with others.

You can determine a person's intelligence in a specific area. How? Ask them questions to see how much or little they know about a topic. For example, in *The Adventure of the Illustrious Client,* Watson impersonated Dr. Hill Barton, an expert in Chinese pottery. Baron Adelbert Gruner, however, saw through his deception. He asked Watson several questions to test his knowledge about ceramics. When Watson refused to answer the questions, Baron Gruner called him an imposter.

Also, how much schooling a stranger has received reveals his or her intelligence. Did the stranger complete grade and high school? Did they attend college or graduate school? Did they get specialized training in a specific field?

What books and newspapers do they read? How is their writing ability? Does the individual communicate through written letters? Typed e-mails? Texts or tweets? The grammar, word usage, vocabulary, spelling and sentence structure may indicate their education level.

You also can tell a lot about a stranger's intelligence from his or her everyday life experiences. Their worldly knowledge reveals what they know. Their worldly experience reveals what they have done. Their common sense or practical intelligence reveals the decisions they make in their lives.

In *The Gloria Scott* case, Holmes described Victor Trevor's father as being a practical, worldly man. His father traveled a lot, worked with his hands and possessed little formal education. His father's practical intelligence or common sense, however, made him a fortune.

A stranger's common sense, knowledge, education and experience are an important part to understanding him or her. All the above factors combined can help you to get a practical, real world sense of a stranger's intelligence.

Eliminate the Personal Equation

Once Sherlock Holmes rated a stranger's intelligence, the second step he took is to make allowances for the 'personal equation'.[41] The personal equation is the natural bias you have when sizing up a stranger. You make allowances for it by understanding the personal factors that influence your judgment. Then you eliminate any prejudices, biases or expectations that you may have.

There are many personal biases that can affect your judgment. For example, you may see only what you want to see about people (confirmation bias). You may believe something about someone only because your friends do (communal reinforcement). You may personally find meaning in something a person does where there is no meaning (personal validation).

---

[41] Wikipedia states: "The personal equation, in 19th- and early 20th-century science, referred to the idea that every individual observer had an inherent bias when it came to measurements and observations."

You may not notice changes about people even when they are right before your eyes (change blindness). You may make excuses for someone because you like them (rationalization). You may block from your mind something a person said because it hurts to think about it (denial). These biases and many others are the modern day equivalent of the personal equation Sherlock Holmes discussed.

You can eliminate personal biases by looking at all sides of an issue. Keep an open mind when dealing with people. Know your prejudices, expectations, motives and correct them. Control your feelings (fear, anger, depression, etc.) and do not let them unduly influence your thinking. Do your own research and check sources. Do not allow a group to think for you. Stick to facts and evidence when evaluating arguments and opinions. Consider with caution hearsay, rumors, gossip and anecdotal stories that people tell you.

Sherlock did all the above when he made allowances for the personal equation. In *The Musgrave Ritual,* Holmes concluded the Butler Brunton possessed a 'first-rate' intelligence (he had above average intelligence). Therefore, Holmes saw no need to look for any bias in himself while interpreting Brunton's actions.

When Sherlock Holmes did not rule out the personal equation, however, he usually met with disastrous results. In *A Scandal in Bohemia,* Holmes did not calculate his personal equation with Irene Adler. He allowed his stereotypical view of women to interfere with his reasoning. Thus, he lost in a duel of wits with her.

In *The Adventure of the Three Gables,* Sherlock Holmes also did not use his personal equation when evaluating Isadora Klein's intelligence. Therefore, he made a mistake when he overrated it. Once he eliminated any personal bias in his thinking about a person, he moved to the third step in his imagination technique.

Holmes Put Himself In The Person's Place

In *The Musgrave Ritual,* Sherlock Holmes described to Watson the third step in his imagination technique. He said: "You know my methods in such cases, Watson. I put myself in the man's place, and, having first gauged his intelligence, I try to imagine how I should myself have proceeded under the same circumstances." Holmes could put himself in another individual's place and see things from his point of view because Holmes possessed highly developed empathy.

Empathy, as defined in this book, is the ability to understand another person's thoughts, feelings and actions. It is the ability to put yourself in their shoes and walk in them. It is the ability to imagine how you would think or feel in the same situation. It is the ability to know what you would do in that exact situation. Although Sherlock Holmes controlled his emotions, he did have empathy for others.

In *The Adventure of the Noble Bachelor,* Sherlock Holmes showed his empathy for Lord St. Simon. He explained to Watson that he understood why Lord St. Simon did not display any gracious conduct towards his ex-wife and her first husband. Holmes mentally placed himself in Lord St. Simon's shoes. Holmes empathized with Lord St. Simon's frustration, pain and anger at losing his ex-wife and her wealth.

In *A Study in Scarlet,* Sherlock Holmes showed his empathy for Jefferson Hope. He stated to Watson: "...from his point of view, any sudden change would be likely to draw attention to himself." Holmes said this after he explained how Hope avoided detection for a murder he committed.

In *The Sign of Four,* Holmes showed his empathy for Jonathan Small. He said to Watson: "...let us put ourselves in the place of Jonathan Small. Let us look at it from his point of view." Holmes said this after he explained how Mr. Small accomplished his deadly mission.

In *The Boscombe Valley Mystery,* Holmes showed his empathy for a young man accused of murder. He stated to Watson: "I shall approach this case from the point of view that what this young man says is true." He said this after he explained his theory on what happened in the case.

But exactly how do you walk in someone else's shoes? What if the person comes from a very different background than you? How do you actually think and feel like they do? How do you look at something from another person's point of view? Simple. Do what Sherlock Holmes did. Use your imagination to put yourself in the stranger's place.

How To Put Yourself In A Person's Place

In *The Adventure of the Retired Colourman,* Sherlock Holmes exposed miser Josiah Amberley as a murderer. He then said to Inspector MacKinnon: "You'll get results, Inspector, by always putting yourself in the other fellow's place, and thinking what you would do yourself. It takes some imagination, but it pays." Holmes then explained to Inspector Mackinnon how he put himself in the murdered man's place:

> "Now, we will suppose that you were shut up in this little room, had not two minutes to live, but wanted to get even with the fiend who was probably mocking at you from the other side of the door. What would you do?"

> "Write a message."

"Exactly. You would like to tell people how you died. No use writing on paper. That would be seen. If you wrote on the wall someone might rest upon it. Now, look here! Just above the skirting is scribbled with a purple indelible pencil: "We we —' That's all."

"What do you make of that?"

"Well, it's only a foot above the ground. The poor devil was on the floor dying when he wrote it. He lost his senses before he could finish."

"He was writing, 'We were murdered.'

"That's how I read it...."

Holmes read from the evidence what the murdered man did because he understood what the dying man *thought*. Once you understand how a person thinks you can then put yourself in his or her place. The ability to do this requires that you create a mental picture with your mind's eye.

Imagination is the mind's eye! It allows you to 'see' what others cannot!

Close your eyes and picture yourself feeling, experiencing, thinking and acting like the person. Visualize what it means to be the person you are trying to understand. Use the mental image to look at things from his or her point of view.

In *The Adventure of the Abbey Grange,* Sherlock Holmes suggested Watson use his 'mind's eye' to visualize several wineglasses. Watson stated that he saw the glasses clearly in his mind. Holmes then explained to Watson his hypothesis regarding the beeswing in the wine glasses. Holmes suggested Watson use his 'minds eye' because he wanted Watson to understand how the criminal who devised the plan *thought*.

Once you use your mind's eye to visualize a mental image, then internalize your mental picture. Use empathy. Mimic the person's behavior, speech and facial expressions to get a sense of what the person is going through. Use the same technique that actors use to get into character. They role-play. An actor that is studying for a character role will *become* the character.

In *The Adventure of the Dying Detective*, Holmes said, "The best way of successfully acting a part is to be it." He then fooled Culverton Smith into believing that he lay dying. Holmes estimated Smith's intelligence, made allowances for any bias, placed himself in Smith's shoes and imagined what it would take to get Smith to admit the murder. Holmes then internalized the mental picture when he became the physical manifestation of the Asiatic disease Smith believed Holmes contacted.

After you internalize your mental picture, then make it personal. When you personalize a mental picture, you add an extra layer of understanding to what you are doing. You are making the stranger relevant to your life through adapting the mental picture to your situation. Often when you personalize what a stranger is saying or doing you can draw a parallel from your own experience. It will help you quickly understand strangers and make it easier to put yourself in their shoes.

How do you make a mental picture personal? Easy. Ask yourself questions such as "How would I think, feel or act under similar circumstances?" "Did I ever have a similar experience?" "What would Sherlock Holmes do?" "Does the person's physical action remind me of something I did or said in the past?" "Does the individual talk or act like someone I know?" "What would the person do next?" Sherlock Holmes did this many times as he looked at things from another person's point of view.

In *A Study in Scarlet*, Sherlock Holmes made his mental picture of Jefferson Hope personal. He explained to Watson how Hope sought to recover a ring:

"Now put yourself in that man's place. On thinking the matter over, it must have occurred to him that it was possible he had lost the ring in the road after leaving the house. What would he do then? He would eagerly look out for the evening papers in the hope of seeing it among the articles found. His eye, of course, would light upon this. He would be overjoyed. Why should he fear a trap? There would be no reason in his eyes why the finding of the ring should be connected with the murder. He will come. He will come. You shall see him within the hour..."

Holmes could predict Hope's thinking; behavior and motives because he personalized what Jefferson Hope would do and thought like him. Holmes then further explained to Watson that Hope worked as a cabdriver. Hope avoided detection by making no sudden changes in his behavior.

In *The Sign of Four,* Sherlock Holmes made his mental picture of Jonathan Small personal. Holmes explained to Watson how Small hid a boat:

"I then put myself in the place of Small and looked at it as a man of his capacity would. He would probably consider that to send back the launch or to keep it at a wharf would make pursuit easy if the police did happen to get on this track. How, then, could he conceal the launch and yet have her at hand when wanted? I wondered what I should do myself if I were in his shoes. I could only think of one way of doing it. I might hand the launch over to some boat-builder or repairer, with the directions to make a trifling change in her. She would then be removed to his shed or yard, and so be effectually concealed, while at the same time I could have her at a few hours notice."

Sherlock Holmes predicted what Jonathan Small had done because Holmes personalized what he would do in a similar situation. He then acted on it. Holmes further explained to Watson how he tracked down the boat by inquiring in all the boat yards until he found it.

In *Silver Blaze,* Holmes made his mental picture of a racehorse personal. Sherlock Holmes explained to Watson where the horse went:

> "...what has become of the horse. Now, supposing that he broke away during or after the tragedy, where could he have gone to? The horse is a very gregarious creature. If left to himself his instincts would have been either to return to King's Pyland or go over to Mapleton. Why should he run wild upon the moor? He would have surely have been seen by now. And why should the gypsies kidnap him? These people always clear out when they hear of trouble, for they do not wish to be pestered by the police. They could not hope to sell such a horse. They would run a great risk and gain nothing by taking him...."

Holmes predicted where the racehorse fled and found his tracks because he personalized what the horse would do. He then followed his mental picture. He said to Watson: "See the value of imagination...we imagined what might have happened, acted upon the supposition, and find ourselves justified." Holmes found the racehorse because he used his imagination to think outside the box.

Think Outside The Box Like Sherlock Holmes

In Chapter 3, you learned about reasoning by elimination and how it could lead you to flawed thinking if you did not consider all possibilities. In Chapter 4, you learned how to use specialized knowledge to provide the raw data you need to visualize more causes that are possible.

When you think outside the box, combine your imagination with your logic and special knowledge. Come up with new angles and points of view that you did not consider before. It is using the imagination scientifically just as Sherlock Holmes stated. He used it during his investigations or to size up strangers. One-way Sherlock Holmes would think outside the box is when a person suggested a wrong theory (typically Watson or Lestrade). It would stir something in Holmes's own imagination to come up with the correct answer.

In *The Adventure of the Creeping Man,* Watson described how he stimulated Holmes's thinking. Watson said: "...I was a whetstone for his mind. I stimulated him. He liked to think aloud in my presence...If I irritated him by a certain methodical slowness in my mentality, that irritation served only to make his own flame-like intuitions and impressions flash up the more vividly and swiftly. Such was my humble role in our alliance."

For example, in *The Hound of the Baskervilles*, Watson deduced several facts from a walking stick left behind by its owner. Sherlock Holmes then examined the stick and corrected Watson. He said: "...Watson, most of your conclusions were erroneous. When I said that you stimulated me I meant, to be frank, that in noting your fallacies I was occasionally guided towards the truth."

Another way Sherlock Holmes stimulated his own creative thinking is he sought input from other people. He often asked Watson, clients, witnesses or rivals what they thought about a stranger or problem even as he formed his own theory. He used this method to increase his chances of being correct when he reasoned by elimination. Many times during his criminal investigations, Holmes would ask: "What do you make of it?" or "Do you have a theory about the problem?" He would then use the person's answer to stir his own thoughts and find a solution.

Sometimes, rather than just ask a question, Holmes would go to the crime scene to stimulate his creative thinking. In *The Adventure of the Bruce-Partington Plans,* Watson describes how Detective Lestrade noticed Holmes, while standing at a crime scene, did not pay attention to the fresh evidence Lestrade had found regarding a young man's death:

> "...Why, whatever is the matter with Mr. Holmes?"

> "My friend was standing with an expression of strained intensity upon his face, staring at the railway metals where they curved out of the tunnel. Aldgate is a junction, and there was a network of points. On these his eager, questioning eyes were fixed, and I saw on his keen, alert face that tightening of the lips, that quiver of the nostrils, and concentration of the heavy, tufted brows which I knew so well."

Holmes used his imagination to think outside the box and visualize a scenario to explain the young man's murder. He focused his mind on the points in the junction and pictured how the young man came onto the train's roof. Watson had no idea what Holmes was imagining. He described how Holmes's facial expressions "showed me that some novel and suggestive circumstance had opened up a stimulating line of thought" in Holmes's mind. Holmes used his imagination, with no evidence, to picture someone placing the young man's body on the train's roof. He then imagined the body falling off during the train speeding to its destination.

In *The Adventure of the Sussex Vampire,* Sherlock Holmes also used his imagination, without any facts or evidence. He thought outside the box regarding a husband claiming his wife sucked their child's blood like a vampire. Holmes stated he already knew what he would find before he left 221B Baker Street. Holmes could say this because he used his imagination, along with his reason and special knowledge, to visualize what he believed had happened. As he told the husband Robert Ferguson:

> "It has been a case for intellectual deduction, but when this original intellectual deduction is confirmed point by point by quite a number of independent incidents, then the subjective becomes objective and we can say confidently that we have reached our goal. I had, in fact, reached it before we left Baker Street, and the rest has merely been observation and confirmation."

But what exactly did Holmes confirm?

First, he rejected the idea immediately that a vampire had anything to do with the matter. Holmes read the letter from the law firm. Holmes then said to Watson: "Rubbish, Watson, rubbish! What have we to do with walking corpses who can only be held in their grave by stakes driven through their hearts? It's pure lunacy."

Second, he used his special knowledge of history to deduce that a queen from England's past had once sucked the poison from a wound.

Third, from it being a South American household Sherlock Holmes observed the arrow and bow. He expected to find the weapons.

Fourth, he understood the connection between the dog, the poison and why someone needed to test it.

Fifth, he used his imagination to put himself in the wife's place. He estimated her intelligence and eliminated any bias, to see that she only sought to save the child's life.

And sixth, he observed the son Jack and understood Jack's motives for wanting to harm the child.

194

Holmes's skill may seem amazing but you already possess this natural ability. It is the ability to think creatively. It is the ability to put your self in someone else's place. It is the ability to use your imagination to tell what someone is thinking. Use the Holmesian imagination technique together with the other principles. Once you do this, you will have a powerful tool for reading a person's mind.

Go to Pages 328 to 330 if you want to practice
the imagination exercises now.

Chapter 8

This Holmesian Tip Works Wonders for Sizing-Up Strangers

*"...the skillful workman is very careful indeed
as to what he takes into his brain-attic.
He will have nothing but the tools
which may help him in doing his work..."*
Sherlock Holmes, A Study in Scarlet

In the *British Broadcasting Corporation (BBC)* crime drama series *Sherlock,* Actor Benedict Cumberbatch plays Sherlock Holmes. In the second season episode entitled *The Hounds of Baskerville,* a young man, Henry Knight, comes to Holmes at 221B Baker Street. Mr. Knight tells him about terrible memories he has regarding his father's death 20 years ago.

The modern day Sherlock Holmes investigates the matter and finds a torn burnt paper with some letters on it. He tells Watson and Dr. Stapleton to leave the room so he can use an ancient memory technique. He then uses the technique to figure out the letters' meaning. The scene in which Holmes searches his mind for information is a brilliant visual representation of the memory technique.

The memory technique Holmes used is so simple anyone can do it. You do not need Einstein intelligence. You do not need a photographic memory. You do not need to be a professional memory champion. You only need to learn a few easy steps because the technique relies on your natural ability to memorize.

In this chapter, you will learn about memory and how it works. You will learn the pros and cons of using it in your everyday life. You will learn how to improve your own memory. You will learn the ancient memory technique Holmes applied whenever he solved a problem. Finally, you will learn how to put it all together to size up strangers.

What Sherlock Holmes Believed About Memory

Sherlock Holmes compared his memory to a storage room where the mind could only hold limited facts and data. He believed in only storing relevant information in his mind that he used to solve crimes. He discarded any other information he believed unnecessary to his work.

In *A Study in Scarlet,* after Watson told him about the solar system, Sherlock Holmes replied: "Now that I know it, I shall do my best to forget it." He then explained his theory about memory in this way:

> "I consider that a man's brain originally is like a little empty attic, and you have to stock it with such furniture as you choose. A fool takes in all the lumber of every sort that he comes across, so that the knowledge which might be useful to him gets crowded out, or at best is jumbled up with a lot of other things, so that he has a difficulty in laying his hands upon it. The skillful workman is very careful indeed as to what he takes into his brain-attic. He will have nothing but the tools which may help him in doing his work. It is a mistake to think that that little room has elastic walls and can distend to any extent. Depend upon it there comes a time when for every addition of knowledge you forget something that you knew before. It is of the highest importance, therefore, not to have useless facts elbowing out the useful ones."

Sherlock Holmes held a common belief about memory popular in the late 19th century. He believed the 'filing cabinet' or 'library' concept where memory resides in a fixed, limited and specific part of the brain. Since that time, however, scientists have learned much more about how memory works.

The Three Types of Memory

Memory, as defined in this book, is the ability to retain and remember information received from the five senses. Contrary to what Sherlock Holmes believed, scientists have discovered the brain actually has flexibility. They have learned memory takes place across the *whole* brain not just one part of it.[42] They understand different areas in the brain come together to form memories.[43] They know that the brain contains over 100 billion neurons and trillions of synapses that link together.[44]

The 19th century psychologist Herman Ebbinghaus classified memory into three distinct categories: sensory, short-term and long-term. The sensory stage begins with using the five senses to create the memory. For example, when you observe a stranger's eyes, hear a stranger's voice, smell a stranger's cologne and touch a stranger's hand, these actions leave a strong sense impression in your mind. In other words, the more senses you use, the more vivid the memory.

As a person forms memories through the five senses, the brain either strengthens already linked nerve cells or creates new links between neurons and synapses. These nerve connections form a 'neural network' that causes chemical, electrical or physical changes in the brain. The nerve

---

[42] *How Stuff Works: How Human Memory Works,* Richard C. Mohs, Ph.D. and Carol Turkington.

[43] *How Stuff Works: How Human Memory Works,* Richard C. Mohs, Ph.D. and Carol Turkington.

[44] A neuron is a nerve cell that specializes in passing signals to other target cells. A synapse is a molecular link that joins nerve cells together and allows nerve impulses containing sensory information to travel between nerve endings within the brain *(see Wikipedia).*

connections directly affect areas in the brain associated with memory such as the cerebral cortex and hippocampus.[45] Once you have formed the memory, then the short-term stage comes into play.

The short-term memory stage begins when the brain stores a sense impression (sight, sound, etc.). This process lasts less than a second. You quickly lose the memory if you do not use it. Most people can retain from one to four items in their minds for up to 20 or 30 seconds.[46] After that, the items vanish from the mind unless the person makes a conscious effort to remember them. You slowly transfer critical information you repeatedly use to long-term memory.

The long-term memory stage begins after it receives information and experiences from the short-term memory. Through repeated learning and training, the long-term memory retains the important information. Long-term memory can hold vital information for a person's lifetime. It has no limits to the amount of information it can retain (but if you do not use it, you will slowly lose it). Once the brain stores the critical sense impression in the long-term memory, the person only has to recall it consciously when needed. You will learn how the memory works to accomplish this below.

How Memories Get Processed

There are three basic ways you process a memory. First, you receive it. You register the memory in the brain. Second, you store it. You retain the memory in the brain for future

---

[45] The cerebral cortex is the area in the brain that plays a key role in memory and other mental functions. The hippocampus is the area in the brain that consolidates short and long-term memories (*see Wikipedia*).

[46] In 1956 Psychologist George Miller published: *"The magical number seven, plus or minus two: Some limits on our capacity for processing information."* Psychological Review 63 (2): 81–97 (see Wikipedia).

reference or use. Third, you recall it. You consciously request the memory from the brain in order to use it.

Scientists describe registering memories as encoding. Encoding, as defined in this book, is simply stamping a memory onto your consciousness. You encode memories through awareness. Paying close attention to information ensures you will receive and imprint it accurately in your mind.

In *The Adventure of the Six Napoleons,* Detective Lestrade asked Sherlock Holmes what to do with a new fact Holmes found regarding a street lamp. Holmes replied: "To remember it — to docket it. We may come on to something later which may bear upon it." This case establishes Holmes *consciously* retained facts and information he needed so he could encode it into his memory for later use.

Once information becomes encoded, it then gets stored in the brain. The storage process, however, does not copy memories like a tape recorder (as most people believe). The brain actually retains information in different areas and reconstructs it on the fly when you need it.[47]

For example, when you meet a stranger, each sense impression you retain — the stranger's face, voice, appearance and behavior — gets stored in a different region in the brain. Without your awareness, each brain area works seamlessly in retaining your total experience in meeting the stranger.

When you need information, you recall it to your mind. The thoughts you think are the means that allow you to recall a memory. Simply think about it and your thoughts will activate an electrical or chemical process in your brain. Different regions in your mind will 'light up' and send the memory fragments they

---

[47] Memory *(Skeptic's Dictionary):* http://www.skepdic.com/memory.html.

hold to your consciousness. You will receive these different fragments as one whole 'memory' of what you sought to recall.

In *The Disappearance of Lady Frances Carfax,* Sherlock Holmes sought to recall a fact he retained in his mind. He said to Watson: "...It was the remark of the undertaker's wife...she had said, "It should be there before now. It took longer, being out the ordinary.' It was the coffin of which she spoke...then in an instant I remembered the deep sides, and the little wasted figure at the bottom. Why so large a coffin for so small a body? To leave room for another body." Holmes had recalled a clue from the deepest parts of his mind, which helped him solve the case.

You can also trigger a memory without thinking about it. Often something you see, hear, taste, touch or smell will remind you of a previous memory. In *The Adventure of the Lion's Mane*, Sherlock Holmes vaguely remembered reading about a deadly jellyfish. He told Mr. Murdoch: "I am an omnivorous reader with a strangely retentive memory for trifles. That phrase 'the Lion's Mane' haunted my mind. I knew that I had seen it somewhere in an unexpected context." The phrase had triggered a memory in Holmes's mind regarding similar information he read.

The ability to receive, store and recall memories comes natural to you. But there are advantages and disadvantages to using it that you should know about. Knowing the facts about memory will make you better at memorizing. It will help you avoid the mistakes many people make when sizing up strangers.

Holmes Understood The Pros and Cons of Memory

Sherlock Holmes had the right idea when he rejected useless information from entering his memory. He always filtered the information he received. No one can absorb all the information they receive in their everyday lives. We all screen, either consciously or unconsciously, what we experience and learn. We all forget most of the daily sense impressions that enter our minds. Holmes simply made a *conscious* decision to filter specific data he needed to do his work. He understood the upside and downside when using his memory.

The upside when using his memory during investigations had many benefits. *Holmes used his memory to remember things because he had a specific goal in mind.* In *The Norwood Builder* case, Holmes informed Detective Lestrade that he had a reason for everything he did after he recalled a thumb mark not being on a wall the night before. *Holmes used his memory to remember important details related to his work.* In *The Valley of Fear,* Detective White Mason expressed admiration at Holmes's skill in naming a specific gun maker from his memory.

Holmes used his memory to remember names, faces, facts and evidence that had bearing on his cases. In The *Charles Augustus Milverton* case, Watson described how Holmes recalled to his memory a beautiful woman who had just committed a murder. *Holmes used his memory to remember experiences, images and words to solve cases.* In *The Adventure of the Bruce-Partington Plans*, Holmes stated how he vaguely remembered seeing windows above a train line while traveling on it.

Holmes used his memory to see clues, patterns and problems. In *The Five Orange Pips,* Holmes relied on his memory to detect a pattern in assassins mailing letters before they arrived to kill the victim. *Holmes used his memory because the knowledge and experience he gained made it easy for him to investigate a case.* In *The Red-Headed League,* Holmes described how hearing events in one case enabled him to use his memory from similar cases as a guide to solving it. Above all else, Holmes used his memory with the other principles in this book.

Sherlock Holmes also understood the downside in relying too much on his memory. *Holmes knew that memory is extremely unreliable and inaccurate.* In *The Adventure of the Noble Bachelor*, Holmes requested Watson remain as a witness during a client interview as a check on his memory. *Holmes knew that stress and emotions could keep him from concentrating and distort his memory.* In *A Scandal In Bohemia*, Watson described how Holmes resisted emotions because they would cast "...doubt upon all his mental results" (his memory being one of them).

Holmes knew that memory is easily manipulated and susceptible to bias. In *The Sign of Four*, Holmes admitted his memory failed him or he would have predicted the small footprints he discovered. *Holmes knew that although he used cocaine, the drug did his memory harm.* In *The Sign of Four*, Holmes admitted to Watson that the drug had a bad physical influence on him.

Holmes knew that outside distractions or new information could easily interfere with his memory. In *The Hound of the Baskervilles,* Holmes described to Watson how each new case he investigated shut out the memories of his old cases. *Holmes knew that memory loss happens quickly if it is not used.* In *The Hound of the Baskervill*es, he also described how he did not remember all the facts in the Hound case due to his not dealing with it anymore.

The memory pros and cons that Sherlock Holmes understood are important to know. They are important because the memories you have gathered throughout your lifetime define you. The life skills and habits you learn come from the memories you have formed. Memories are the total of all your experiences. They make you who you are. You draw your knowledge from them. As a result, focus on using and improving your memory to better size up strangers.

How To Improve Your Memory Like Sherlock Holmes

Most people know their memory works because they use it every day. But no one *really* knows *how* it works. Scientists and other experts are still conducting research and tests to determine the answers. Although they have not found all the answers to how memory works, you do not need to understand it fully to improve your own memory. All you need to do is use mnemonic techniques to have a memory like Sherlock Holmes.

Mnemonic techniques are memory enhancers that help you remember. Professional memory champions often use them to remember large groups of complex numbers and subjects. They are natural memory aids that anyone can use. Some tips below use mnemonic techniques. Other tips are simply common sense. But all the following tips will improve your memory:

1. **Pay Attention.** Sherlock Holmes's intense interest in people is what made him successful in memorizing things about them. You remember what is important to you. Show interest in learning what you want to memorize. Your attitude will determine more than anything else what you remember. If you pay close attention in the first place when you see or hear something, you are less likely to forget it.

2. **Meditate.** Sherlock Holmes often meditated when he needed to stimulate his memory and recall things. Meditation helps relax your mind and makes it easier to remember things. Take ten to fifteen minutes to meditate while you are in the office or at home. Practice breathing through slowly inhaling and exhaling. Do it at a time when no one will disturb you.

3. **Exercise.** Although Sherlock Holmes did not exercise frequently, he often engaged in activities, which required him to use lots of energy. For example, once he vigorously beat a dead body with a stick to see the bruises. Another time he furiously stabbed a dead pig

with a harpoon in a butcher shop.[48] Studies have shown that keeping fit improves your memory. Working out daily stimulates the areas in the brain that influence your ability to retain or recall information. It also slows down memory loss. Stretching, calisthenics, jogging and lifting weights are all exercises you should regularly do.

4. **Sleep.** Sherlock Holmes often went hours without sleeping. That is one Holmes example you should not follow. Getting the proper rest helps improve your memory. Scientists state that while you sleep, the brain processes the sense impressions, experiences, thoughts and feelings you had during the day. The areas in the brain responsible for memory remain active while you sleep. Eight hours sleep daily is the recommended amount the average person needs. Anything less could result in you forgetting things more often.

5. **Socialize.** Sherlock Holmes stayed to himself and did not normally socialize. When it suited his purposes, however, he socialized to get information he needed. Researchers at the *Harvard School of Public Health* conducted a study, which found that the more active you are socially the less memory loss you have.[49] Outgoing, positive and friendly people build more friendships than people who stay to themselves. Scientists say social relationships stimulate the brain. Whenever you stimulate the brain, you strengthen the areas in the brain that use memory and make it perform better. Your memory benefits from this stimulation because you use it every day to remember faces, names, places and things.

---

[48] Holmes beat a dead body in *A Study in Scarlet* and stabbed a dead pig in *The Adventure of Black Peter*. He later said: "There can be no question...of the value of exercise before breakfast."

[49] *"Effects of Social Integration on Preserving Memory Function in a Nationally Representative U.S. Elderly Population,"* Karen A. Ertel, M. Maria Glymour, Lisa F. Berkman, *American Journal of Public Health*, July 2008, Vol. 98, No. 7.

6. **Enjoy Life.** Sherlock Holmes rarely laughed, but when he did, he would have fits of laughter. Laughing and having fun stimulates areas in the brain responsible for memory. Getting in touch with your positive feelings through activities that give joy will help improve your memory. Listening and telling jokes, dancing and playing games such as volleyball will fire up your memory. Find your own enjoyment in life and live it to the fullest.

7. **Diet.** Sherlock Holmes did not follow a proper diet. He sometimes went days without eating while investigating a case. Science has since revealed that going without food for long periods is unhealthy. You should also not follow his example. Studies have shown that eating the proper foods can improve your memory. Eating small meals and avoiding unhealthy foods will help you remember things more easily. A diet consisting of fruits, vegetables, nuts, fish and other healthy food products will give your memory a boost. Omega-3 fatty acids and other supplements will stimulate your memory-related brain functions.

8. **Reduce Stress.** Whenever Sherlock Holmes experienced stressful situations, he would play his violin or attend the Opera. Everyday stress can affect how you remember things and people. Depression, anxiety, fear, worry, anger and negative thinking reduce your ability to memorize. You cannot eliminate stress from your life, but you can control it. You control it through thinking positive, getting expert advice and following through on it.

9. **Use Your Five Senses.** Sherlock Holmes developed his five senses to the fullest during his investigations. It is one of the reasons he possessed such a good memory. The more you rely on your senses, the better your memory will get. Using your three primary senses:

seeing, hearing and touching are the main ways to improve your memory. Your secondary senses: smelling and tasting, although equally important, come into play less frequently.

10. **Exercise Mentally.** Sherlock Holmes exercised his mind by working out the solutions to secret writings, codes and ciphers. Nothing simulates the memory like reading, puzzles, logic games or learning something new. Just as you exercise the body, you must exercise the mind. Read a challenging book. Figure out a crossword puzzle. Challenge yourself to a game of logic. Learn to play the piano or guitar. Study Spanish or French. All these activities and many others can stir your brain and boost your memory.

11. **Use Association.** Sherlock Holmes often looked for similar memory clues to help him figure things out when he met a stranger or solved a problem. One key to effective memory is to associate what you want to remember with something you already know. Association applies the mnemonic technique of using similar things to remind you about the image, word or person. Pinpoint a stranger's unique facial or body feature. Maybe the stranger has a big nose or tiny feet. Focus on these distinguishing features and link them with someone you already know.

12. **Visualize.** Sherlock Holmes often visualized people and situations before he even encountered them because he used his mind's eye. Visualization is a basic mnemonic memory technique. You can develop a better memory through picturing things in your minds eye. A clear image will stick in your mind faster than a vague one. Picture what it is you want to remember. Be specific and make the image vivid. You are more likely to recall a distinct picture than one that is foggy in your brain.

13. Use Peg Words. Sherlock Holmes applied this mnemonic technique although he did not realize it at the time. Memory experts suggest using peg words to improve your memory when you need to remember something in specific order. Peg words help you to remember the place each item is in on a list. First, memorize each item on the list. Second, create a mental picture of each item in your head. Third, associate each item with a number to make it easy to visualize. For example, if you wanted to provide a description of someone, you would give each feature about the person a number and associate it with a peg word. The person's nose would get number one. The person's eyes would get number two and so forth. Then picture each feature with an image. The person's nose could get a clown's red nose. The person's eyes could get the all Seeing Eye on a dollar bill. Fourth, associate the features with their peg words to recall them.

14. Group Things Together. Holmes often memorized things by grouping them together. Memory experts call grouping things together 'chunking.' It is a mnemonic memory technique used to help people remember a list of random items. The basic idea is to lump similar things together to make them easier to remember. For example, if you notice a crowd of people, you could mentally group all the women, men and children separately. Then add how many are in each group to help you remember them, such as 7 women, 5 men and 3 children.

15. Use Jingles. Sherlock Holmes did not use jingles or rhymes, but he would have if he had known about them. Memory experts suggest you can improve your memory by using a jingle or rhyme. Most people use this mnemonic technique naturally. Children learn their ABCs and simple grammar or math problems with rhymes. A catchy jingle will stick in your mind. Singing a jingle to music will help you remember basic information better.

16. **Use Acronyms.** No record exists in the Canon that has Holmes using acronyms but memory experts say they are great mnemonic memory aids. An acronym is a word abbreviation that makes it easier to remember something. It takes the first letter in a key word or idea and creates a new word. You can create an acronym to help you remember a stranger's appearance. For example, the word HUGS could help you remember a person's **H**at, **U**nderwear, **G**loves and **S**ocks.

17. **Use Acrostics.** Holmes did not use acrostics but they would have improved his memory dramatically if he did. An acrostic is a sentence that uses the first letter in each word to help you remember something. Use it to memorize words in specific order. For example, if you wanted to remember the eight principles you can make up an acrostic sentence that combines them all. Use the sentence: "**I K**now **D**etails **I**n **M**y **L**ife **O**n **E**arth" to remember each principle: **I**ntuition, **K**nowledge, **D**eduction, **I**magination, **M**emory, **L**istening, **O**bservation and **E**xperience.

18. **Use Your Surroundings.** Sherlock Holmes often used his environment to help him remember. You can use your environment to help you memorize important things. Anything that can trigger a memory can help you remember something. Simply change a thing's location and it will jar your memory. For example, if you need to remember to take your smartphone in the morning to work, move a pot onto a kitchen countertop rather than the stove. When you see the pot on the countertop in the morning, you will sense something is out of place. It will cause you to remember to take the smartphone.

19. **Speak aloud.** Sherlock Holmes often said things aloud to improve his memory as he investigated a crime scene. Memory experts suggest you can remember better if you say out loud what it is you want to memorize. The technique is to repeat aloud what you want to remember. This mnemonic tip uses your hearing to make the memory more vivid. Use the tip to describe out loud the strangers you see during your daily activities. For example, while in a car waiting for the traffic light to change, observe pedestrians strolling on the sidewalk. Describe their features and appearance aloud.

20. **Focus Your Memory.** Sherlock Holmes always focused his memory when he needed to remember something. Memory experts suggest you concentrate on what you want to remember. Do not get distracted or think about other things. You can forget a memory quickly if you do not think about it. One way to avoid distractions is to organize things to help you remember better. For example, use your smartphone to record dates on a calendar, create a to-do list or record phone numbers. It frees your mind from routine things and helps you memorize other less routine things better.

21. **Understand What You Memorize.** Sherlock Holmes often explained his ideas to Watson to help himself remember and understand a problem. You can also explain what it is you are memorizing to someone else. You will help yourself understand it better. Rather than just memorizing something by rote, seek to understand in detail what you want to remember. When you comprehend what it is you want to remember, it makes the memories more vivid. Study and research the person or subject to increase your understanding. Learn the basic ideas when memorizing difficult things.

22. **Use Repetition.** Holmes repeatedly memorized things until he did it without thinking about it. Some things you want to remember do not require that you understand them. For example, if you need to remember a list of words or names for short-term use. In these cases, it is better to memorize through repetition. Simply repeat what you want to learn continually. Do it until it becomes a habit. Constantly repeating something over in your mind is one sure way to remember it. It will stick in your mind and you will recall it easier. Repeat what you want to remember for a few minutes at a time. Do not cram everything in several hours of memorizing.

23. **Be Creative.** Sherlock Holmes used his creativity to remember things and people. Use your imagination to invent strange or silly associations that help you remember something. Often these weird associations will only make sense to you but they will help you remember things. For example, in the online article *"The Key To Memory,"*[50] Memory Champion Joshua Foer suggests you create a link between a person's name and face. He writes: "If it's a woman named Abby, imagine a bee stinging her eye. If it's a guy called Bill, imagine him with a duckbill for a mouth. If it's someone named Barbara, picture a crown of barbed wire around her head. Create these images in your mind's eye with as much color, action and meaning as possible. For example, don't just picture a bee stinging Abby's eye. Hear the bee buzzing, imagine her eye swelling, and try to feel how painful it would be. The more senses you can use, the better." The more bizarre or out languish the association, the easier you will remember it.

---

[50] Read the article at: http://www.huffingtonpost.com/joshua-foer/the-secret-to-remembering. Mr. Foer is also the author of *Moonwalking with Einstein: The Art & Science of Remembering Everything.*

24. Prioritize. Sherlock Holmes did this when he used his memory. No one can remember everything. Few people have photographic memories. We all screen, either consciously or unconsciously, the impressions we receive through our five senses. Make a conscious effort only to memorize the things that are important to you. Remember what is useful and reject what is useless. Anything else you need to know, you can always consult other people, books or the Internet.

25. Be Patient. Sherlock Holmes always had patience when he conducted his investigations or sized up strangers. Improving your memory will not happen overnight. It takes time for you to learn these memory tips. You must have patience. Practice the memory suggestions in your everyday life. Know that they will work if you give them a chance.

The above memory tips and techniques can help you remember people, places, things, numbers and words. Sherlock Holmes relied on a similar memory technique hinted at in the beginning of this chapter. In fact, it is the most famous of all memory techniques.

The Sherlock Holmes Memory Technique

The memory technique Sherlock Holmes used relies on the *Method of Loci.*[51] The method of loci is an ancient Greek mnemonic memory technique that uses locations to help you remember. It comes from the concept that people can easily memorize places they already know.

---

[51] The method of Loci (meaning place or location from the Latin plural *Locus*) comes from ancient Roman and Greek treatises such as *Rhetorica ad Herennium* and Cicero's *De Orator.* Common English phrases "in the first place," "in the second place" likely came from the Loci method (see *Wikipedia*).

In *The Valley of Fear,* Holmes used a version of the method of loci when he stayed in a room at the Manor House of Birlstone. Holmes said: "I shall sit in that room and see if its atmosphere brings me inspiration. I'm a believer in the genius loci."

Sherlock Holmes called the method of loci the 'brain attic.' Others call it the 'memory palace.' This book calls it the 'memory temple.' No matter what name you call it, the method of loci mnemonic memory technique works the same. And you can learn exactly how to use it by following these simple steps:[52]

1. **Pick a Memory Temple.** Choose a place that you know well. The more familiar you are with the location, the easier you will remember it. Most people choose where they live, such as their house or apartment. Others choose where they work or a place they go to often such as a park or school. The larger your memory temple, the more things you can fit in it to remember. For example, you could fit more memories into your 'house' than you could fit into your 'bedroom.'

2. **Decide on a Path.** Once you have chosen a specific location, chart a route that you will travel. You can then physically walk the path to note each object you will focus on. This step is good if you need to remember things in order. If you need to memorize things randomly, you can skip this step.

3. **Create Memory Markers.** Each location in your imaginary temple will have a signpost to identify it. Memory experts call these identifiers memory 'pegs.' Think of these pegs as folders or storage boxes for what you want to remember. Make sure each marker is unique so that you do not confuse it with something else in your

---

[52] The steps have been adapted from Wikihow.com: *How to Build a Memory Palace* at http://www.wikihow.com/Build-a-Memory-Palace.

memory temple. Visualize each object in your memory temple and use the peg to identify it.

4. **Place Related Information into Categories.** The information you place in the memory temple should be important to you. Some people place 'things' in their locations. Other people place actual individuals they know in their folders. Still other people place numbers, facts or words in their folders. The key is to place related information into the same category. That way, you will retrieve it easier when you need it.

5. **Memorize Your Temple.** Practice memorizing each specific place where you have mentally stored information. You can draw a map of the actual route to help you remember it. Make the map specific. Visualize every detail along the route and check it against your map. Commit the mental map to your memory so you can remember it easy.

6. **Use Memory Triggers.** A memory trigger is a symbol or other representation that you use to help you memorize something. Use it to jog your memory and easily picture what you want to remember. For example, certain songs you remember may trigger memories of specific times and people in your life. A specific perfume may trigger your mother, sister or girlfriend's image. A picture may help you recall a fond time in your life.

7. **Use Other Mnemonic Aids.** You can increase the memory temple's effectiveness by combining it with other mnemonic techniques. For example, you could speak aloud as you identify each marker. You could also use music or rhymes to help you remember objects along the path.

8. **Take a Mental Walk in Your Temple.** Once you have mapped out a familiar route and identified each location, take a mental walk along the path. Do this to check that each physical location matches up with its' mental counterpart. As you take the mental walk, visualize each location in your mind's eye.

9. **Use Your Memory Temple.** Practice recalling the information you have memorized by mentally looking at each location. Drill yourself to start from any place along your path. Train your mind to recollect specific information when you need it. You can do this if you practice traveling in your memory temple on a daily basis.

10. **Create New Temples.** You can build as many memory temples as you need. Construct some memory temples for information you will remember only briefly. Develop other memory temples to hold information that will last for months or years. The important thing is that you know how long you want to memorize the information then build the right memory temple for it.

The Sherlock Holmes memory temple technique is a powerful tool for storing information for later recall. You just have to use it in combination with the other memory tips and techniques to succeed at sizing up strangers.

Put It All Together Like Sherlock Holmes

Sherlock Holmes used his memory for one purpose only — to solve crimes and size up strangers. Every essential fact he gathered he committed to his memory to achieve that goal. He took mental notes of everything he observed and heard. He built stock images in his memory temple from the strangers he met. Each location in his temple contained similar images of people he met. He compared the strangers he encountered with these images to quickly size them up.

You can build stock images by placing micro expressions, emotions, body language, eye movements, faces, personalities, body types, fashion and inferences into different locations in your memory temple.

For example, in Chapter 2 you learnt about spotting facial expressions and body language. You could place all facial expressions such as smiling and frowning into a memory location in your minds eye. You could place physical gestures such as folding your arms or crossing your legs into another memory location. Each memory location will help you size up the people you meet.

Chapter 5 instructed you to meet all kinds of people from all lifestyles. The purpose in meeting all kinds of people is so you can memorize their personalities, traits, mannerisms and compare these factors to other strangers you meet. Look at similar people you meet daily for factors that will trigger your memory with a person or experience from your past.

For example, in the cable TV show *Lie To Me,* Actress Monica Raymund played Rita Torres, a natural who could read micro-expressions without any technical or educational training. In a deleted scene from the episode *Moral Wavier,* she observed a fear micro expression on a man's mouth. It triggered a similar memory of a fear micro expression she had as a young girl with her abusive father. As a result, she could tell that the man was hiding something.

The key to triggering your memory is to use your imagination to put yourself in a person's place. You have already learnt how to do this from Chapter 7. What you need to do now is create a link between your memory and the information you need to remember. Use your memory to draw a mental sketch of a stranger's personality. Then imagine how the stranger would

217

behave in the future.[53] Sherlock Holmes did this through habit and self-training.

To develop a memory like Sherlock Holmes you must also make the memory techniques habitual through training yourself. You must practice everything about memory that you learned in this chapter. You will learn exactly how to do that in Chapter 12.

Go to Pages 330 to 335 if you want to practice
the memory exercises now.

---

[53] *"The New Power of Memory"* by Shirley S. Wang, *The Wall Street Journal*, Tuesday, March 12, 2013, *Personal Journal* Section, Pages D1 & D4.

Chapter 9

Use This Sherlockian Tip
To Instantly Size-Up Strangers

"But do you mean to say," I said, "that without leaving your room you can unravel some knot which other men can make nothing of, although they have seen every detail for themselves?"

"Quite so. I have a kind of intuition that way..."
Sherlock Holmes, A Study in Scarlet

What do *"A Study in Scarlet," "Silver Blaze," "The Adventure of the Abbey Grange," "The Adventure of the Cardboard Box,"* and *"The Adventure of the Norwood Builder,"* have in common? They are all cases in which Sherlock Holmes used his gut feelings and hunches to size up a stranger or solve a problem.

Sherlock Holmes is not famous for using intuition. He built his reputation on using observation and deduction. Contrary to his reputation, however, Holmes often used his 'sixth sense' when investigating cases he found interesting.

In *Silver Blaze,* Watson describes Holmes as having "a sudden idea" which made Holmes lean forward and touch a young man on his sleeve. He asked the young man a seemingly unimportant question about sheep. The hunch about the sheep later helped Holmes crack the case and find a missing racehorse.

In *The Adventure of the Abbey Grange,* Holmes "instinct" warned him that a seemingly closed case had more to it than it first appeared. He told Watson: "I simply *can't* leave that case in this condition. Every instinct that I possess cries out against it. It's wrong — it's all wrong — I'll swear it's wrong." Holmes then refocused his mind on the case and solved it.

In *The Adventure of the Cardboard Box,* Holmes had a "flash of insight." He observed a respectable lady and a portrait, which revealed she had two sisters. The old lady had received a box with two severed human ears in it. He told Watson: "It instantly flashed across my mind that the box might have been meant for one of these." Holmes used his hunch regarding the box to solve the case eventually.

In *The Adventure of the Norwood Builder,* Holmes had a "gut feeling" about a housekeeper that was contrary to the facts and evidence. Holmes believed the housekeeper did not reveal everything she knew. He told Watson: "I *know* it's all wrong. I feel it in my bones." Then Detective Lestrade unwittingly showed Holmes a thumb mark, which helped Holmes solve the case and confirm his gut feeling.

All these cases establish that Sherlock Holmes relied on flashes of insight far more frequently than most people believe. The sudden thoughts that came to him are common to everyone. We all have had similar hunches and gut feelings.

In this chapter, you will learn about the intuition Sherlock Holmes used and where it comes from. You will learn the pros and cons of using it and how you can apply it in your everyday life to size up strangers. After you have learnt these things, you will discover that Sherlock Holmes is not that much different from you after all. The intuition he used — you have also used!

The Sherlockian Sixth Sense

It is clear that Sherlock Holmes valued intuition and recognized its' importance in solving difficult cases. In *The Sign of Four,* client Mary Morstan had a gut feeling Holmes might need additional papers and brought them with her to give him. Holmes complimented her when he said: "You are certainly a model client. You have the correct intuition."

In *The Adventure of Wisteria Lodge*, Sherlock Holmes discovered that Inspector Barnes had arrested the wrong man to throw the real suspect off guard. He put his hand on the inspector's shoulder and said: "You will rise high in your profession. You have instinct and intuition."

Intuition, as defined in this book, is any thought, idea or feeling that suddenly flashes within your mind without any logical analysis or rational thought. Often when you get a sudden flash of insight, it is hard to explain how you *know* what you know. In *A Study in Scarlet*, Holmes explained it to Watson in this way: "It was easier to know it than to explain why I know it. If you were asked to prove that two and two made four, you might find some difficulty, and yet you are quite sure of the fact." So, it is with intuition. You may not know why you know it but you *know* it.

In the *Study in Scarlet* case above, Holmes also famously explained to Watson: "I *knew* you came from Afghanistan." That is how intuition works. Most of the time, the individual who receives a hunch is not conscious of it until it hits him or her unexpectedly. When it hits, the individual *knows*. Although you may be unaware as you go about your daily routine, your unconscious mind is always aware. Many people do not know this and believe certain myths about intuition.

Three Myths about Intuition

The belief that Sherlock Holmes only used observation, deduction and not intuition in his thinking is one myth that many people accept as true. A second myth many people also believe is that women are naturally more intuitive than men. In fact, both Watson and Holmes believed this second myth.

In *The Boscombe Valley Mystery*, Watson describes how Miss Turner rushed into a room and glanced at Watson. She then fastened her gaze upon Holmes and "with a woman's quick intuition" spoke to him first. Watson's description of the woman's actions relies solely on her *gender*. It also reveals his oversimplified view of women's intuitive ability.

Like Watson, Holmes' also unintentionally exposes his stereotyped view of women common in the 19th century. In *The Man with the Twisted Lip*, Holmes states: "I have seen too much not to know that the impression of a woman may be more valuable than the conclusion of an analytical reasoner." The truth is both men and women have the capacity to use intuition equally. The level of accuracy relies on each individual's *desire* to improve his or her intuitive abilities. Studies have show that it has nothing to do with a person's gender.[54]

The third myth many people believe is that intuitions come from outside the mind, through a connection with a supernatural power. They call this power "The Force," "Supreme Being," or "God." They claim it is responsible for the sudden flashes of inspiration or insight that human beings receive. These are the same claims that psychics and believers in the paranormal, ESP and telepathy put forth to the gullible. The truth is hunches or gut feelings do not pop into the mind from an outside source; they originate from *within* your mind.

The Unconscious – The Warehouse of the Mind

Scientists have verified through scientific studies that intuitions come from the brain.[55] The brain is where the

---

[54] *"Where Is Women's Intuition"* by Dr. William Ickes. http://www.psychologytoday.com/blog/everyday-mind-reading/200901/where-is-womens-intuition.

[55] See Linköping University. *"Intuition Can Be Explained."* ScienceDaily. *ScienceDaily*, 2 July 2008. <www.sciencedaily.com/ releases/2008/07/080701135820.htm>.

unconscious exists. The unconscious is like a warehouse where an individual's thoughts, memories, feelings, images, urges and experiences are stored. The unconscious collects stimuli from the five senses and stores it in the mind without the person's awareness.

When encountering good or bad situations or people, the unconscious springs into action, often without the individual realizing it. Sherlock Holmes said as much in *A Study in Scarlet*, when he described how he sized up Watson: "From long habit the train of thoughts ran so swiftly through my mind that I arrived at the conclusion without being conscious of intermediate steps."

The unconscious mind thinks automatically. It makes no distinction about the data it receives from the five senses; it collects both positive and negative stimuli. The stimuli may seem trivial and minuscule (micro facial expressions and gestures, slight variations in voice tone, etc.), but your mind picks them up without your conscious knowledge. The stimuli received into your unconscious from your five natural senses — seeing, hearing, touching, tasting and smelling — activate a 'sixth sense' when they are mixed with thoughts, images, feelings, urges or impulses residing in the unconscious.

The unconscious processes the stimuli and relays it back to your conscious mind in the form of a 'feeling," "thought" or "physical sensation." It happens lighting fast and normally occurs without using reason or logic. It explains the positive or negative "vibe," "feeling" or "gut" reaction you get when you meet a stranger.

When you hear someone say: "I got a bad feeling about him," "I'm getting a good vibe from her," or "I'm feeling strange in my stomach" this vibe, feeling or physical sensation is nothing more than your unconscious mind sending you an alert message.

These intuitive messages can help or hurt you depending on how you use them.

The Pros and Cons of Sherlockian Intuition

Intuition can help you by pointing you in the right direction when the person, situation or problem you are facing is unknown. Intuition works best when you are unsure of the outcome or you do not have time to analyze a problem. In *The Adventure of the Lions Mane,* Sherlock Holmes tried to figure out how both a man and a dog suddenly died in the same place. He said: "Some dim perception that the matter was vital rose in my mind...I had just reached the top of the path when it came to me. Like a flash, I remembered the thing for which I had so eagerly and vainly grasped..."

In addition, intuition can help you see the big picture even when all the facts are seemingly against you. In *The Bruce-Partington Plans*, Mycroft Holmes listened to Detective Lestrade's theory regarding the missing submarine plans. He then cried to his brother Sherlock: "All my instincts are against this explanation." Mycroft *sensed something was not right* even though all the evidence pointed otherwise. He urged Sherlock to go to the crime scene and investigate the matter. Mycroft's instincts proved correct when Holmes solved the case.

Moreover, intuition can warn you of impending danger. It allows you to anticipate another person's actions and make a quick decision on the spot, while under pressure, to counter it. In *The Valley of Fear,* John Douglas sensed danger the moment he entered his study. He told Sherlock Holmes and Inspector MacDonald: "I guess when a man has had dangers in his life — and I've had more than most in my time — there is a kind of sixth sense that waves the red flag. I saw the signal clear enough, and yet I could not explain why..."

In *The Final Problem*, Professor Moriarty unexpectedly entered Holmes's study at 221B Baker Street. Holmes later told Watson: "The fact is that upon his entrance I had instantly recognized the extreme personal danger in which I lay...I slipped the revolver from the drawer into my pocket and was covering him through the cloth." Holmes instincts allowed him to anticipate Professor Moriarty's intentions and he quickly countered him.

Following your instincts, however, can also lead you astray. Often snap judgments based on instinct are unreliable because they result in wrong impressions. These impressions usually come from bias, prejudice, stereotypes or false perceptions. Although your intuition may seem right in a given situation, it often turns out wrong. Sherlock Holmes recognized this fact in *The Problem of Thor Bridge.* In this case, he said to Watson: "you have seen me miss my mark before, Watson. I have an instinct for such things, and yet it has sometimes played me false."

Like Holmes, recognize that the hunches and gut feelings you get are not always right. In *A Study in Scarlet,* Detective Gregson of Scotland Yard made a mistake when he followed the wrong clue from a hat. He relied on his gut and arrested the wrong man. He explained to Holmes after interrogating the suspect's mother and sister: "...I began to smell a rat. You know the feeling...when you come upon the right scent — a kind of thrill in your nerves." His instincts proved wrong because he arrogantly believed his inner voice.

If you become brash with your sixth sense and believe that you are never wrong, your hunches will fail you. Listening to your inner voice can sometimes fool you because often all the facts are not available when making a quick decision.

In addition, strong emotions can interfere with intuition. Fear and anger not kept in check will keep intuitions from springing forth. It in turn will hurt your imagination, which is

225

necessary to size up strangers. To avoid this, you must fine tune your intuition and make it work for you.

The ability to fine tune your intuition is easy to do because it is something that comes natural to you. Therefore, you should have no problem in following the instructions below to use your intuition as Sherlock Holmes did.

How To Use Your Intuition Like Sherlock Holmes

In previous chapters, you learnt about several practical principles you need to size up strangers as Sherlock Holmes did. You have now reached the part in the book that reveals how to use your intuition or sixth sense, along with these principles, to make your assessments regarding strangers more accurate.

Intuition is the final clue to the secret for which you are searching!

Intuition holds the key to the secret because often you must use the secret either before or after you receive your hunches. Holmes would use the secret either before or after he had a sudden flash of insight regarding a stranger or problem. You can control what you imagine. You can control how you think. You can control your memory. You cannot control your intuitions. Intuitions pop from within your mind without warning. They come and go as they please. You can, however, prepare your unconscious to release them.

Like a farmer that fertilizes the soil to ensure it produces the crops he wants to grow, you can fertilize your unconscious to make intuitions more likely to appear. You fertilize your unconscious by observing and listening, by getting knowledge and experience, by memorizing and using imagination as you study and train in the specific topic or field that interests you.

Then, in the critical moment when you need it most, without any conscious thought or effort from you, the unconscious will spring into action and produce the "hunch" you need. Just as Sherlock Holmes did, you can then, if you choose, use the secret to verify your hunch. It is that simple. And the tips below will show you how Holmes did it so that you can follow his example.

Holmes Used His Five Senses. Most people have lost their highly developed sense of smelling, hearing or seeing. They no longer use these senses to the fullest in their modern life. In primitive times, hunters relied on their five senses for everything. They used their sense of sight to track game. They used their sense of taste to detect good or bad food. They used their sense of hearing to listen for potential threats. They used their sense of touch to examine things. They used their sense of smell to detect sweet or foul odors in people or animals. Unlike the average person today, Holmes never lost his highly developed five senses.

Sherlock Holmes developed his five senses through constantly using them in his daily activities. He did it through habit until his sharpened senses became automatic. In *A Study in Scarlet,* Watson describes Holmes using his sense of touch to examine a body at a crime scene: "...his nimble fingers were flying here, there, and everywhere, feeling, pressing, unbuttoning, examining."

In *The Man with the Twisted Lip,* Holmes demonstrates his sense of hearing. He whispers to Watson to keep his voice very low in an opium den because "...I have excellent ears." In *The Adventure of the Blanched Soldier,* Holmes used his sense of smell to deduce a missing man had Leprosy. He used his nose to detect "...a faint but incisive scent..." on brown leather gloves.

In *The Adventures of Charles Augustus Milverton,* Watson describes how Sherlock Holmes used his sense of sight to see in the dark as he and Watson stealthy entered into Milverton's house to steal important papers. Holmes once told Dr. Watson: "Observation with me is second nature."

In *A Study in Scarlet,* Watson describes how Young Stamford explained Holmes's readiness to use his sense of taste. Holmes would test a vegetable alkaloid on his own tongue just to see its' effects. As a result, through Holmes developing his five senses to the fullest, he unconsciously obtained the stimuli he needed to fuel his intuitions.

Holmes Obtained Expertise. Most people learn how to use intuition from everyday living. As they go through life, they acquire knowledge and experiences that the unconscious draws upon when needed. Holmes accumulated vast amounts of specialized knowledge and practical experience, which resided in both his conscious and unconscious, and came forth from his mind as intuitions when he needed them most. Chapters 4 and 5 have already revealed how to obtain this knowledge and experience. These two principles gave Holmes the expertise he needed to instantly size up strangers.

Researchers from several universities conducted two studies in which they found that you could usually "trust your gut" when you have expertise in a specific subject or field.[56] In one study, the researchers found that study participants could intuitively tell the difference between a real and fake designer handbag based on their prior handbag ownership.

In other words, the more knowledge and experience you have in a specific area, the more likely you will have correct intuitions. It is self-evident that Sherlock Holmes used his vast knowledge and experience of crime to develop his expertise as a consulting detective.

---

[56] Rice University. *"In Decision-making, it might be Worth Trusting Your Gut."* *Science Daily*, 14 Dec. 2012. Web 18 Jun. 2013.

Holmes Memorized Relevant Data. Holmes believed in the 'mind attic' principle and used it to release his intuitions. He would store relevant information in his head and rely on his memory to retrieve it when the situation called for it.

In *The Disappearance of Lady Frances Carfax,* Holmes unconsciously stored a detail in his mind that he heard regarding the undertaker's wife. Holmes explained it to Watson this way: "...My night was haunted by the thought that somewhere a clue, a strange sentence, a curious observation, had come under my notice and had been too easily dismissed. Then, suddenly, in the gray of the morning, the words came back to me." Holmes then instantly remembered the coffin itself, which led to his sudden intuition that the coffin was too big for the small body.

Intuition and memory go hand in hand. When you memorize specific people, places or things your mind stores them for future reference and recall. You can retrieve what you need just by thinking about it. Your memory will then send it to you in the form of a thought impulse, image or feeling. Other times you may not know what you need but your unconscious taps into your memory and relays it to you as an intuition. The more relevant memories and experiences you have, the bigger your memory database and the more accurate your intuitions!

For example, an experienced chess prodigy who memorizes 100,000 different moves will instantly *know* his next move. How? He immediately compares the move he is considering with the thousands of chess moves already in his memory. In the online article: *"How to Use Intuition More Effectively,"* Associate Professor of Psychology Ben Newell explains how Psychologists De Goot, Simon and Chase "...demonstrated that a signature of chess expertise is the ability to identify promising moves very rapidly."[57] According to the article, beginners slowly

---

[57] Chase, W. G., and Simon, H. A. (1973). *The Mind's Eye in Chess.* In W. G. Chase, ed., Visual information processing, pp. 215–281. New York: Academic Press.

weight each move because they do not have a vast memory bank to draw upon. Like the experienced chess prodigy, Sherlock Holmes investigated hundreds of criminal cases and could rapidly draw from his memory information he needed.

Holmes Trusted His Gut Feelings. Most of the time, when Holmes sized up strangers he used *reason* as the basis for his conclusions. On the occasions when he did not use reason, he trusted his gut and instincts. Holmes knew *when* to listen to his inner voice and *when* to reject it. He trusted his inner voice when he knew, based on his prior knowledge or experience that he had dealt with a similar situation, stranger or problem. Holmes used his intuition to reveal patterns and similarities so he could act instantly upon them during his investigations.

As Sherlock Holmes conducted his investigations, ideas or thoughts would suddenly come to him. In *The Adventure of the Speckled Band*, he examined a room for evidence. He stated: "The idea of a snake instantly occurred to me." The idea led to his solving the case. On other occasions, he anticipated situations, people and things before he encountered them.

In *The Adventure of the Sussex Vampire*, he left Baker Street to conduct his investigation regarding an alleged vampire mystery. Holmes stated: "My instinct felt the presence of those weapons upon the wall before my eyes ever saw them." Holmes usually trusted his instinct when it suddenly came upon him.

In *The Adventure of the Abbey Grange,* Holmes interviewed witnesses and examined the evidence that Detective Stanley Hopkins presented to him regarding a murdered man. All the facts and evidence corroborated the witnesses' story. Holmes had a nagging feeling, however, that *something was not right,* because he observed three half full wine glasses. He trusted his instinct even though the facts and evidence seemingly contradicted it. Why? Because he realized before arriving at the murder scene, that he had allowed the story he heard and the witnesses he questioned to warp his judgment.

Trusting your intuition as Sherlock Holmes did is important. Depending on your intuition when you meet a stranger is also critical because its gives you the quick insight you need to make a decision on the spot. In situations that require snap judgments or fast decisions, relying on your hunches is a successful strategy. Often when you spend too much time thinking about a stranger or problem, rather than following your gut, you miss important data and opportunities.

Holmes Verified His Hunches With Reason. Whenever Sherlock Holmes had a sudden hunch, he checked it against his logic. He always used cold, hard reasoning to determine whether he had correct intuitions. In *The Adventure of the Abbey Grange,* after Holmes had a bad feeling about the case, he went over the facts and evidence in his mind again with *reason* to figure out the truth!

Sometimes Holmes would use reason *before* he received a sudden intuition. He did it in *The Naval Treaty,* where he thought deeply about a solution until as Watson described it: "some new possibility had dawned suddenly upon him." Other times Holmes would use reason *after* he received a sudden intuition. He did it in *The Adventure of the Norwood Builder,* where he had a hunch something did not seem right regarding an alleged murder. After Detective Lestrade had discovered a thumb mark, Sherlock Holmes reasoned someone had placed it on the wall during the night. Either way, he relied on logical thinking to guide him to the correct conclusions.

When you receive an intuition sometimes you have to act on it immediately because you have no time to analyze it. These types of intuitions are often right because they rely on your prior knowledge and experience. In other situations, you may have more time to figure out if your hunch is correct. You can then use the rules of deduction from Chapter 3 to determine its validity. The key is to balance your intuition with your logic and use the appropriate one at the right time.

Holmes Thought Hard About a Problem. Whether he thought about a problem for a few minutes, a few hours or a few days, Holmes always devoted his complete attention to it. He would focus and concentrate upon the problem, looking at it from every angle, weighing the pros and cons, thinking about the possibilities and probabilities, until he reached a theory that explained all the facts.

On these occasions, Watson described Holmes as being lost in thought, with his eyes closed. Sometimes he curled up in a chair. Sometimes he slowly paced the floor with his chin on his chest and hands in his pockets. Sometimes he stared at the ceiling in total silence as he turned the problem over in his mind. Then suddenly, he would spring to life with an idea or thought. Sherlock Holmes used deep thinking to release his creativity to help him solve the mystery.

In *The Adventure of the Beryl Coronet,* Watson describes how Holmes "...hardly spoke a word the whole way out to the southern suburb, but sat with his chin upon his breast and his hat drawn over his eyes, in the deepest thought." In *Silver Blaze,* Watson describes how Holmes leaned back in the carriage he rode in "...with his eyes fixed upon the sky in front of him, entirely absorbed in his own thoughts."

In *The Musgrave Ritual,* Holmes describes to Watson how he analyzed a mystery. "I sat down upon a keg in the corner and thought the whole matter carefully over." In *The Naval Treaty,* Watson describes how Holmes "...sank back into the state of intense and silent thought from which he had emerged." All these cases establish that Holmes thought hard about a problem whenever someone presented a complex case to him.

Some individuals need an aid to help them concentrate and focus. In *A Few Good Men* (*1992*), Actor Tom Cruise portrayed a military lawyer who did his best thinking while swinging a baseball bat. Similarly, Holmes often used a pipe to help him concentrate and focus. In *The Red-Headed League,* to aid him in thinking Holmes smoked for fifty minutes with his pipe. He described it to Watson as a "three pipe problem."

Sherlock Holmes also believed a change of atmosphere would help him concentrate. In *The Valley of Fear,* he stayed in the study alone and stated: "I shall sit in that room and see if its atmosphere brings me inspiration." In *The Hound of the Baskervilles,* Holmes also stated: "I find that a concentrated atmosphere helps a concentration of thought."

But sometimes even when he thought hard over a problem, Holmes could still not find a solution. He would hit a brick wall and come to a standstill. In these occasions, Holmes would seek to break the mental logjam. He would use the next mental technique to stimulate his intuition.

Holmes Relaxed His Mind. When Holmes did not have enough data to reason from a hypothesis, he simply took his mind off the problem. He did it to jump-start his creative mind. In *The Adventure of the Norwood Builder,* he played his violin. In *A Study In Scarlet,* he went to a concert. In *The Adventure of the Cardboard Box,* he meditated. In *The Adventure of the Speckled Band,* he turned his mind to more cheerful matters as he smoked a pipe. In *The Adventure of the Devil's Foot,* he took a walk along cliffs with Watson to ease his mind.

Watson described how Holmes relaxed his mind. In *The Hound of the Baskervilles,* Watson states:

> "Sherlock Holmes had, in a very remarkable degree, the power of detaching his mind at will. For two hours the strange business in which we had been involved appeared to be forgotten and he was entirely absorbed

in the picture of the modern Belgian masters. He would talk of nothing but art, of which he had the crudest ideas, from our leaving the gallery until we found ourselves at the Northumberland Hotel."

Watson also described how Holmes could tune out present problems by focusing his mind on something else. In *The Adventure of the Bruce-Partington Plans,* Watson states:

"One of the most remarkable characteristics of Sherlock Holmes was his power of throwing his brain out of action and switching all his thoughts on to lighter things whenever he had convinced himself that he could no longer work to advantage. I remember that during the whole of that memorable day he lost himself in a monograph which he had undertaken upon the Polyphonic Motets of Lassus."

In *The Adventure of the Retired Colourman,* when Sherlock Holmes faced a difficult problem, he told Watson: "Let us escape from this weary workaday world by the side door of music. Carina sings to-night at the Albert Hall, and we have time to dress, dine, and enjoy."

In *The Adventure of Black Peter,* after examining a cabin, Holmes said: "...I can do nothing more. Let us walk in these beautiful woods, Watson, and give a few hours to the birds and the flowers." Sherlock Holmes did not hesitate to take his mind off a problem and do something else in order to stimulate his thinking and intuitions. When you take your conscious mind off a problem and do something else, it releases your unconscious to process the information and find an answer.

How many times have you tried to solve a problem but could not do it? When you took your mind off it and thought about something else, the answer came immediately to you. Sometimes you can release intuitions and hunches by simply keeping your mind off what you are thinking about. Focus on

234

something else. Read a book. Exercise. Watch TV. Listen to music. Go to a movie. Play with your kids. Relax your mind and you will find hunches coming more easily to you.

The hunches will come easier because using intuition is an ability that comes natural to you. As Sherlock Holmes did, when you get a hunch, know when to use reason and when to follow your gut. It is the key to your success in sizing up strangers or solving any problem.

Go to Pages 336 to 339 if you want to practice
the intuition exercises now.

Chapter 10

How to Size-Up Strangers
By Studying Their Personal Items

*"...it is difficult for a man to have any object in daily use
without leaving the impress of his individuality upon it
in such a way that a trained observer might read it..."*
Sherlock Holmes, The Sign of Four

M ost people at one time or another have come across a lost item belonging to an unknown person. You may have found a watch, hat, coat or other object and wondered who owned the item. Sherlock Holmes used his method to reconstruct a person by examining the individual's personal property.

One practical reason for developing this skill is so that you can return a lost item to its rightful owner. Or a detective may use this method to identify and track down a witness, victim or criminal. Holmes believed that deducing an owner's characteristics by examining his or her personal property is a learned skill that anyone could teach himself or herself.

He believed people who use personal items every day such as a hat; cane or eyeglasses leave clues to their personalities on the objects they own. He also believed certain items leave more clues than others to the trained observer. In *The Yellow Face* case, he told Dr. Watson: "...pipes are occasionally of extraordinary interest...nothing has more individuality, save perhaps watches and bootlaces."

In *The Adventure of the Golden Pince-Nez*, Holmes told Dr. Watson that: "...it would be difficult to name any articles which afford a finer field for inference than a pair of glasses."

Throughout his career, Sherlock Holmes examined several personal items left by strangers. He then read the owners' characteristics to Dr. Watson.

Holmes often challenged Watson to tell him the stranger's personality and background from a personal item that the stranger left behind. In *The Adventure of the Blue Carbuncle,* he asked Watson: "...What can you gather yourself as to the individuality of the man who has worn this article?"

In *The Hound of the Baskervilles,* Holmes asked Watson, "...What do you make of our visitor's stick...Let me hear you reconstruct the man by an examination of it." When Watson failed the test, Holmes would then take the item, closely examine it and tell what he found.

The skeptical Dr. Watson once requested Holmes read a watch he had in his possession so that he could test Holmes's skills. Holmes scrutinized the watch and shocked Dr. Watson with his conclusions. The method he used to read the watch relies on the same questions and principles you have learned in the previous chapters. The only difference is that in this chapter you will learn how to apply the method to an *inanimate object* rather than a living person.

How Holmes Sized-Up People by Studying Their Property

Physical items such as watches, canes, pipes, hats or eyeglasses are the best-empirical evidence for deducing an unknown person's character. The reason is that the person who lost the personal property most likely used it daily. He or she also probably unintentionally left clues on it.

Many people adapt personal objects to their own tastes and peculiarities, which make the personal property very individual in nature. The personal object often reflects the owner because he or she may hold, use or wear it a certain way. The owner may add extra accessories to the object to make it unique or extravagant. A trained observer will pick up the subtle clues in the physical evidence and draw conclusions from it.

The personal items strangers' carry can also tell you about their prior activities and reveal things about them. The following is a list of personal items and the things to look for when seeking to size up strangers:

1. **Watches:** What kind of metal? Gold? Silver? Titanium? What kind of case? Leather? Suede? Metal? Plastic? Is it a man or woman's watch? Does it have abbreviations? Monograms? Inscriptions? Is it a designer watch? Sports watch? Business watch? Child's watch? How expensive is it? Is the watch manual, digital or electronic? In *The Sign of Four,* Holmes analyzed a watch and deduced it belonged to Watson's older brother.

2. **Rings:** What kind of metal is it? Is it a man's or woman's? What style is it? What is the setting? What kind of stones and how many stones does it have? Does it have initials or other marks? Does it have symbols? What does it cost? Is it an engagement ring? Graduation ring? Wedding ring? Sorority or other organizational rings? In *A Study in Scarlet,* Holmes used a ring found at a crime scene to lure a suspect to his room. The suspect duped Holmes, however, when the suspect sent an accomplice who fled with the ring.

3. **Chains:** What kind of metal is it? Gold? Silver? How long is it? How much does it weigh? What kind of link or style? How much does it cost? Is it real or fake? Does it have anything attached to it like a name, symbol or design? In *The Red-Headed League,* Holmes deduced a man had been in China by a Chinese coin dangling from his watch-chain.

4. **Earrings or studs:** Is a male or female wearing it? What type of metal is it? Gold? Silver? Diamonds? What style is it? Is it a screw? Coil? Drop? How many stones does it have? What does it cost? How many earrings or studs are in the ear? Is the stranger wearing an earring on one or both ears? In *The Red-Headed League,* Holmes observed a witness had a pierced ear.

5. **Jewelry:** What kind of jewelry is it? What kind of metal or material? How much does it weight? What kind and number of stones? Does it have initials? Inscriptions? Monograms? Is the maker's name on it? What does it cost? In *The Naval Treaty*, Sherlock Holmes deduced a man as not being a family member by the monogrammed initials on the man's locket.

6. **Pocketbooks, Handbags, Suit Cases, Wallets:** Is it a designer brand? Is it leather? Suede? Cloth? What is the size? Color? Shape? Does it have initials or other marks on it? What does it cost? What is it being used for? What are the contents? Is it male or female? Is it new or worn? Is it real or fake? In *The Adventure of the Three Gables,* Holmes spotted labels on several trunks and suitcases to deduce the owner came from Italy.

7. **Furs, Coats, Jackets:** Is it real fur or fake? Is it a designer name? What is the material? Color? Style? Size? Length? What does it cost? Is it new? Used? In *The Adventure of the Speckled Band,* Holmes observed mud on a client's jacket to determine she traveled by a horse cart.

8. **Animals:** What kind of animal is it? Dog? Cat? Horse? Is it a big animal? Small? What is the color or distinctive marks? What is its' age? Is it male or female? Is it friendly or aggressive? Does it have an ID tag? In *The Adventure of the Creeping Man,* Sherlock Holmes stated: "...a dog reflects the family life. Whoever saw a frisky dog

in a gloomy family, or a sad dog in a happy one? Snarling people have snarling dogs, dangerous people have dangerous ones. And their passing moods may reflect the passing moods of others."[58]

9. **Cars/Trucks/Bicycle:** What is the make? Model? Color? Style? Distinctive marks? Year? Does it have any dents or scratches? Any accessories or improvements such as grills, rims, bumpers? Any monograms? Labels? Symbols? License plates? In *The Adventure of the Priory School,* Holmes deduced from a bicycle tire track the specific bicycle a man rode.

Observing a stranger's personal property can help you evaluate him or her. It can also give you clues to their personality, character, attitude, mood and prior activities. Holmes always looked at a stranger's personal property on an individual basis. He looked for indications on the object that were unique to that individual to reach his conclusions.

Sherlock Holmes did not prejudge the object but instead let the object reveal itself to him. He knew that common, everyday objects provided the best clues because the owner used them daily, leaving trace evidence of their ownership behind. But how did Holmes do this? Read further to learn the Master's method.

Holmes Looked Closely At The Personal Property

The first step in reconstructing an individual from his or her personal belonging is to look at the item closely. Unlike when you glance at people, when you observe an inanimate object, you can stare at it for a long time.

---

[58] In *The Adventure of the Creeping Man,* Holmes deduced from a dog attempting to bite his owner that the owner had used a drug, which made the owner act like a monkey. In *The Adventure of Shoscombe Old Place,* Holmes deduced that a brother impersonated his dead sister from her favorite dog's reaction to the brother.

In *The Adventure of the Noble Bachelor,* Holmes examined a locket. Dr. Watson describes how he did it:

> "Holmes gazed long and earnestly at it. Then he closed the locket and handed it back..."

In the *Sign of Four,* Holmes examined a watch. Dr. Watson describes how he did it:

> "...he balanced the watch in his hand, gazed hard at the dial, opened the back, and examined the works, first with his naked eyes and then with a powerful convex lens..."

In *The Adventure of the Blue Carbuncle,* Holmes examined a hat. Dr. Watson describes how he did it:

> "...he picked it up and gazed at it in the peculiar introspective fashion which was characteristic of him..."

In *The Yellow Face,* Holmes examined a pipe. Dr. Watson describes how he did it:

> "...Holmes was turning the pipe about in his hand, and staring at it in his peculiar pensive way...He held it up and tapped on it..."

In *The Adventure of the Golden Pince-nez,* Sherlock Holmes examined a pair of eyeglasses. Dr. Watson describes how Holmes did it:

> "...Sherlock Holmes took the glasses into his hand and examined them with utmost attention and interest. He held them on his nose, endeavored to read through them, went to the window and stared up the street with them, looked at them most minutely in the full light of the lamp...."

In *The Hound of the Baskervilles,* Holmes examined a cane. Dr. Watson describes how he did it:

> "...he now took the stick from my hands and examined it for a few minutes with his naked eyes...and carrying the cane to the window, he looked over it again with a convex lens..."

Just as Sherlock Holmes did, you can use a magnifying glass or reading glasses with high magnification to look over an item. If the item is small like a watch or ring, balance it in your hand to get a feel for it. If the item is large like a hat or cane, pick it up and look it over carefully.

Visualize the owner holding or wearing the item. You can also use or wear the item to get a 'feel' for it. For example, wear a hat or watch to see how it fits. When examining clothing, compare your size to the owner's size to determine the owner's approximate body shape, height or weight.

Holmes Focused on Specific Details

The second step is to look for specific details about the item. Dr. Watson described how Sherlock Holmes looked for specific details on a personal object to reconstruct the owner's personality and background. In *The Yellow Face* case, Holmes noticed the pipe the owner left behind had an expensive tobacco mixture in it; had a charred mark all down the right side and had deep bite marks on it.

In *The Adventure of the Golden Pince-nez* case, Sherlock Holmes noticed that the owner's eyeglasses were delicately mounted in solid gold. He noticed it had wide clips, concaved with high strength and had a tiny worn band of cork on the clip. In both cases, Holmes's attention to detail helped him to reach accurate conclusions about the owners' personality and physical characteristics.

You can follow Holmes's example by examining the personal item that you have found from every angle. Hold it up in the light. Look at every part of the item. Look at it from the top to bottom and bottom to top. Notice anything unusual or insignificant about the item.

For example, if the personal item were a watch, you would note the kind of metal it has and a description of the case. You would note whether it belongs to a man or woman, whether it has abbreviations and whether it has initials, monograms or inscriptions on it. All of these details can tell you about the owner's age, gender, race, right or left-handedness, financial status, education level and so forth.

Holmes Expected to Find Data

In *The Sign of Four,* Watson handed Sherlock Holmes a watch and said: " I have here a watch which has recently come into my possession. Would you have the kindness to let me have an opinion upon the character or habits of the late owner?" Holmes took the watch, and after examining it closely, handed it back to Watson. "There is hardly any data." Sherlock Holmes said with a crestfallen expression. He then suggested someone recently cleaned the watch, "...which robs me of my most suggestive facts."

Watson conceded someone cleaned the watch before he received it. He felt in his heart, however, that Holmes used it as an excuse to cover up his inability to read the watch. Watson thought to himself: "What data could he expect from an unclean watch?" What Watson did not know is when you look at an unknown owner's personal item; there *are* specific data you can expect to find when the item is worn or dirty.

Below is a list of common sense details to watch for when you decipher a personal object left by a stranger:

- Scratches, dents and markings may indicate the owner is careless.

- No scratches, dents or markings may indicate the owner is neat or organized.
- Dirt may indicate the owner is lazy, unclean or arrived from another location.
- Letters or initials may indicate the owner's name, location, organization.
- Dents or stains may indicate the owner is impulsive or reckless.
- Faded or worn marks may indicate the owner had the item for a long time.
- Expensive items may indicate the owner's social or financial status.
- Cultural items may indicate the owner's race, religion, gender or social status.
- Style of item may indicate owner's gender, age, race, social or financial status.
- Repairs may indicate owner values item, has foresight and economic status.
- No repairs may show owner does not value item or financial status declined.
- New or recently cleaned items may indicate owner had item for short time.
- Dates may indicate how old item is or how long the owner possessed it.
- Clothing or shoes may indicate the owner's weight, height, gender and age.
- Item location may indicate whether owner is right or left handed.

Do not write the above data details in stone. Use them with caution. They are only indications of what the object *may* show, not what it will show. There may be other explanations for indications left on an item. For example, in *The Adventure of the Blue Carbuncle* case, Sherlock Holmes analyzed a hat. He inferred from details on the hat that the man's wife did not love him anymore and he had fallen on bad times.

Yet the man could have been a bachelor, he could have purchased the hat at a flea market or he could have borrowed the hat from a friend. Often more than one explanation for a thing exists but usually only one explanation is correct. Always consider alternative explanations that fit the item and are consistent with what it means. You can determine the correct meaning by carefully studying the inanimate object, looking at the most-probable cause and then checking your inferences.

Holmes Made Inferences From the Details

The third step is to draw meaning from details you find on the object that will imply something about the owner. This step relies on using reason, logic and common sense. You also must balance the most-probable explanation and use the simplest one. Use the explanation that seems most natural and reasonable under the circumstances.

Take into consideration the time and place where you found the item or how the person presented it to you. Form a theory regarding the owner and start to reconstruct the person based on the data, facts and evidence in front of you. You can also use the same questions and principles you learned from the previous chapters to uncover clues about the item.

In *The Yellow Face* case cited above, Holmes reasoned from all the details he found on the pipe. He inferred that: "...the owner is obviously a muscular man, left-handed, with an excellent set of teeth, careless in his habits, and with no need to practice economy..."

In *The Adventure of the Golden Pince-nez* case also cited above, Holmes reasoned from all the details he discovered on the eyeglasses. He inferred that the owner was a woman of good address, attired like a lady, with a thick nose, close eyes, puckered forehead, rounded shoulders and had seen an optician twice in the last few months.

In *The Sign of Four*, Sherlock Holmes drew inferences from an unclean watch Dr. Watson asked him to examine. Holmes explains how he did it below:

> "...I should judge that the watch belonged to your elder brother, who inherited it from your father...the W. suggests your own name. The date of the watch is nearly fifty years back, and the initials are as old as the watch; so it was made for the last generation. Jewelry

usually descends to the eldest son, and he is most likely to have the same name as the father. Your father has, if I remember right, been dead many years. It has therefore, been in the hands of your eldest brother....he was a man of untidy habits — very untidy and careless. He was left with good prospects, but he threw away his chances, lived for some time in poverty with occasional short intervals of prosperity, and finally, taking to drink, he died. That is all I can gather..."

In *The Adventure of the Blue Carbuncle*, Watson claimed he could see nothing after examining an old hat. Sherlock Holmes replied: "On the contrary, Watson, you can see everything. You fail, however, to reason from what you see. You are too timid in drawing your inferences."

Holmes often made bold educated guesses based on the facts he observed. Dr. Watson then described how Holmes drew inferences from the old black hat that its owner had left behind:

"...this hat is three years old. These flat brims curled at the edge came in then. It is a hat of the very best quality. Look at the band of ribbed silk and the excellent lining. If this man could afford to buy so expensive a hat three years ago, and has no hat since, then he has assuredly gone down in the world...putting his finger upon the little disc and loop of the hat-securer. "They are never sold upon hats. If this man ordered one, it is a sign of a certain amount of foresight, since he went out of his way to take this precaution against the wind. But since we see that he has broken the elastic and has not troubled to replace it, it is obvious that he has less foresight now than formerly, which is a distinct proof of a weakening nature. On the other hand, he has endeavored to conceal some of these stains upon the felt by daubing them with ink, which is a sign that he has not entirely lost his self-respect..."

In *The Sign of Four,* Holmes examined Watson brother's watch. Holmes then said to Watson: "What seems strange to you is only so because you do not follow my train of thought or observe the small facts upon which large inferences depend." In all four cases above, Holmes used his rules of deduction to reason from what he saw. He then reached highly accurate conclusions about the characteristics of the item's owners.

Holmes Always Checked His Conclusions

The fourth and final step is to test your theory to ensure its validity. Sherlock Holmes always verified his conclusions by testing them out, predicting an outcome or if possible, checking with the original source.

In *The Sign of Four,* Holmes verified that the watch he deduced had belonged to Watson's older brother. Watson confirmed that the brother inherited it from their father. In *The Adventure of the Blue Carbuncle,* Holmes verified that a hat belonged to its owner. He placed an ad in the local paper and waited for a man to pick it up. When the man arrived, he fit Holmes's description exactly.

In *The Yellow Face,* Holmes checked that a pipe belonged to its owner by waiting for the man to return to 221B Baker Street. When the man came back, he fit Holmes's description exactly. In *The Adventure of the Golden Pince-nez,* Holmes verified that the pair of eyeglasses he deduced belonged to a woman. He later discovered her hiding behind a bookcase in a secret room.

In *The Hound of the Baskervilles,* Holmes verified that he had correctly reconstructed a walking stick. He did it after speaking to the owner when the owner arrived at 221B Baker Street to claim his cane.

Scientists verify facts all the time using the scientific method. You may also note that the four steps above mirror exactly the scientific method's four simplified steps: observe and collect data; form a theory; test it and then reach a conclusion. A scientist uses reason, based on the scientific method, to discover the smallest details and uncover the most trifling clues.

Holmes used his own version of the scientific method whenever he sought to reconstruct an owner from his or her personal property. On many occasions, Holmes stated to Dr. Watson that he had trained himself over the years to attain his highly developed deductive skills.

Practice Reading Everyday Items

Sherlock Holmes would often say: "surely my deductions are simplicity itself..." in describing his ability to deduce an owner's personality or background from inanimate objects. Although Holmes made this ability seem easy, without practice and self-training, it is not as easy as it sounds. You can train yourself to read a stranger's personal items but you must frequently practice to become proficient at it. You can practice studying with a commonly used personal item. Then verify your conclusions by questioning the owner.

Five everyday personal items that you can start with are the same ones Holmes analyzed: a hat, eyeglasses, cane, pipe and watch. Use the five stories that these items appeared in as a starting point and guide. Acquire and practice with these five items and ask yourself questions about them. Study and draw inferences about them by observing any details you find. Write down your inferences and then check them.

In *The Elementary Methods of Sherlock Holmes*, author Brad Keefauver makes the point that although technology has rendered such things as horse drawn carriages obsolete, you can still apply the methods Holmes used today. Mr. Keefauver illustrates his point by describing how to reconstruct a stranger from a common set of keys:[59]

> "...were a modern-day client of the detective to leave his keys behind, there would be a wealth of data to be had. There are the obvious deductions, such as what the make of the client's car is, or how security-minded he may be. But beyond those, just imagine what Sherlock Holmes could do with a set of keys. A single door key might indicate an apartment dweller. Copies of keys can reveal a large family. Certain types and numbers of keys can point out job characteristics and status. And the key chain or ring can be helpful as well. Is it too big for a man's pocket? Then the client must be a woman carrying a purse. Is there a trinket or charm attached to the ring? If so, is it an older piece with sentimental value or a faddish bauble?"

In the British TV show *"Sherlock,"* on the episode *The Great Game*, Actor Benedict Cumberbatch portrays Sherlock Holmes. He deduces specific details about an owner from a modern pair of sneakers. Holmes examines the training sneakers closely and then reconstructs the owner to Watson:

Holmes: "The owner loved these. Scrubbed them clean, whitened where they got discolored, changed the laces three...no, four times. Even so there are traces of his flaky skin where his fingers have come into contact with them, so he suffered from eczema. The shoes are well-worn more so on the inside, which means the owner had weak arches. British made, 20 years old. They're not retro, they're original. Limited edition, two blue stripes, 1989."

---

[59] *The Elementary Methods of Sherlock Holmes; Chapter 10: The Walk-In Information Source Updated;* Quotes from Pages 77-78.

Watson:	"But there's still mud on them. They look new."
Holmes:	"Someone's kept them that way. Quite a bit of mud caked on the soles. Analysis shows it's from Sussex with London mud overlaying it."
Watson:	"How do you know?"
Holmes:	"Pollen. Clear as a map reference to me. South of the river, too, so the kid who owned these trainers came to London from Sussex 20 years ago and left them behind."
Watson:	"So what happened to him?"
Holmes:	"Something bad. He loved those shoes remember. He'd never leave them filthy, wouldn't let them go unless he had to. So a child with big feet...Carl Powers..."

What the above two examples establish is that Sherlock Holmes would have read a stranger's personal property just as easily in modern times as he did in 1887. The principles Holmes used to read inanimate objects never change. They remain just as practical today as in his time.

Sizing up a stranger by reading his or her personal belongings is a skill that you can master with enough practice and self-training. Chapter 12 contains additional exercises that you can practice with to develop your skill to its fullest potential.

Go to Pages 340 to 343 if you want to practice
reading personal property exercises now.

Chapter 11

How To Size-Up Strangers
By Analyzing Their Handwriting

"Have you ever had occasion to study character in handwriting?
What do you make of this fellow's scribble?"
Sherlock Holmes, The Sign of Four

In *Sherlock Holmes: A Game of Shadows (2011),* Sherlock Holmes enters Professor James Moriarty's study where he finds Moriarty has just finished a lecture. Holmes asks Moriarty to autograph a book Moriarty wrote entitled: *"The Dynamics of an Asteroid & Lecture Notes."* Professor Moriarty takes the book, signs it and hands it back to Holmes. As they politely but subtly threaten each other, Holmes asks Moriarty if he is familiar with the study of Graphology. When Moriarty says no, Holmes analyzes his handwriting. Holmes then says it reveals Moriarty as a creative genius with a meticulous nature but prone to egotism, narcissism and insanity.

The movie portrays Sherlock Holmes as using his skill to decipher a stranger's character and personality traits from handwriting. The stories throughout the Canon depict him as an expert at evaluating written statements or analyzing important documents to decide if they are genuine. But in the real world, can you really size up strangers by analyzing their handwriting? In real life, can you really tell if a signature or document is fraudulent just by looking at it?

This chapter will answer the above questions. It will show you how Sherlock Holmes used three basic approaches to analyze handwriting. Then it will reveal the truth about handwriting analysis. Finally, it will show you how to use handwriting analysis in a practical way to size up strangers.

Sherlock Holmes Applied Graphology

The first approach Sherlock Holmes used is *Graphology*. Graphology is the analysis of handwriting to determine a person's personality and character. Graphologists believe that particular writing elements, such as a letter stroke or slant, reveal specific personality traits.[60] They claim by evaluating these writing elements you can uncover hidden emotions, unseen behavior and unknown character traits. Holmes believed this. He relied on Graphology writing elements whenever he sized up a stranger or investigated a case.

In *The Reigate Puzzle*, Holmes examined a torn paper that implicated a father and son in a murder. Holmes stated:

> "It may be obvious to you in the Greek e's but to me there are many small points which indicate the same thing...I am only, of course, giving you the leading results now of my examination of the paper. There were twenty-three other deductions which would be of more interest to experts than to you."

According to Sherlock Holmes, Graphology experts look for 23 handwriting elements to properly analyze handwriting. These writing characteristics or 'small points' are visible in everyone's handwriting. Holmes never revealed the 23 handwriting deductions that he used to decipher the torn paper. You can, however, review several case histories from the Canon to discover them. The following is a list of elements Holmes used to analyze handwriting:

1. **Tool.** Whenever Holmes examined a person's handwriting, he always looked at the writing tool the

---

[60] *The International Graphoanalysis Society (IGAS)* states this on its website at www.igas.com.

person used. Was it a pen, pencil or marker? Is the pen fine or ballpoint? What color is the ink? In *The Adventure of the Missing Three-Quarter*, Sherlock Holmes observed a client wrote a note with a quill pen rather than pencil. He then became excited when he took an impression from the paper. In *The Adventure of the Cardboard Box*, Sherlock Holmes noticed a client received a package written with a broad-pointed pen in inferior ink. In several other cases, he noted the type of tool used before he studied the handwriting.[61]

2. **Surface.** After Sherlock Holmes examined the writing tool, he would examine the writing surface. A writing surface is anything on which you can write. In *A Study in Scarlet*, Holmes determined a man's height from his handwriting on a wall. In *A Scandal in Bohemia*, Holmes determined a man's German nationality after studying the paper quality and sentence construction in the man's handwritten note. Holmes often looked for clues to a writer's identity from the paper quality before he studied the handwriting.

3. **Style.** Sherlock Holmes often deduced a writer's gender and nationality from their handwriting style. In *The Adventure of the Lion's Mane*, Holmes recognized a woman's penmanship from her "scrawling, feminine hand." In *The Adventure of Wisteria Lodge*, Sherlock Holmes analyzed a note and stated, "The writer of this note is certainly English." Holmes would look at the handwriting style for clues such as whether the person wrote in script, print or decorative. He then examined the

---

[61] In *The Hound of the Baskervilles*, Holmes deduced that an address had been written in a hotel because he reasoned a hotel would normally have an empty pen and inkbottle. In *The Adventure of the Three Students*, Holmes noted a suspect wrote furiously with a soft lead pencil until he broke the tip. Holmes then analyzed the pencil and predicted to College Lecturer Hilton Sloames that once he found the pencil, Mr. Sloames would find the suspect.

lettering for angles, curves, humps and arches to determine the writing style.[62]

4. **Margin.** According to graphologists, how a person fills a paper with writing reveals how the writer's fills his or her own life. Margins indicate a writer's mood, disposition and how he or she relates to society in general. A left narrow margin reveals the writer's past, a balanced margin means the writer has a balanced life and a right wide margin means the writer is afraid of the future. The top margin reveals how goal oriented and ambitious the writer is. The bottom margin reveals a writer's drive and instincts. Critics state, however, that no empirical evidence exists for these claims and that margins are just for making writing readable.[63] In *The Adventure of the Empty House,* Holmes used the margin from his index of biographies to write that Colonel Sebastian Moran was the second most dangerous man in London.

5. **Stroke.** Sherlock Holmes analyzed individual letter strokes when he scrutinized a stranger's handwriting. Stroke types are associated with personality traits and energy. For example, an angular stroke is associated with aggressiveness while a backward stroke is associated with immaturity. Holmes would look at backward and forward strokes, up and down strokes, sharp and angular strokes; altered and connected strokes, flourished strokes and writing with no upstrokes to identify each type of stroke and associate it with a personality trait.

---

[62] *"Handwriting Styles & Want They Mean"* an online *eHow* article by Catherine Copeland discusses handwriting styles such as Arcade and Garland. See it at: http://www.ehow.com/info_8439297_ handwriting-styles-mean.html.

[63] An assertion that no empirical evidence exists could also apply to the other 22 elements that analyze personality traits from handwriting as well.

6. **Slant.** According to graphologists, the slant in a letter reveals the writer's feelings. A vertical slant (|) indicates the writer controls his or her feelings and lives in the present. A left slant (\) indicates the writer is shy, dwells in the past and is indifferent. A right slant (/) indicates an outgoing, social personality with strong feelings and tends to look to the future. Varying slants (|, \, /) indicates the writer is moody, unpredictable and emotionally unstable. In *The Valley of Fear,* Sherlock Holmes receives two letters from a confidential informant. He tells Watson: "...Porlock is evidently scared out of his senses — kindly compare the writing in the note to that upon its envelope...The one is clear and firm. The other hardly legible." You can infer from this case that Sherlock Holmes deduced the writer's emotional state of mind when he analyzed the letter slants in the writer's handwriting.

7. **Pressure.** When Sherlock Holmes analyzed handwriting, he looked for any impressions left on the paper. The impressions on the paper revealed to Holmes how much pressure the writer used as he or she wrote. According to Graphology, pressure represents an individual's energy level. Heavy pressure may mean a writer has a lot of energy, is intense, aggressive or has stress. Medium pressure may mean the writer has a balanced energy level. Light pressure could mean the writer is passive, laid back and has little or no energy. In *The Reigate Puzzle,* it is clear Holmes is talking about writing pressure. He says to Watson: "When I draw your attention to the strong *t*'s of 'at' and 'to,' and ask you to compare them with the weak ones of 'quarter' and 'twelve...the 'learn' and the 'maybe' are written in the stronger hand, and the 'what' in the weaker." As a result, Holmes deduced two different individuals wrote on the paper using alternate words.

8. **Size.** How big the lettering is reveals a writer's confidence level and ability to concentrate. Sherlock Holmes no doubt analyzed the size of each letter as he analyzed handwriting. In *The Sign of Four,* Sherlock Holmes scrutinized several letters from a man's writing and stated, "Look at his long letters...that *d* might be an *a*, and that *I* an *e*. Men of character always differentiate their long letters, however, illegibly they may write. There is vacillation in his *k's* and self-esteem in his capitals." A person who writes with very small or tiny letters may have low self-esteem, be shy and quiet yet respectful. This person is usually intelligent, pays attention to details and can concentrate. A person who writes with average or medium size letters is usually has average concentration and confidence. A person who writes with large or huge letters probably is very confident, a showoff, loud, extroverted, needs lots of attention and narcissistic.

9. **Spacing.** Sherlock Holmes's skill in examining word spacing is what enabled him to solve a murder in *The Reigate Puzzle*. In this case, he noticed the peculiar word spacing in a torn note, which revealed two individuals wrote it. Holmes explained it this way:

> "If you examine this scrap with attention you will come to the conclusion that the man with the stronger hand wrote all his words first, leaving blanks for the other to fill up. These blanks were not always sufficient, and you can see that the second man had a squeeze to fit his 'quarter' in between the 'at' and the 'to', showing that the latter were already written...."

According to Graphology, letter, word or sentence spacing reveals a writer's social personality and mood. A writer with little or no letter or word spacing indicates a people-person, who is warm and very social. A writer with average or normal spacing is socially balanced and fair. A writer with wide spacing indicates trouble dealing with others socially, independent, reserved and intelligent.

10. **Speed.** In *The Man with the Twisted Lip,* Sherlock Holmes sought to figure out whether a missing man still lived. He questioned the man's wife (who still believed him alive). She gave Holmes a letter; to prove her husband still lived. Sherlock Holmes examined the letter and asked her if she really believed her husband wrote it. She stated her husband wrote differently when he had to rush. Holmes thought everything over, while sitting on five pillows and smoking an ounce of shag throughout the night, and eventually found her husband alive. When a person writes in haste the writing is usually illegible or unclear. The hurried person often writes impulsively without thinking. Fast writers usually are fast thinkers with a lot of energy whose writing tends to not have dotted 'i's or crossed 't's. Slow writers tend to think slowly, have less energy and are methodical. A person who writes at a normal pace indicates a balanced personality with a normal energy level.

11. **Baseline.** In *The Adventure of the Abbey Grange,* Sherlock Holmes received a letter from Inspector Stanley Hopkins requesting he come immediately to a crime scene. Holmes deduced murder as the reason for the urgency because he noticed: "Hopkins's writing shows considerable agitation, and he is not an emotional man." How could Holmes tell from the inspector's writing that he was 'agitated'? Simple. He studied the baseline in the inspector's writing. The baseline is the line on which a person writes words and the natural direction they flow. Movement to the right suggests moving forward. Movement to the left suggests falling backward. Sometimes the paper has lines that guide the writer. Other times the paper is blank with no lines. The baseline

in writing reveals the writer's emotional health. A very uneven or wavy baseline indicates the writer is emotionally insecure and unpredictable. A straight baseline reveals the writer is in control emotionally, tense and rigid. An even baseline means the writer's feelings are balanced. A baseline that travels upward or is ascending reveals a writer who is hopeful, enthusiastic or optimistic. A downward or descending baseline indicates someone who is moody, depressed or thinks negative.

12. **Alignment.** In *The Adventure of the Cardboard Box*, Sherlock Holmes noticed that a package he inspected had an "address printed in rather straggling characters." The irregular letters revealed to Holmes that the writing had improper alignment. Normal letter alignment ensures all characters are the same size and remain straight on the baseline. It makes a document easy to read. Most people learn from a young age to properly align the letters they write to the page. Holmes reasoned from this clue that the man who wrote the address had limited education (no lessons in penmanship) and knew little about the town of Croydon (incorrect spelling).

13. **Clarity.** In *The Adventure of the Norwood Builder*, Sherlock Holmes deduced a man wrote a Will while in a train because in certain parts, the Will had good writing and in other parts, it had bad writing. Good handwriting is any writing that is easy to read, simple to understand and facilitates communication. The spaces are even, the margins are balanced, the letters are neat, the words are distinct and the sentences are well organized. Bad handwriting is any writing that is hard to read, impossible to comprehend and hinders communication. The writing is messy, the letters are tangled, the words are confusing and the message is mixed or hard to understand. Clarity in writing indicates sharp thinking and good communication skills. Slovenly writing

suggests the writer does not care about communicating and puts little or no thought into what he or she writes.

14. **Shape.** In *The Valley of Fear,* Sherlock Holmes studied a slip of paper. He recognized a spy from Professor Moriarty's criminal organization wrote it. Holmes stated: "It is Porlock's writing...I can hardly doubt that it is Porlock's writing, though I have seen it only twice before. The Greek *e* with the peculiar top flourish is distinctive." What made Holmes so sure the spy Porlock wrote the letter? Simple. Holmes identified Porlock by the distinctive way he shaped his letters while writing. People train very early in life to write letter shapes. They practice making angular, round and flourished letter shapes in their writing. As they grow older, they develop a particular style in shaping each letter and transition into cursive script writing. A graphologist sees a person who writes with pointed letters as aggressive, highly intelligent, intense and strong willed. He sees a person who writes with rounded letters as meek, submissive, creative and soft. He sees a person who writes with flourish letters as creative, imaginative and artistic.

15. **Zone.** Graphology has three zones, which express different aspects of the writer's personality. The upper zone expresses a writer's *mind* — intelligence, spiritual nature, ambitions and confidence. People usually write the letters 'l', 'h', 't', 'b' and 'd' in this zone. The middle zone expresses a writer's *emotions* — daily habits, ego and sense of self, feelings and practical nature. People usually write the letters 'a', 'm', 'n', 'o' 'u', 'e' 'i', 's', 'v', 'c', 'r', 'w', 'x' and 'z' in this zone. The lower zone expresses a writer's *body* — physical nature, sexual desires, material and unconscious urges. People usually write the letters 'f', 'g', 'j', 'p' and 'y' in this zone. In *Sherlock Holmes: A Game of Shadows (2011),* Holmes used zone analysis when he scrutinized Professor Moriarty's handwriting.

261

Holmes stated: "...The upward strokes on the 'p', the 'j', the 'm', indicate a genius level intellect, while the flourishes in the lower zone denote a highly creative, yet meticulous nature."

16. **Loops.** When Sherlock Holmes analyzed handwriting, he studied the loops in writing. People usually write the loops in one of the three zones. When a person writes a loop in a particular zone, the loop becomes associated with the trait in the zone. For example, when a person writes a loop in the upper zone, it represents the writer's intelligence and spiritual attributes. Tall loops represent the writer's interest and desires. Wide loops reveal that a writer is broadminded and smart. An excessive loop indicates a person who dwells in fantasy. A short loop means a writer may be materialistic and want money. A narrow loop means a person is narrow minded with little or no imagination. A writer with no loops could mean the person is serious and practical.

17. **Pattern.** Whenever Sherlock Holmes analyzed handwriting, he looked for patterns in the writing. He would look at the way a person normally writes and note the way he or she formed their letters and words. He knew over a period of time the writing would develop into a predictable pattern. He would then look for any changes in the pattern to spot clues for further investigation. A person who normally prints their words but now suddenly starts writing script would draw Holmes's suspicion. A person who normally writes neatly but suddenly starts writing sloppy would raise a red flag in Holmes' mind. In *The Adventure of the Red Circle*, Holmes became suspicious when he discovered a landlady only received *printed* notes from a secretive tenant. As Holmes stated to Watson: "Seclusion I can understand; but why print? Printing is a clumsy process. Why not write?" Holmes always stayed alert to the

arrangement, form and movement of writing on a page when analyzing handwriting.

18. **Connection.** One of the most important things Sherlock Holmes looked for when he analyzed handwriting is the connection between letters. As an expert in Graphology, Holmes would have noticed that letters did not touch or whether all the letters connected and flowed into each other. Letters that do not touch each other reveal a writer who acts impulsively, is creative and thinks independently. When some letters connect this reveals a writer who is intuitive and less logical. All letters connecting together reveals a person who is careful, alert and analytical.

19. **Signature.** According to Graphology, a writer's signature is their public image and the way they want people to see them. The signature size, legibility and style reveals a lot about the writer. A small signature may mean the writer is shy and reserved. A clear and legible signature may mean the writer is comfortable with his or her self. A fancy or elaborate signature may mean the writer is a showoff or seeks attention. An illegible or hard to read signature may mean the writer is secretive or private. A left-handed writer is usually very independent. A right-handed writer is usually intelligent and creative.

In *A Case of Identity,* Sherlock Holmes deduced a man had a hidden agenda with his female client because the man *typed* his signature rather than *signed* it. Holmes then solved the case and exposed the schemer. Holmes said to Watson: "My suspicions were all confirmed by his peculiar action in typewriting his signature, which inferred...that his handwriting was so familiar to her that she would recognize even the smallest sample of it."

20. **Deviation.** When Sherlock Holmes analyzed handwriting he looked for missing or altered letters, changes in wording and unnatural penmanship. He looked for pen lifts, unsteady lines, unusual letter formations, 'i's not dotted and 't's not crossed. He looked for inconsistent slants and strokes and no natural writing flow. In *The Adventure of the Cardboard Box,* Sherlock Holmes noticed in a package he inspected that the letter 'i' had been changed to 'y' in the word 'Croydon'. Holmes knew that no two people write alike or the same person's writing may vary. Holmes therefore looked for subtle telltale signs that deviated from normal handwriting.

21. **Quality.** According to Graphology, the quality in people's writing can reveal a lot about them. Quality in writing is about the consistency and fluidness in the words and sentences. It measures the writing flow, which reveals its rhythm and movement. Specific or vague wording, paragraph balance and structure are also components of quality. Deterioration in quality usually reveals itself in poor handwriting that is illegible or stiff.

In *The Adventure of the Priory School,* Sherlock Holmes investigated a young boy's disappearance. He questioned the school's principle Thorneycroft Huxtable about the Duke of Holdernesse's stiff handwriting on an envelope. Holmes then met the Duke and his secretary and questioned them further on the letters they wrote and mailed before the boy's disappearance. He would later discover what happened to the boy and solve the German schoolmaster's death.

22. **Structure.** Sherlock Holmes could read a writer's background from his or her handwriting. One of the ways he did this is by scrutinizing the writing structure. In *The Adventure of the Creeping Man,* Holmes deduced one writer's foreign background from his "crabbed" hand and

the other writer's educational background from the structure in his writing. The format on a page gives the writing its' structure. Some people organize their writing structures, while other writing structures ramble. The space or gaps between lines is what makes the line, paragraph and sentences seem structured. The more lines on a page, the less gaps or spacing. The fewer lines on a page, the more gaps or spacing. Wide line spacing means the writer is confidant and a visionary. Even line spacing suggests the writer is balanced and good at planning. Closed line spacing reveals a writer who stays to his or her self and is afraid to open up to others. Uneven spaced lines suggest the writer is moody and unpredictable.

23. **Lettering.** In *The Sign of Four,* Holmes determined the same person wrote several papers in a disguised hand. He looked at the each letter formation in the papers to know the authorship. Graphologists also look at letter formations when analyzing handwriting but associate them with personality traits. To graphologists, each letter in the alphabet has a meaning.

Round letters mean a person is carefree, calm and a good citizen. Block letters mean the person is hardworking and meticulous. Angular letters mean the writer is aggressive, forceful and a leader. Moderate letters suggest the writer is wise, balanced and loving. Capital Letters reveal the writer's self confidence, self-worth, importance and how they want others to see them. A person who writes in all capitals seeks to hide his or her true nature and is secretive. A person who writes in small capitals usually is shy and timid. A person who writes in large capitals means they are ambitious, creative and success oriented. A person who writes in extra large capitals is egotistical and arrogant. Normal capitals suggest a person who is thoughtful and fair.

Sherlock Holmes used the 23 elements listed above in various combinations to analyze handwriting and deduce a stranger's personality and character. In addition to using Graphology to size up strangers, Holmes also applied a second approach to analyze handwriting.

Sherlock Holmes Studied Statements

The second approach Holmes used is he studied written statements. Today experts call it *Statement Analysis.*[64] It is the word-by-word analysis of the content in a person's statement. It determines whether he or she is being forthright and complete with the information given.

When modern day investigators apply the techniques in statement analysis, they look for linguistic clues in a person's written statements. They seek out inconsistencies, which will help them during the interview and interrogation process to spot deception or obtain a confession.

The major premise an investigator using statement analysis operates under is that a truthful statement has different discernable factors than a deceptive statement. [65] The investigator then applies written speech analysis and looks for extraneous information. He will spot whether conviction is present in the statement and examine the statement for balance to get at the truth.

---

[64] Statement analysis is also known as *Scientific Content Analysis (SCAN).* Avinoam Sapir, a former Israeli police polygraph examiner, created it and operates the *Laboratory of Scientific Interrogation, Inc. (LSI).*

[65] German psychologist Udo Undeutsch published a hypothesis in which he stated: "Statements that are the product of experience will contain characteristics that are generally absent from statements that are the product of imagination." Steven W. Horowitz, *"Empirical Support for Statement Validity Assessment,"* Behavioral Assessment 13 (1991): 294-295.

The specific techniques the investigators use include, but are not limited to, establishing a baseline for the truthful statement. They also identify when a written word or phrase deviates from it. They analyze a person's written speech for past and present tense language. They look for pronouns, nouns and verbs. They recognize writing that includes non-essential information and writing that has important information left out. They spot whether or not the person is fully committed to their narrative and determine whether the statement is balanced.

In the article *"Statement Analysis: What Do Suspects' Words Really Reveal?"* [66] FBI Agent Susan Adams describes a statement analysis technique. In the article Ms. Adams states:

> "To analyze a statement, investigators first need to examine the individual parts of speech, particularly pronouns, nouns, and verbs, and to establish the norm for each. If a deviation from the norm appears, they then should ask, "Why?"

Sherlock Holmes used the same technique over a hundred years ago in *The Adventure of the Three Gables.* Holmes applied statement analysis when he noticed from a sheet of paper that the person who wrote it changed the pronouns in the writing. Holmes described it this way:

> "Queer grammar!" said Holmes with a smile as he handed the paper back to the inspector. "Did you notice how 'he' suddenly changed to 'my'? The writer was so carried away by his own story that he imagined himself at the supreme moment to be the hero."

It is clear from his analysis of the content of the paper that Holmes had established a baseline and noticed any deviations from it. He also scrutinized the writer's grammar, picking up on the change from the pronoun 'he' to 'my.'

---

[66] FBI Law Enforcement Bulletin, October 1996, 12-20.

Moreover, Holmes saw the writer had conviction because as Holmes stated, the writer imagined himself at the critical instant as the hero in the incident. Studying written statements, such as the one in the *Three Gables* case above, naturally led Holmes to the third and final approach.

Sherlock Holmes Examined Documents

The third approach Holmes used is he examined documents during his investigations. Today, experts call this *Questioned Document Examination (QDE).*[67] QDE is the study of signatures and documents to determine their authenticity. A document examiner seeks to answer questions as to a disputed document's origin, author, source, condition and completeness.

The document examiner looks for three main factors whenever he examines a document.[68] The first factor he looks for is *habituation*, the routine way individuals write out of habit. It is the person's penmanship style, which develops, through time, into predictable and discernable writing patterns.

The second factor the examiner looks for is *complexity.* It is the variations in how each person writes the letters in the alphabet. A trained document examiner can spot the differences in lettering because every person has their own way of writing each letter.

The third factor the examiner looks for is *uniqueness*, the one of a kind writing style no one else has. The examiner seeks to identify a document's author by eliminating writing that is not exactly the same as the author's.

---

[67] Wikipedia at: *http://en.wikipedia.org/wiki/Questioned_document _examination.*

[68] *The Application of Forensic Document Examination Techniques to the Writings of J. S. Bach and A. M. Bach. Understanding Bach, 3, 87-92.*

A document examiner will scrutinize the writing instrument used. He will examine the ink and paper. He will identify any marks or symbols. He will note handwriting characteristics and look for alterations, deletions or additions. He will study the document's condition (torn, burnt, wet, etc.) and compare the findings against known documents or signatures. Holmes often did exactly this when a client presented a signature or document to him for examination.

In *The Sign of Four,* Sherlock Holmes examined an envelope and letter client Mary Morstan gave to him. Holmes looked to determine the identity of the writer from examining the questioned documents. Watson describes Holmes's reaction when he first examined the envelope:

> "Post-mark. London, S. W. Date, July 7, Hum! Man's thumb mark on corner — probably postman. Best quality paper. Envelopes at sixpence a packet. Particular man in his stationery. No address."

Holmes looked at the date, the post-mark, the paper quality and the thumb mark left on the envelope's corner for clues to the writer's identity. Watson then describes how Holmes examined additional papers Miss Morstan gave him:

> "He spread out the papers upon the table and gave little darting glances from one to the other. " They are disguised hands, except the letter," he said presently; "but there can be no question as to the authorship. See how the irrepressible Greek *e* will break out, and see the twirl of the final *s.* They are undoubtedly by the same person...."

Holmes questioned the client as to her husband's handwriting to gauge a baseline against which he could compare the documents with each other. He also observed several letter characteristics such as strokes, slants and shapes to determine who wrote the paper.

In the same case above, Holmes inspected a map with his double lens. Watson describes how he did it:

> "Holmes unfolded the paper carefully and smoothed it out upon his knee. He then very methodically examined it all over with his double lens. "It is paper of native Indian manufacture," he remarked. "It has at some time been pinned to a board. The diagram upon it appears to be a plan of part of a large building with numerous halls, corridors and passages. At one point is a small cross done in red ink, and above it is '3.37 from left,' in faded pencil-writing. In the left-hand corner is a curious hieroglyphic like four crosses in a line with their arms touching. Beside it is written, in very rough and coarse characters, 'The sign of the four — Jonathan Small, Mahomet Singh, Abdullah Khan, Dost Akbar'.... it is evidently a document of importance. It has been kept carefully in a pocket-book, for the one side is as clean as the other."

Sherlock Holmes scrutinized the map just like a modern day document examiner. He closely inspected the ink and paper. He noted the paper had been pinned to a board. He identified relevant marks and symbols. He examined the rough, coarse handwriting. Holmes pointed out how both sides of the paper stayed clean.

In *The Man With the Twisted Lip,* Holmes examined the ink in a letter to determine if anyone forged the letter. Holmes described his analysis to his client Mrs. St. Clair this way:

> "The name, you see, is in perfectly black ink, which has dried itself. The rest is of the grayish color, which shows that blotting paper has been used. If it had been written straight off, and then blotted, none would be of a deep black shade."

In *The Adventure of the Cardboard Box,* Holmes analyzed a package delivered to retired spinster Miss Cushing. Watson described how Holmes examined the yellow cardboard box, brown paper and its contents:

> "...Holmes examined, one by one, the articles which Lestrade had handed to him...Brown paper, with a distinct smell of coffee...address printed in rather straggling characters: 'Miss S. Cushing, Cross Street, Croydon." Done with a broad-pointed pen, probably a J, and with inferior ink. The word 'Croydon' has been originally spelled with an 'I,' which as been changed to 'y'...The box is a yellow, half-pound honeydew box, with nothing distinctive save two thumb marks at the left bottom corner. It is filled with rough salt of the quality used for preserving hides and other of the coarser commercial purposes. And embedded in it are these very singular enclosures."

Sherlock Holmes analyzed the box, how the paper smelled, how the characters were printed, the type of pen used and the ink quality. Most importantly, Holmes determined a word had been altered and noted two thumb marks at the box's left bottom corner — all elements a modern day document examiner would have looked for.

The Truth About Handwriting Analysis

As stated at the beginning of the chapter, Sherlock Holmes used three approaches to handwriting analysis: Graphology, statement analysis and document examination. But just because Sherlock Holmes used these approaches to analyze handwriting, does not automatically make him right. You can admire Sherlock Holmes's handwriting analysis skills without letting them blind you to the truth.

To do this, you must not allow your admiration for Holmes to bias your judgment. You cannot allow your desire for Holmes to be right to lead you astray. You must not make excuses for him. You must use the same cold logic Holmes used to reject anything he could not prove — even if it means rejecting arguments Holmes himself presented.

It is clear from stories in the Canon that Sherlock Holmes held the belief that Graphology reveals a person's character and personality. Holmes was wrong. Experts state many scientific studies have shown that Graphology is not a reliable indicator of personality or character. [69] Most scientists have rejected Graphology and state it is a pseudo-science.

Most courts do not recognize Graphology as a science or accept it as evidence. Most reputable colleges and universities do not include Graphology in their teaching curriculums or award degrees for it. Recognized experts such as Magician/Skeptic James Randi and Scientist Barry Beyerstein reject Graphology. They contend it is fake science.[70]

It is equally clear Sherlock Holmes used statement analysis during his investigations. Holmes was wrong again. Experts state statement analysis is a skill, which relies more on art than science. They also assert it relies more on wishful and magical thinking than cold facts. They contend no research or studies support proponents' claims regarding statement analysis.[71]

---

[69] Study#1: Jennings, D. L., Amabile, T. M., & Ross, L. (1982), *Informal Covariation Assessment: Data-based versus theory-based Judgments. In D. Kahneman, P. Slovic, & A. Tversky (Eds.), Judgment under uncertainty: Heuristics and biases*, Cambridge, England: Cambridge University Press, pp. 211–238. Study#2: Bayne, R., & O'Neill, F. (1988), *"Handwriting and personality: A test of some expert graphologists' judgments", Guidance and Assessment Review* (4): 1–3.

[70] James Randi did a famous experiment with a graphologist to expose the flaws in graphology. You can see the test Mr. Randi conducted at http://www.youtube.com/watch?v=NeYkOHQ683k. Scientist Barry Beyerstein wrote an online article titled: *"How Graphology Fools People."* You can read the online article at: http://www.quackwatch.org /01QuackeryRelatedTopics/Tests/grapho.html.

[71] *The Skeptic Dictionary* features an online article that debunks statement analysis. The article discusses statement analysis and the lack of scientific

Many courts do not accept statement analysis testimony as evidence. No peer-reviewed periodicals have published valid scientific research to support it. *The Laboratory of Scientific Interrogation, Inc.*, has taught Scientific Content Analysis (SCAN) to law enforcement agencies and private security firms worldwide. No reputable colleges or universities, however, teach the course. Many experts reject statement analysis because it has not yet proven its' scientific validity.

Although critics claim Sherlock Holmes incorrectly used Graphology and statement analysis, they concede he stood on solid ground with questioned document examination. Of the three approaches to handwriting analysis, critics argue questioned document examination is the most reputable and scientifically based.[72]

They contend Courts permit expert testimony based on its' findings and it is taught in several colleges and universities. Most experts agree it is a scientifically valid form of handwriting analysis because scientists can objectively test it. Sherlock Holmes clearly believed and applied questioned document analysis successfully to solve several cases.

What the three approaches to handwriting analysis tell us is that pseudoscience can influence even an intelligent individual like Sherlock Holmes. But Holmes' using pseudo-sciences does

---

research or studies to support it. You can review it at http://www.skepdic.com/ statementanalysis.html. You can also check out *The Skeptic Society* at http://www.skeptic.com/.

[72] Some critics even believe that QDE is not scientifically based. An April 2003 online article on *The Straight Dope* website entitled: *"Is Handwriting Analysis a Legit Science?"* answered a reader's question regarding QDE. Writer Cecil Adams claimed: "...while forensic handwriting analysis may not be quackery, it's not exactly science either." The article cited various court cases such as *Daubert* v. *Merrell Dow Pharmaceuticals* (1993) and *United States* v. *Saelee* (2001) to support its' argument that questioned document examination has not proven itself scientifically.

not diminish his stature in our eyes because, like us, it only makes him more human.

During the late 19th Century, Graphology became a popular 'science.' Holmes made Graphology even more popular by tying it to his own scientific persona. It seems likely Holmes (being a scientific man) embraced Graphology because the known science at the time gave it credibility. He also believed it could help him solve crimes.

Scientific consensus, however, has since established Graphology as a pseudo-science similar to astrology and phrenology. So why go through the whole explanation in this chapter about how Holmes applied Graphology and statement analysis if it they are scientifically incorrect?

The answer is Sir Arthur Conan Doyle devoted much time to emphasizing Holmes's Graphology and statement analysis skills. This chapter pays tribute to what Doyle did. It also points out how these so-called sciences look and sound scientific but really are not. Therefore, you can avoid Sherlock Holmes's mistake by applying handwriting analysis in a practical way.

How To Analyze Handwriting in Everyday Life

Sherlock Holmes lived during the late 19th century when most people wrote letters, notes or correspondence to communicate with others. In the last several decades', however, technology has dramatically changed the way humans communicate through the hand written word. With the advent of personal computers, tablets and smartphones, Graphology has slowly lost its relevance because people no longer write as much. Instead of writing letters or postcards like in the past, now people send text messages, e-mails, 'tweets' and communicate through social media websites.

As a result of these new ways to communicate, fewer opportunities will exist during your everyday activities for you to observe a stranger's hand written correspondence. In other words, you are more likely to see strangers with mobile phones texting or tweeting, than you are to see them writing notes or letters. When an opportunity presents itself, however, you can analyze a stranger's handwriting once you learn how to do it correctly. The practical way to apply handwriting analysis in modern everyday life is to do the following:

Ask Questions About the Handwriting. The same questions you use to size up people, you can use to size up handwriting. *What* is this document? *Where* did it originate? *Who* wrote it? *Why* did the person write it this way? *When* did the person create it? *How* did the person make it? These are the first questions that should flash within your mind before you analyze handwriting, statements or documents. Holmes asked a similar question in *A Scandal in Bohemia* when he said to Watson: "...the note itself. What do you deduce from it?"

Keep It Simple and Obvious. A simple approach is noticing *what* people write not the *way* they write. Is the spelling correct? Are there any grammatical errors? Is the vocabulary appropriate? Is slang or profanity used? Does what the writer says make sense? Is it credible? Is it reasonable from your understanding of human experience? What point is the writer trying to make? Is the paper torn? Scented? Smudged? Sometimes you can tell more about handwriting by focusing on *what* a person writes than you can from the *way* they write it.

Use Common Sense. Do not look for complex personality traits from the slants or strokes in handwriting. Instead, pay attention to the common sense things about it. Look for minor personal characteristics that may reveal natural tendencies. Keep in mind, however, that your accuracy will only be a little greater than tossing a coin. Ask yourself questions such as: Is the handwriting from a child or adult? Is the person educated or illiterate? Is stranger writing hasty or too slow? Is the individual's writing neat or sloppy? Is the writer left or right handed? Often using common sense will reveal more about the writer than any specific handwriting analysis ever could.

Look at the Content. Graphologists claim they analyze handwriting for personality traits independent of the written content. They claim to interpret a person's unknown characteristics from the specific loops and letter formations in the handwriting. Rather than do this, a better approach is to *look at the writing content itself for clues to the individual's personality and character.* Does the writing reveal facts or details about the writer? Can you tell the writer's age, gender, race, job, education, religion or cultural background from the writing? Has the writer unwittingly left any clues in the writing? Often you can find out more by analyzing the writing content than you can from the writing style itself.

Use Your Knowledge and Experience. The more you know about a person, the easier it is to spot discrepancies or inconsistencies in his or her handwriting. You are more likely to notice missing but relevant information from handwriting or a statement when you have prior training, knowledge and experience. For example, an experienced detective will interrogate a suspect based on a statement the suspect wrote only after he has interviewed witnesses. He will first examine the crime scene evidence and gather other pertinent information. Only then will he interrogate the suspect. At that time, he will have a clear picture of the facts at hand. He will know when the suspect is lying or leaving out incriminating information because he did his homework first.

Apply Reason to the Writing. Critically evaluate the statement, handwriting or document. Do not use free association to determine that because a letter slants backwards, the person is reserved or because the writing pressure is heavy, the person is aggressive. Instead, simply apply reason and logic to the handwriting. Use the Sherlock Holmes rules of deduction. For example, in *The Man with the Twisted Lip* Sherlock Holmes reasoned with common sense. Sherlock Holmes determined Ms. St. Clair's husband was alive because she observed her husband's hurried writing in one part of a note and his normal writing in the other part.

Make Practical Predictions. Do not make far-fetched predictions about a writer's future work performance or potential for criminal activities. Instead, make practical predictions that are limited by the writing itself. In *The Reigate Puzzle* Sherlock Holmes states: "the deduction of a man's age from his writing is one which has been brought to considerable accuracy by experts." Indeed, some experts state you can deduce a person's age, education and nationality from their handwriting.[73] Other experts say you can reasonably predict a person's gender from their handwriting.[74] To do this, look for clues to the writer's background from the handwritten text. Often without realizing it, the writer will leave clues such as the time, place or phrasing.

Look at Handwriting for Genuineness. In *The Stock-Broker's Clerk*, Sherlock Holmes figured out forgers needed a copy of the clerk's handwriting to steal securities from a famous financial house. Holmes informed the clerk: "Someone wanted

---

[73] *The Write Stuff: Evaluations of Graphology: The Study of Handwriting Analysis* (Beyerstein and Beyerstein, editors, 1992). Research from various studies establishes that people with no training can guess a writer's sex and intelligence with up to 70 percent accuracy. Many experts expect just 50 percent accuracy with blind chance. Document examiners, however, state they cannot make predictions about peoples' age, gender, personality or intent based on written documents. See *Handwriting Examination: Meeting the Challenges of Science and the Law,* Forensic Science Communications, October 2009—Volume 11—Number 4, at: http://www.fbi.gov/about-us/lab/forensic-science-communications/review /2009_10_review02.Htm/.

[74] Hartley, James, "*Sex Differences in Handwriting: a comment on Spear*", *British Educational Research Journal* 17 (2): 141–145.

to learn to imitate your writing and had to procure a specimen of it first." Holmes then explained to the clerk the forger's motives for having the clerk write out a declaration for services with the fraudulent company.

Just as Sherlock Holmes did, you should examine handwritten documents for authenticity. Do not look at handwriting for personality clues. Instead, examine it for possible changes, alterations or forgery. Use the 23 handwriting elements to determine genuineness not character traits. Compare the known features in the writing with the disputed handwriting to identify the writer.

The tips for analyzing handwriting you have learned above are not perfect or foolproof. They do, however, rely on practical abilities you already have and can use in your everyday life. If you use the tips wisely when analyzing handwriting, you will have an advantage over Sherlock Holmes. How? Simple. Unlike Holmes, you will not use pseudoscience to size up strangers by their handwriting. Therefore, you will base your deductions on common sense rather than nonsense.

Go to Pages 344 to 346 if you want to practice
the handwriting exercises now.

Chapter 12

Follow Sherlock's Example To Scan Strangers Accurately

"...Much practice has made it second nature to me."
Sherlock Holmes, A Study in Scarlet

Summary of The Sherlock Holmes Method

The Four Basic Questions:

What do I observe? – Watch the stranger (gather facts, details evidence)
What can I deduce? – Make an educated guess (form a hypothesis)
How can I verify it? – Check the guess (conduct an experiment/predict a result)
What do I conclude? – Make sure the result (confirm your conclusion)

Additional Questions:

Who? What? Where? Why? When? How?

The Eight Principles – Practical Application of Holmes's Method:

Observation – Knowing what to look for
Deduction – Reasoning from what you see
Knowledge – The key to information
Experience - Life's best teacher
Listening – Hearing spoken and unspoken words
Imagination – Putting yourself in someone's place
Memory – The storeroom of the mind
Intuition – The sixth sense

You have learned from the previous chapters what you need to size-up strangers. You will see and meet strangers as you go about your everyday activities — doing your job, shopping at a store, waiting at the bus stop, riding the subway, sitting in the park, walking in the street, and so forth.

As a result, you will have many opportunities to put what you have learned in the previous chapters to the test. Now you must use these skills daily so you can become proficient at them. The most important advice you can learn from Sherlock is to follow his example — *practice and train!*

It cannot be over emphasized how important it is to practice constantly and train yourself in the questions and principles. It is so important that this whole chapter is devoted to exercises you can use to improve your skills. The exercises are easy to follow and you can use them while you are going about your daily routine.

Many exercises you can do on your own without any assistance from anyone. Some exercises you can perform with a friend. Other exercises require that you confirm your conclusions by checking with the sources. The chapter also provides a Sherlock Scan checklist that you can use to take notes while you practice and train.

The science of deduction and analysis requires long and patient study. It is a lifelong process to learn how to accurately and systematically size-up strangers as Sherlock Holmes did. You will not become proficient in it overnight. You must keep at it and practice the skills you have learned every day.

You must continually hone your skills through self-training, even after you have read the entire book and completed all the exercises. For without constant practice and training, you will never size up strangers accurately. The exercises that you will complete below are just the beginning. Use them as the starting point from which you will develop your skills to your greatest potential.

Keep in mind that not every suggestion or exercise will apply to you. You may not be interested in debating or speed dating. You may not want to go to an séance or learn about magic. You must develop and adapt each exercise to your individual personality and situation.

You should do your own research to determine which exercises in this chapter can work for you. Absorb what you find useful. Reject what you find useless. Add specifically what is your own. Then do the exercise to see if it works for you. If it works, then use it. If it does not work, then try another exercise.

The exercises will help you get better at using the principles. The principles will help you get better at applying the four basic questions. The four basic questions will help you get better at sizing up strangers. By reading the book up to this chapter, you have accepted the challenge to discover the secret presented to you in the book's introduction. You owe it to yourself to find and recognize the secret so you can pass the challenge.

Through the pages in this book, you have learned The Sherlock Holmes Method. Now complete the exercises and discover the secret (if you have not already). Then go out into the world and use his simple system of asking questions and applying principles to size up strangers. Or as Sherlock Holmes himself would say: *"You know my methods. Apply them!"*

QUESTION EXERCISES

Asking the right questions is the starting point to sizing up strangers. You can train yourself in the Sherlock Holmes Method by asking questions. Simply practice the exercises below to improve your questioning skills.

1. **Practice Thinking Positive**. You must develop a positive but realistic attitude when using Sherlock's method. If you start to believe that it is too hard to size up strangers as Sherlock Holmes did, then your thoughts will make what you believe a reality. Read the books *Think and Grow Rich* by Napoleon Hill and *The Power of Positive Thinking* by Norman Vincent Peal. These two books will help you understand why a *positive mental attitude* is so important in sizing up strangers.

    Whenever you observe people *think positive* and *expect* to find something interesting about them. Here is an exercise you can do to develop a 'Sherlock Consciousness.' Each day, for the next 30 days, as you go about your daily activities, look for one detail or fact about each stranger you see or meet. Ask yourself questions to obtain these details or facts. For example, you could ask yourself as you watch people: "Is this person wearing a wedding ring?" "Does this person have a tattoo?" "Does this person wear glasses?" "Is this person a smoker?" "Are they right or left handed?" Once you find a detail or fact, simply reaffirm in your mind that you found it. Following this instruction will reinforce the positive belief that the Sherlock Holmes Method works and you can use it successfully.

2. **Why Do You Want To Size Up People?** Everyone has a motive for wanting to size up someone. Are you doing it to screen job applicants? To select a jury? To determine a suspect's guilt or innocent? To tell if someone is lying? To select a partner for a date or marriage? Follow this exercise: write down your reason for sizing up a stranger. Be specific with it. Set a goal and it will motivate you to become better at evaluating people. Each day look at the goal you wrote down and reaffirm that you will reach it.

Then put it into action by following the rest of the exercises in this chapter.

3. **Practice Asking Questions.** Learn the four basic questions by heart. Practice asking yourself the questions until they become automatic and you ask them without thinking. Each day, as you go about your routine, ask yourself the four questions whenever you see or meet a stranger. "What do I observe?" "What can I deduce?" "How can I verify it?" "What do I conclude?" Then ask yourself the additional questions: "What?" "Where?" "Why?" "Who?" "When" and "How?"

The website *Changing Minds* has an excellent section devoted to the different types of questions. The website gives a good analysis of open, closed, probing, leading and unexpected questions to ask. It also discusses specific methods such as "Columbo" and "Socrates" questioning. Go to www.changingminds.org for more details. Then apply the various questioning methods in your daily life with the strangers you meet.

4. **Practice Asking Questions About Peoples' Hands.** Whenever you meet a person, observe their hands. Look closely at them. Ask the following questions whenever you meet a stranger:

Are the hands clean? Dirty? Groomed? Swollen?
Do the hands have minor cuts? Are they soft? Rough?
Do the hands have stains on them?
What kind of stains? Food? Blood? Chemical? Nicotine? Ink?
Is one hand bigger or more developed than the other?
Are the stranger's hands ashy?
Do the hands have wrinkles?
Are they wearing gloves? Bandages? Why?
What kind of gloves or bandages?
Do they have any rings on their fingers?
What kind of rings? How many?

283

Are the nails painted?
Are their nails yellow? Polished? Cracked? Long?
Are the knuckles worn? Bruised?
Do the hands have calluses? Where are the calluses?
Are the backs of their hands discolored? Spotted? Disfigured?
Do their hands have any marks on them?
What kind of marks? Tattoos? Burns? Scratches? Scars?
What are they doing with their hands? Hiding them?
Showing them off? Carrying or holding something?
Is stranger using his or her hands to express themselves?
Are their fingers short and stubbly?
Are they long and tapered?
Are their fingers thick and strong?
Are they missing any fingers?
How does the stranger shake your hand? Is their handshake weak and limp? Is their handshake firm or strong?
Do they grasp your hand in a friendly manner?
Is the handshake aggressive and threatening?

Dr. Joseph Bell believed you could tell a lot about a stranger from their hands. He would deduce things about strangers from observing the calluses on the fingers, palms and thumbs. He then stated their occupations and prior activities. Practice this exercise: when you are on the street or in a park look at each person's hands. Try to figure out the person's job, health, education, social or financial status from his or her hands. Study each person's hands once a day for 30 days.

5. **Practice Asking Questions About Peoples' Footwear.** Studies have shown that you can estimate a stranger's personality and character with 90% accurately from the type of shoes they normally wear. In a study from the *University of Kansas*, researchers established that you could tell an individual's gender, age, income and even their emotional stability from the type of shoes they routinely wear. Sherlock Holmes studied dirt, mud, scuff marks, quality, style and wear and tear on shoes to determine the owners' personality and character.

Practice this exercise: when you are on the subway or bus, look down at each person's footwear. Try to figure out the person's job, health, education, social or financial status from his or her shoes. Ask the following questions:

What type of footwear is the person wearing?
Boots? Sneakers? Shoes? Sandals? Stilettos? Pumps?
Is the footwear in style or out of style? Is it casual?
Trendy? Designer? Classic? Sports? Business? Outlandish?
Is the footwear clean? Dirty? New? Worn?
Does the footwear have any scuffmarks?
Rips? Holes? Stains? Scratches?
Are shoes square toe? Pointy toe? Round toe? Open toe?
What color is the footwear?
Does the footwear have lifts?
Did the person resole the footwear?
Is the footwear too big or small for the person's feet?
Do the shoes have laces? Did the person tie the laces?
How did the person tie the laces?
Does the footwear match the person's clothing?
Is the footwear appropriate for the person's age?
Body shape?
Is the footwear expensive? Cheap? Reasonably, priced?
Does the footwear seem comfortable on the person?
Is it too tight?
Are the heels low, medium or high? Are the heels worn?

Once you have taken a good look at the person's shoes, make deductions about them. According to the study, people who wear expensive shoes tend to have high incomes. People who wear flashy shoes tend to be outgoing. People who wear practical and functional shoes tend to be agreeable and friendly. Analyze the people and the shoes they wear. Ask your own questions about them. Then test your deductions.

For example, you could go to a shoe store or shoe department in a major store like *Macys.* Observe people as they buy shoes. Watch sales personnel as they interact with customers. What type of shoes are people buying? What image do the people hope to project by the shoes they buy? You could compliment a woman in the street on her shoes and see her reaction. Is she an extrovert? Does she tell you where she purchased the shoes? How much they cost? How often she wears them? Why does she wear them? The more questions you ask, the better you will become at sizing up people by their shoes.

6. **Practice Asking Questions About Eye Movements.** Peoples' eye movements reveal their interests, thoughts, motives and other factors. Ask a friend, family member or co-worker questions then closely watch their responses. Ask yourself questions about people as you watch them. What are they looking at? How are they looking? Where do they look? Why are they looking? How long are they looking? How often do they look? Watch a person's eyes as another person passes them. You can notice this with men as a woman walks pass them. You can notice this with women as another woman walks pass them. Practice watching people in different situations, contexts and circumstances. Do people pay more attention to others while in a bar? At a club? At a business function? Make a mental note of everything you observe or record it in a personal journal for future use. For more information, you can review the online article: *"Eye direction and Lying"* at http://www.blifaloo.com/info/lies_eyes.php.

OBSERVATION EXERCISES

The purpose of the following exercises is to help you develop a mindset that makes you aware and alert to the people, places and things that you see. The following exercises will sharpen your observational skills and help you notice details about strangers that you did not see before. Practice the exercises as much as you can. Remember the first basic question: *"What do I observe?"* as you do the exercises.

1. **Practice Using Your Five Senses.** (a) Close your eyes and listen to the sounds around you. (b) Follow the tips in Chapter 2 on observation and this chapter to sharpen your observation skills. (c) Use your sense of touch to tell the subtle difference in things you physically feel. (d) Use your sense of taste to detect the difference in flavor (expert wine tasters and chefs usually have an acute sense of taste). (e) Use your sense of smell to detect different odors on people and animals (body odor, perfumes, food, etc.). Once a day for 30 days, whenever you meet a stranger use your five senses.

2. **Practice Controlling Your Feelings.** Emotions are powerful stimulators. They lay under the surface in conversations. They influence our thoughts. They affect our senses. Practice looking for emotions in yourself and the strangers you meet. Pay attention to your feelings as you observe people. What emotions do they arouse in you? Are you easily angered? Do you tend to worry? Are you fearful of strangers? Are you happy go lucky? Your feelings may influence what you see with people. You can control them by making yourself aware they exist and looking for them while observing people. Once a day for 30 days, practice watching for emotions in yourself and the strangers you see and meet.

3. **Practice Concentrating on What You See.** Learn to focus on specific details about people. Do not let yourself get distracted by unimportant sights, sounds, attitudes or behavior. Practice observing people and concentrating on them only. Once a day for 30 days, pick a different stranger and focus on everything about the stranger. Block out anything from your mind that will keep you from concentrating. As you focus on the stranger, do not

lose sight of why you are observing him or her. Do not get sidetracked by what other people are doing or saying, or events that may be happening around you. Keep your mind on what you are doing and you will get better.

4. **Practice Scanning People.** Each day for 30 days, while you are in public or at work, scan strangers. Look them up and down quickly, noticing any details in their facial expressions, their body language, their fashion, their speech and so forth. Practice scanning them at both short and long distances (5 to 15 feet). Then make a mental inventory of what you see. Do this until you can scan a stranger quickly and spot more details each time.

5. **Practice Watching the People Around You.** Go into an establishment such as a bar, restaurant or store. Look around at everyone. Watch people casually without drawing attention to yourself. What are they doing? What drinks are they sipping? What are they eating? What are they buying? What are they wearing? Where are they sitting? Standing? How many people are in the establishment? How many men? Women? How old are they? Open your eyes and look for as many details as possible. Do this once a day for 30 days in the different places you go.

6. **Practice Speaking What You See.** Verbalize what you are seeing and you will more likely remember it. You can practice speaking what you see aloud as you describe people. Look out your window as people walk pass in the street. State verbally the things you see, such as "I see a 20 year old male black. He is 5'8", weights 165 pounds and has a lean built. He has black hair with a tattoo on his neck. He is wearing a white t-shirt, blue jeans and black Nike sneakers. He is carrying a smartphone."

288

7. **Practice Noticing the Small Things.** Practice watching people on the subway, bus or in the park. Observe what they are wearing, holding, reading or doing. Look for any identifying marks, tattoos or jewelry. Make a mental note of what you see. Then speak to the stranger to test and confirm what you have observed. Once you get good at watching one stranger, increase the number of strangers you observe. Look at two or three strangers at the same time. Look for as many details as you can on them. Time yourself to see how much you can observe. Size up the strangers in less and less time.

8. **Practice Looking at Familiar Things.** In the online article *"Observation Still Matters,"* writer Ronald Mendell talks about looking at familiar things. He states that once you observe things that are familiar to you, the differences will leap out at you. Practice looking at similar things. Notice what is different about them. You will begin spotting little details the more you look. Associate new people with people you already know. With practice, you will spot more and more details. Practice this once a day for 30 days. You can see the article at http://www.pimall.com /nais/n.obser.html.

9. **Practice Observing Unfamiliar Things.** The other side to observing familiar things is to watch unfamiliar things. Practice observing things that are strange to you. The more you look at strange people, places and things, the more familiar you will be with them in the future. Look at strangers from a new perspective. For example, pretend you are the stranger. Imagine his or her train of thought. What are they saying or doing? Think like the stranger: "What will I do today?" "Where will I go?" "Who will I see?" Develop your own personal system of looking at people. Use the first basic question and observation principle consistently when you scan strangers. The

more you use the observation principle, the more details you will discover.

10. **Practice On People You Know.** Ask a family member, relative, friend or co-worker to help you improve your ability to read people. Ask them to present themselves to you and see what you can deduce from their appearance and behavior. Can you guess where they have been? What were they doing? What they are about to do from what you see? After making your educated guesses, then have them tell you whether you are right or wrong. Study your hits and misses. Practice this exercise every chance you can.

11. **Practice Observing Your Surroundings.** When you enter a store, a bar, a park, a house or anyplace, practice looking at everything around you. Stay aware to where things are placed. Keep alert to where people are sitting or standing. Notice the small details in your environment such as the color of the walls, the condition of the floors, whether the windows or open or shut, and so forth. You can tell a lot about people through the things they own, the places they live and the things they do. Keep your eyes open and maintain an active attention to your surroundings. When you return to these places, look for any changes. Do this every day until it becomes a habit and you do it without thinking about it.

12. **Practice Skepticism.** Do not believe everything you see with people. You cannot always accept a stranger at face value. Practice looking for proof when you meet people. You do not have to say it outright, but always seek evidence before you believe someone. Use reason to determine if the evidence they present is accurate and credible. Make your suspicions and doubts second nature to you. Ask questions about anything that does not make sense. Do this with everyone you meet.

13. **Practice Identifying Strangers.** Whenever you meet people, practice getting an accurate description of them. Look for basic things first such as their height, weight, race, gender, age and body type. Then notice their most-prominent features such as a scar or tattoo. Observe their clothing and body language. Train yourself to do this each time you meet someone. After the person has gone, see if you can describe the stranger accurately to a friend, co-worker or family member. What did you get right? What did you miss? Practice doing this until you can accurately describe a stranger to another person. Do this until you become consistently successful at it.

14. **Practice Observing Clothing.** Whenever you meet a stranger, quickly look at what they are wearing. Pay attention to the overall way they are dressing. Notice the style and fashion. Look at the clothing color and quality. Observe whether the clothing is coordinated and suitable for the occasion. Note whether the clothing is appropriate for the stranger's age and body type. Determine whether the stranger is going to work, hanging out, attending a sports event or doing some other activity. Most people scrutinize clothing naturally, but you are doing it more so to improve your observational skill. Therefore, do it every chance you get.

15. **Practice Noticing Personal Belongings.** Whenever you meet a stranger, look rapidly at their personal property. These items can reveal a lot about them. A pen a stranger frequently uses might have bite marks, indicating the person may have stress. A designer handbag might be a fake, indicating that the person is not as financially well off as they appear. Look closely at what the person is carrying, holding or wearing. Train yourself to notice whether the personal property is new, worn, damaged or used. Glimpse inside a woman's handbag or a man's

291

wallet. What do you notice? Cash? Makeup? Job ID? Credit Cards? Drivers License? Often the contents can give you clues to the strangers' occupation, personality, background and previous activities. Practice looking at strangers' personal items every chance you get.

16. **Practice Watching Specific Clothing Areas.** Whenever you meet a stranger, one of the first places you should look is at their pockets. A person's pocket holds many things and can reveal a lot about them. For example, pockets can hold smartphones, wallets, keys, weapons, cash, coins and so forth. Then look at the stranger's outerwear, footwear, headwear and hand wear. Look for any bulges in their pockets, any signs of wear and tear on their shoes, any stains or rips on their hats or coats. These things are clues to what they have recently done or are about to do. Train yourself to look for these small details whenever you encounter strangers as you go about your daily activities.

17. **Practice Noticing First Impressions.** Whenever you meet a stranger, get a sense of their overall appearance and behavior. Stay aware of your reaction. In general, people make judgments about others within a few seconds after meeting them. The judgments can be positive, negative or a combination of both, depending on the overall sense or feeling you get. Train yourself to check your first impressions to verify that they are accurate. To do this, simply follow up after meeting or interviewing the stranger. Check out sources, look into the person's background and so forth. Then review everything you learned to determine your accuracy. Practice doing it each time you meet people and you will show improvement at getting accurate first impressions from strangers.

18. **Practice Taking Mental Inventory.** Whenever you meet people, do not be afraid to place them into categories after you have observed them. Practice labeling strangers. You should base the categories you place them into on your knowledge and experience. Avoid stereotypes by keeping an open mind and staying aware to any perceptual biases, you have. Practice relying on the stranger's facial expressions, body language and gestures to help you fit them into the category you have created. Do this once a day for 30 days.

19. **Practice Observing Micro-Expressions.** In your everyday activities practice watching for micro-expressions with the people you meet. You can do this during your daily conversations or when you are interacting with people. Pay close attention to the muscles around the face to pick up the fleeting expressions of joy, sadness, contempt, anger, fear, surprise and so forth. Each day watch a family member, friend, relative, co-worker or stranger to see if you can notice a micro-expression. Pick one expression (such as anger) and focus on it for the entire day. The next day pick another expression. You will see many expressions as you go about your daily routine so this exercise should not be hard. Do this until you get good at it.

20. **Practice Reading Body Language.** The only real way to become good at reading peoples' body language is to do it. You do it already so it is natural to you. The only difference now is to make yourself *aware* of what you are doing. Every chance you get, observe people going about their daily routines. Closely watch their body movements to determine what non-verbal messages they are sending. Each day go out and focus on one particular area such as the torso, arms, legs, feet or hands. Read body language books to get you started such as *The Definitive Guide to Body Language* by Allan and Barbara Pease. You will find

several more reading suggestions in the back of this book to get you started. The important thing is that you watch for the body language signals with everyone you meet. The more you do it, the better you will get.

21. **Practice Observing Creatively.**   To really understand something, you must understand the thinking that went into making it. If it is an object, you can ask yourself: "What is its purpose?" If it is a person, you can ask yourself: "What does this person want?" To do this, practice thinking outside the box and looking at the person or object from a different point of view. Observing strangers from different angles and perspectives can often help you see things about them that others miss.

22. **Practice Studying Photographs.**   Acquire a family member or friend's photograph. Study it for 30 seconds. Write down everything you see. Look away for a minute or two. Then look at the picture again to see what details you missed. Do it repeatedly until you pick up every detail quickly. You will get better through trial and error. You can also look at magazine covers and celebrity photos for any signs of editing through Photoshop.

23. *Practice Reading Health in Strangers' Faces.* Foxnews.com has an online video clip that discusses the various ways you can read a stranger's health status in their face. Dr. Phillipa Cheetham discusses how the face can show signs of disease. The video clip shows indicators that reveal a stranger's health such as seeing anemia and jaundice in the eyes. Or a vertical crease in the ear lobe that reveals an increased risk of cardiac disease. You can view it at http://video.foxnews.com. Search for the article: *"State of Your Health Written All Over Your Face."* You can also get more information at www.drcheetham.com. Whenever you meet a stranger

look for signs of health on their faces. Most people do this instinctively. You are just increasing your awareness. Do this once a day for 30 days.

24. **Practice Recording People On Video.** Paul Ekman and other professional deception detection experts record people on video. They will watch their clients' faces and bodies for micro-expressions and gestures. You can do the same thing with your smartphone or tablet. Record your friends, family, relatives and co-workers (with their permission of course). Then practice watching the video again in slow motion to see if you can spot their micro-expressions and gestures.

25. **Practice Watching Movie Mistakes.** There are websites such as www.moviemistakes.com and www.*InternetMovieDatabase.com* that point out movie mistakes. The errors you can look for are continuity, revealing, visible crew/equipment, audio and factual mistakes. A continuity mistake occurs when there is no consistency between scenes. For example, in one scene a car may have a dent on the right side. In the next scene, the dent is gone. A revealing mistake occurs when props are visible in the scene that should not be visible. For example, someone leaves a dummy in camera view. A visible crew or equipment mistake occurs when a crewmember or piece of equipment accidently remains in the scene. For example, you see a crewmember or extra walking pass. An audio mistake occurs when you hear something you are not supposed to hear or sounds do not match up with the scene. For example, an actor's lips move but you hear no words. A factual mistake occurs when the scene does not match with reality or the laws of physics and nature. For example, a rifle shot may sound like a machine gun or an actor may fall several stories from a building with no broken bones. Practice looking at movies for errors and see if you can spot them. Then go

to the websites and check your observations. Try to find as many mistakes in the movies as you can before checking at the websites for the answers.

26. **Practice Watching TV/Cable Shows.** You can learn a lot from TV shows such as *"Lie to Me," "Law & Order: Behavioral Science Unit", "Sherlock"* and *"Elementary."* The shows usually have an expert on set to ensure that the information conveyed is accurate and factual. A TV show such as *'Lie to Me'* often reveals tips on how to read peoples' body language, facial expressions, tone of voice and other gestures. TV Shows such as *'Law and Order'* can give you psychological insight into people by showing how the experts size them up. TV Shows such as *'Sherlock'* and *'Elementary'* place Sherlock Holmes in our modern world. They help you visualize how his methods would work in the present times. Cable channels such the *History Channel* and *Discovery Channel* present shows such as *The 1ˢᵀ 48 Hours* and *Crime Scene Investigation (CSI)*. These reality programs show how actual experts work in their fields. Watch these programs for real life examples on how to size up strangers. Subscribe to services such as *Netflix, HuLu* or *Amazon* to find TV shows such as *To Tell The Truth* and *Brain Games* to hone your deception detection skills.

27. **Practice Playing Match Games.** Computer or app games such as *'Spot the Difference'* and *'Hidden Pictures'* teach you how to spot the difference in various pictures that the computer presents to you. These games are usually on a timer, which forces you to quickly look at the smallest details in the picture to find the match. You can down load these games onto your desktop computer, notebook, tablet or smartphone from online media stores such as iTunes. At the PBS website you can play the free *"Sherlock Observation Game."* The game has five pictures that challenge you to spot differences while on a timer.

When you make a mistake the game penalizes you. Check it out at www.pbs.org/wgbh/masterpiece /sherlock /observation.html. You can also play the photo analysis challenge at https://www.cia.gov /kids-page/ games/photo-analysis-challenge. It has several levels: intermediate, advanced and expert. In addition, read brain game books such as *Picture Puzzles,* which challenge you to spot the differences in various photos.

28. **Practice Noticing Appearance and/or Behavioral Changes.** Whenever you are around people watch how they normally act and dress. Practice watching how people act naturally to get a 'feel' for them. Then you will notice subtle changes in their attitude, appearance and behavior when the changes occur. Most men do not pick up subtle changes that a woman makes in her appearance. She may change her perfume, make up or buy a new dress. Or a man may start working late, hanging out with friends more or going to the gym. Any sudden changes that are not normal usually are a sign that something is amiss.

29. **Practice Taking Face Reading Test.** Dr. Paul Ekman has developed several tests that can help you read a stranger's facial expressions. On Dr. Ekman's website http://www.paulekman.com you can buy and down load his METT or SETT micro-expression software from $20 up to $120. For a free example of how the software works, go to the website http://www.cio.com/archive /120104/faces.html and take the short test.

30. **Practice with Change Blindness Demonstrations.** Retired Professor and Researcher J. Kevin O'Regan has a website that lists several demos of change blindness. You can practice with demos to improve your skills in recognizing change blindness. You can find the demos at

Professor O'Regan's website: http://nivea.psycho.univ-paris5.fr/#CB.

31. **Practice Watching Videos on YouTube.** Search for topics on reading body language, facial expressions, fashion, Sherlock Holmes, shoes and other subjects. You can find almost any topic or subject you are interested in on *YouTube.*

Search for the following videos to test how observant you are. Simply type in the name of the video and see if you can spot the changes:

   a. **The Amazing Color Changing Card Trick Video.** This video tests your ability to observe details. Watch it closely to see you what you spot and miss.

   b. **The Basketball Team Pass Trick Video.** This video tests the average person's tendency to miss changes in a person or situation while observing people, places and things. The makers of this video, published a book entitled *The Invisible Gorilla: How Our Intuitions Deceive Us,* which shows how many people miss seeing things that are right before their eyes.

   c. **The Who Dunnit Video.** This video will test your observation skill in spotting subtle changes in characters and scenery during a murder. Pay close attention to the trifling details and you will pass the test.

   d. **The Change Blindness Video.** This video tests your ability to detect changes as they occur. Most people, because their brains naturally filter out information, fail to see changes right in front of them.   Stay alert to the subtle changes; pay attention to details and you will pass this test.

32. **Practice Watching Movies.** Several movies have scenes where a character uses the Sherlock Holmes Method to size up a stranger. Watch the movies (on YouTube, DVD or Netflix), note how the character does it and try to figure out how he or she reached the conclusion. For example, in *Sherlock Holmes* (2009) Holmes sizes up Watson's fiancée, Mary with just a glance at her. In *Young Sherlock Holmes (1985)*, a youthful Sherlock sizes up a teenage Watson upon first meeting him. Some more examples of characters in films that performed the Sherlock Method are listed below:

Baggage Claim (2013) - Montana Moore sizes up men at an airport
Her (2013) - Theodore & Samantha size up strangers at a park
Temptation (2013) – Harley and Judith size each other up
The Wolverine (2013) - Wolverine sizes up fake monks
GI Joe Retaliation (2013) - GI Joe Jaye sizes up a fake U.S. President
Skyfall (2012) - James Bonds sizes up Severine in a casino.
Collateral (2004) - Taxi Driver Max sizes up a female lawyer
Bourne Identity (2002) - Jason Bourne sizes up a man in a cafeteria
XXX (2002) - Xander Cage sizes up undercover agents in a diner
Poolhall Junkies (2002) – Johnny sizes up Mike as a pool player
Baby Boy (2001) - Yvette sizes up Jodi to see if he is cheating on her
Wild, Wild, West (1999) - Jim West sizes up a fake President Grant
L. A. Confidential (1997) - Hooker Bracken sizes up Officer White
Sprung (1997) Gold digger Adina sizes up men at a party
The Devil's Advocate (1997) – Lawyer Lomax sizes up a jury
Men in Black (1997) - Agent J sizes up a little alien girl
Silence of the Lambs (1991) - Dr. Lecter sizes up FBI Agent Starling
Return of Sherlock Holmes (1987) – Holmes sizes up Watson
Arthur (1981) - Butler Hobson sizes up Linda's father
Annie Hall (1977) - Alvy and Annie size up people in a park

33. **Go to a Psychic.** Attend an séance to see how psychics perform their craft. The psychic will 'communicate' with your dead loved one. As the psychic is performing the séance, observe the psychic and analyze the mentalist techniques he or she is using. See if you can spot the

techniques. In the movie *Ghost (1990),* spiritual adviser Oda Mae Brown held an séance with a widow seeking to know about her dead husband. Oda Mae used several mentalist techniques to make the woman believe she communicated with him. Try to guess which ones Oda Mae used. Watch TV shows such as *"The Mentalist"* and *"Psych."* Then find more information on the TV shows at www.TV.com and www.TVsquad.com. You can also check out renowned mentalist Joe Riggs at his website http://theworldofjoeriggs.com/blog/.

34. **Watch/Play Poker.** Poker games are all about strategy and bluff. You play the person not the hand. Most expert poker players are good at reading people. They learn how to read an opponent's 'tells' to win the game. According to *pokertell.com* a 'tell' is "...any clue, habit, behavior or physical reaction, that gives other players more information about your hand." There are whole websites devoted to reading a player's tells. Go to a website such as www.poker-tells.com or read a book such as *The Pocket Idiot's Guide to Poker Tells* by Andy Bloch and Bobbi Dempsey. Go to these sources and research reading tells. Then watch poker games on Cable TV or go to a casino and watch poker players in action. You can learn to read tells by playing poker and watching your friends, family and co-workers. In addition, you can see examples of tell reading from watching movies like *Casino Royale (2006),* where James Bond sizes up a woman on a train, plays poker and reads another player's tells. Also, in the movie *Rounders (1998),* poker player Mike sizes up several players at a poker table.

35. **Use The Sherlock Scan Checklist.** Pages 347 to 348 contain an evaluation form that lists specific things to look for while asking questions and using the principles. Make copies of the form. Use it like a field journal to record what you see and deduce. You can approach a

stranger and say you are doing a study or survey. Then ask the person to verify what you put on the form. As you get better at sizing up strangers, stop using the form and mentally list the things you see in your mind. Do this until you do not need to use the checklist.

36. **Watch/Learn Magic.** Magicians and illusionists exploit the brain's tendency to focus on certain areas. They make you believe you are seeing everything while simultaneously making you miss the most important thing about the trick. The great magicians such as Harry Houdini and David Copperfield rose to fame and great wealth using these magic stunts and mind tricks. There are whole websites devoted to learning magic secrets. Some websites include www.martinsmagic.com and www.elmwoodmagic.com. Go to these websites and research magic to understand it. You can also watch movies like *Now You See Me (2013)*. In this film, four illusionists use magic to perform heists and fool law enforcement authorities. One magician, Jack Wilder, says to an audience: "The more you think you see, the less you'll actually notice" and "The closer you look the less you see." Expert magicians follow these maxims all the time. They know your eyes can deceive you. Practice watching magicians and illusionists as they perform magic. See if you can spot their tricks. The only way to avoid a magician fooling you is to stay alert, use reason and common sense as you watch them. Then search on *YouTube* for *Magic's Biggest Secrets Finally Revealed* and learn how they did it.

37. **Practice Photo Analysis.** Collect old and new photographs. Use your smartphone or computer to review the pictures. Study the people in the photographs. Look for meaning, themes and relationships in the photographs. Gather a few pictures that contain many details. Look at each picture for one minute. Observe as

many details in the picture as you can. See how many details you can remember. Practice observing the pictures with less time until you can remember many details in only one or two seconds. You can also read *Photo Language* by Robert Akeret and *Phototherapy Techniques* by Judy Weiser (both on Amazon.com). Also, go to websites such as http://www.cyberbee.com /quicklessons/photo.html for more observation tests. In addition, search and research the word 'photo analysis' on *YouTube, Wikipedia* and *Google.*

38. **Practice Watching Optical Illusions.** The best eagle-eyed observers know that their eyes can fool them. Therefore, they are constantly aware that everything is not as it seems. They practice and train to recognize potential perception mistakes by studying optical illusions. Read *The Ultimate Book of Optical Illusions* by Al Seckel and *The Art of the Illusion* by Terry Stickels and Brad Honeycutt (available on Amazon.com). Also, go to websites such as http://www.moillusions.com and http://www.eyetricks.com for sample optical illusion tests. In addition, search and research the word 'optical illusions' on *YouTube, Wikipedia* and *Google.*

REASONING/LOGIC EXERCISES

The purpose of the following exercises is to help you develop a mindset that makes you think logically. The following exercises will improve your ability to think critically and reason accurately. Remember the second basic question: *"What can I deduce?"* as you do the exercises.

1. **Study Critical Thinking.** Several online websites such as commonsenseathesim.com and www.criticalthinking.org focus on accurate thinking. These websites provide information on thinking straight, avoiding crooked thinking and evaluating facts and evidence. One website

www.butte.edu/departments/cas/tipsheets /thinking /reasoning.htm, has a section devoted totally to critical thinking and the biases that affect it. You can also study books such as *Becoming A Critical Thinker* by Robert Todd Carroll and *Don't Believe Everything You Think* by Thomas E. Kida to improve your critical thinking skills. Social media websites such as *Facebook* and *Twitter* have areas devoted to critical thinking. Use your smartphone or tablet computer to search for applications you can download that focus on improving critical thinking skills.

2. **Practice Mill's Reasoning Method.** The 19th Century philosopher John Stuart Mills created several ways to spot cause and effect. An online article entitled *"Mill's Methods"* discusses the different ways: looking for common factors, looking for differences, looking for variety and looking for left over effects (residue). These terms have technical sounding names but people use them in everyday, common sense reasoning to determine causality. You can learn Mill's method and answer the four comprehension questions at: www.wwnorton.com /college/phil/logic3/ ch15/millmeth.htm.

3. **Practice Deducing Yourself.** The easiest person to deduce is you. You know yourself better than anyone else does. Practice analyzing the things you do everyday. Look at yourself in the mirror. Ask yourself what might a stranger see when they look at you. Can they tell by your clothing the type of work you do? Can they determine by your height, weight and appearance, how old you are? Look at details on yourself such a tattoo or scar and try to figure out if you can tell something about yourself from it. The good thing about deducing yourself is that you can verify what you deduce. Then apply what you learn about yourself to the strangers you meet.

4. **Practice Deducing With A Friend.** Sherlock Holmes played deducing games with his brother Mycroft Holmes. They would see strangers and size them up. Practice deducing people with a friend, co-worker or family member. You can do it while at a park, restaurant, bar or party. First, you make a deduction about the stranger. Then your friend makes one. Next, the two of you continuously try to top the other by the making more accurate deductions. Finally, check with the stranger to confirm your deductions. The one who gets the most deductions right wins the game.

5. **Practice Deducing Strangers.** Whenever you see or meet a stranger, look for specific physical cues that you can make inferences from. For example, common sense deductions such as lipstick on a man's collar might reveal he is having an affair. A deduction such as bruises on a man's knuckles might reveal he is a boxer or martial artist. A deduction such as a cliff mark on the side of a woman's neck might reveal she plays the violin. Observe physical indicators like these to make deductions about strangers. Do this as you go about your daily activities.

6. **Holmes Riddles.** Some newspapers such as the *New York Daily News* publish puzzles using Sherlock Holmes as the theme. Practice solving these puzzles to increase your reasoning skills. First, write down the puzzles on paper. Second, as you get more proficient, do the puzzles in your head. Last, try solving the puzzles mentally and timing yourself to do them faster each time. You will get better the more you do it.

7. **Study Advertising for Logical Fallacies.** Advertising seeks to persuade people to buy things based on emotion and crooked thinking. Learn about the many marketing tricks advertisers use to manipulate your thinking. Practice watching TV commercials. See if you can spot

the logical fallacy the commercial uses to persuade you to buy the product. Some advertisers use commercials to appeal to your feelings. Other advertisers use commercials to appeal to your reason. The website *Critics and Builders of Culture* contains great examples of advertising fallacies. The video clips shows 30 second commercials. The website then explains the logical fallacy each ad uses to persuade you to buy. Analyze the commercials to figure out the advertiser's illogical pitches and appeals. Then review the website at: criticsandbuilders.typepad.com/amlitblog/logical-fallacies/. In addition, you can research the Internet. Also, read such books as *Humbug! The Skeptic's Field Guide to Spotting Logical Fallacies in Thinking* by Theo Clark, and *Nonsense: Red Herrings, Straw Men and Sacred Cows: How We Abuse Logic in Our Everyday Language* by Robert J. Gula.

8. **Review Logical Fallacy Websites.** Look at websites such as www.skepticsfieldguide.net and http://www.logicalfallacies.info/ to learn about logical fallacies. Also, check the *Fallacy Files* and *Changing Minds* websites, which have a list of tactics, grammatical ambiguities, oversimplifications, and formal fallacies you can study to improve your logical fallacy detection skills. Simply go to http://www.fallacyfiles.org and www.changingminds.org to review the list. Then practice spotting logical fallacies in your everyday activities: during conversations, debates and arguments.

9. **Review Fact-Checking Websites.** Several websites fact-check the information that you hear and see. Get in the habit of using fact-checking websites whenever you need to verify information. Fact checking websites such as www.factcheck.com and www.politifact.com rely on the same questions and principles you have learned in this book. Use them to increase your reasoning and logic

skills. Websites such as www.thestraightdope.com, www.truthorfiction.com and www.snopes.com seek to answer questions; dispel rumors, gossip, hearsay and weird stories circulating on the Internet.

10. **Review List of Biases.** Human beings are naturally biased. They naturally prejudge people, places and things. In order to limit your own prejudicial thinking, check the list of biases at *Wikipedia.com* and *The Skeptics' Dictionary* at www.skepdic.com/hiddenpersuaders.html. Wikipedia lists over 160 cognitive biases with definitions. Skepdic.com lists 63 biases (called hidden persuaders) with definitions and explanations. Study the ones that may apply to you and eliminate them. You can eliminate a personal bias by recognizing you have it. Then look for opposite viewpoints, facts or evidence that are different from yours. Doing this will improve your personal equation discussed in Chapter 7.

11. **Read about Holmesian Style Deductions that Others Make (websites).** On *http//boards.straightdope.com*, *http//www.tumblr.com.tagged/a-guide-to-deduction* and *http://www.reddit.com/r/roomdetective* you can read about other people who make Holmesian styled deductions in their everyday lives. Read the comments and learn what others think about making Sherlock Scans. For example, www.tumbler.com contains a section it calls *'Deduce this,'* where participants send in photos of their desks, rooms, closets and so forth. Others then deduce the participants by what they see in the photos. They look for clues from the items in the room (books, photos, posters, clothing, etc.). Then they deduce the person's gender, age, interests, personality, education level, where they live, whether they are right or left handed and many other things. Before you read what the participants deduce, practice looking at the photos to see if you can deduce things about the photo's owner. Then read the

participants answers to see if you are correct. Do this once a day for 30 days.

12. **Analyze Holmesian Style Deductions That Others Make.** In your everyday travels, you will meet people who make Sherlock styled deductions. Practice analyzing how they do it and keep a journal. I keep a journal on my smartphone. Whenever I observe a person performing a Sherlock Scan, I write down what they do and learn from it. People make Sherlock method type deductions everyday in their normal lives. For example, while researching this book in the library, two young men sat at my study table. I deduced them both as gay and listened to their conversation. One young man said to the other: "You just ate a sandwich." The other young man replied: "How did you know that?" The first young man replied: "I saw the breadcrumbs between your teeth." Practice doing this once a day for 30 days.

13. **Watch/Participate in Debates.** You can increase your logic and reasoning skills by watching people in formal debates. Analyze how they present their arguments, their strengths, weaknesses and the strategies they use. See if you can spot invalid arguments, logical fallacies and crooked thinking. You can also join a debating team and learn first hand how they do it. You can read such books as *Basic Debate: 4th Edition* published by McGraw-Hill, *The Debaters Guide* by Jon M. Ericson and *Pros and Cons: A Debater's Handbook* by Trevor Sather. You can also go to websites such as http://www.createdebate.com, http://www.forandagainst.com and http://www.debate.org to learn more about debating. Movies such as *The Great Debaters (2007)* and *Abe Lincoln in Illinois (1940)* highlight debaters in action. You can also find debating videos on *YouTube* and learn more about debating on *Wikipedia*.

14. **Play Chess.** Chess is a thinking person's game. It teaches strategy, mental agility, control and creatively. Practice playing chess to develop your mental strength. To build your chess game, read books such as *Bobby Fischer Teaches Chess* by Bobby Fischer, *My System* by Aron Nimzowitsch and *Chess For Dummies* by James Eade. You can also go to websites such as www.chess.com, www.chesstempo.com and http://gameknot.com/ to learn more about the chess game.

15. **Read Solve-It-Yourself Mysteries.** You can learn to think logically by practicing solving mysteries. For example, test yourself with the following mysteries:

   a. **Logical Mystery #1:** Two teams are playing baseball. It is the bottom of the ninth inning with the home team losing 4 to 1. A batter comes up with the bases loaded and hits a grand slam homerun. Yet, there are no men on base. The home team wins the game 5 to 4. How is that possible?

   b. **Logical Mystery #2:** One snowy night, Sherlock Holmes was in his house sitting by the fire. All of a sudden, a snowball came crashing through his window, breaking it. Holmes gets up and looks out the window just in time to see three neighborhood kids who were brothers run around a corner. Their names were John Crimson, Mark Crimson and Paul Crimson. The next day Holmes receives a note on his door that read: "?Crimson. He broke your window." Which of the three Crimson brothers should Holmes question about the incident?

c. **Logical Mystery #3:** Sherlock Holmes examines a crime scene. The victim is the owner who is slumped dead on a chair and has a bullet hole in his head. A gun lies on the floor and Holmes finds a cassette recorder on the table. On pressing the play button, Sherlock hears the message "I have committed sins in my life and now I offer my soul to the great lord"...following a gunshot. Sherlock smiles. Of course, it is a murder. Why did he think so?

Read the following books to improve your mystery-solving skills. The authors leave clues within the books so you can solve the mystery: *The Westing Game* by Ellen Raskin, *And Then There Were None* by Peter Foreman and *Encyclopedia Brown, Boy Detective* by Donald J. Sobol. Also, go to the following websites to test your ability to solve mysteries http://www.theproblemsite.com, http://playwithyourmind.com and http://www.braingle.com. The answers to the above three mysteries are below. [75]

16. **Challenge Yourself with Riddles and Puzzles.** Improve your ability to think logically and reason accurately by challenging yourself with riddles, puzzles and brainteasers. For example, test yourself with the following riddles:

a. **Riddle #1:** What is greater than God, more evil than the devil, the poor have it, the rich need it, and if you eat it, you will die?

b. **Riddle #2:** If you put a coin in an empty bottle and insert a cork into the neck of the bottle, how could

---

[75] Answers to mysteries: Mystery #1: All women were playing. Mystery #2: question mark (?) means to question Mark Crimson. Mystery #3: A dead man cannot rewind the tape himself.

you remove the coin without taking the cork out or breaking the bottle?

c. **Riddle #3:** A man looks at a photograph and says: "I have no brothers or sisters, but the person in the photograph is my father's son." What is the relationship between the speaker and the man in the photograph?

Read the following books to increase your reasoning skills: *399 Games, Puzzles & Trivia Challenges Specially Designed to Keep Your Brain Young* by Nancy Linde, *The Big Book of Brain Games* by Ivan Moscovich and *The World's 200 Hardest Brainteasers* by Gary Gruber. These websites will test your ability to solve problems: www.brainbashers.com, www.thinkriddles.com, and www.mindcipher.com. The answers to the above three riddles are below.[76]

17. **Practice Analyzing Movie Plots.** Many scenes in movies simply do not follow logic. A plot mistake occurs when the plots and story lines do not match up with the characters' words and actions. Often movies simply defy common sense and appeal to the viewer's emotions, instincts, biases and assumptions. Watch movies to analyze the plot. Think about the actions and emotions the characters display. For example, in *Sherlock Holmes (2009)* the English Court hangs Lord Blackwood. The logical thing to do after you hang a person is to check his or her neck to see if it is broke. Yet, Dr. Watson checks Lord Blackwood's pulse to confirm he is dead! It does not make sense. Watch a movie, to see if you can figure out a movie plot flaw. Then check your results on the website

---

[76] Answers to riddles: Riddle #1: The answer is "Nothing." Riddle #2: Push the cork into the bottle and shake the coin out. Riddle #3: The man holding the photograph is the father of the man in the photograph. The man in the photograph is his son.

www.movieplotholes.com. This movie plot hole website is especially interesting. It points out contradictions in movie plots. Use it to improve your powers of logical reasoning. Practice this once a day for 30 days.

18. **Practice Deductive/Inductive Thinking.** Critically evaluate arguments. Do the premises support the conclusion? Are the premises true? Watch the movie *A Few Good Men (1992)*. Analyze the courtroom scene where Lieutenant Daniels cross-examines Colonel Jessup regarding a code red order he gave that results in the death of a new cadet. Study the deductive arguments both attorneys give for and against giving the code red. You can also watch the House episode where House deduces a man's tendency for suing doctors simply from asking the man two questions. You can find an excellent study guide at www.*factchecked.org* that analyzes the deductive arguments from *A Few Good Men* and the *House* episodes. The study guide explains House's thinking as he makes inductive arguments and highlights how the films make both types of arguments.

19. **Practice Thinking Fast.** In *The Adventure of the Speckled Band*, Watson described Holmes as having "rapid deductions, as swift as intuitions." The following exercises will help you practice reasoning quickly:

    a. **Play Speed Chess/Checkers.** Playing speed chess and/or checkers will increase your ability to think fast under pressure. You will need a timer, a chess or checkerboard and to practice. You can watch speed checker or chess players in parks or at clubs that specialize in it. Read about it and watch videos on it on YouTube to get started. You can also watch movies such as *Searching for Bobby Fischer (1993)* and *Fresh (2002)* for a glimpse on how it works. But the best way to learn speed chess or checkers is to actually do it. Learn the basics then go out and practice. Do this as many times as necessary.

b. **Time Yourself.** You can increase your ability to reason quickly and think on your feet by timing yourself. Use a stopwatch, smartphone or clock to see how fast it takes you to analyze a puzzle or observe a stranger. The more you practice, the better and faster you will get. Practice this as many times as necessary.

c. **Play Rubic's Cube.** Practicing with a Rubic's Cube is an excellent way to increase your mental speed. You can learn the basics of figuring out the Cube by reading a book such as *Speed Solving the Cube* by Dan Harris. Then go on *YouTube* to see how players do it. Learn the tricks of the trade and then practice using a Rubic's Cube to make yourself better.

d. **Speed-Read People.** As you go about your daily activities practice speed-reading people. Try to learn as much as you can about them in the first few seconds of observing or meeting them. Take a quick glance at them and see how much you can deduce. Notice a woman with a big belly? She is probably pregnant. Notice a man with a black eye? He probably just had a fight. These are obvious common sense observations you make everyday. Get into the habit of asking questions when you are making deductions. Ask yourself: is the stranger a smoker? A nail biter? A drinker? Right or left handed? A drug user? Then ask yourself what is the simplest answer that explains all the available facts. Do this in less and less time until you can learn a lot about a stranger in only one or two seconds. You do not need to check with the person since you are only verifying things that are visible on them. Do this once a day for 30 days.

SPECIALIZED KNOWLEDGE EXERCISES

The purpose of the exercises below is to help you gain the specific knowledge you need to size up strangers. The following exercises will improve your ability to acquire specialized knowledge in particular areas and subjects. Practice each exercise for as long as it takes to master it. Remember the third basic question: *"How can I verify it?"* as you do the exercises.

1. **Study Psychology.** Psychology is the study of the human mind. There is a branch of psychology for every human behavior — criminal, child, abnormal, sales, sports, industrial, crowd, political — you name it, and a psychological field exists for it. You do not need a degree to study human psychology but you should have a basic understanding how it works. You can read books, watch videos and study. Read online articles from www.*psychologytoday.com* or subscribe to the *Psychology Today* magazine. But the best way to learn psychology is actually to interact with people and learn what makes them tick. Practice looking for denial, depression, rationalization, projection and other psychological processes in the strangers you meet.

2. **Study Fashion.** Clothing communicates messages to people. It can tell you about the wearer's self-image, self-esteem, style, finances, occupation and many other things. When you study fashion design, you will learn how clothing fits, the fabric that is used, what message the wearer is sending, what the stranger is trying to reveal or conceal and many other things. Learn fashion design by studying in an accredited school or college, reading books on fashion and studying videos on *YouTube.* One

excellent way to study fashion design is simply to watch what everyone is wearing. What are the clothing trends, the colors, the fabric, the cut and style? You can do this as you go about your daily activities. You will see people dressing in different styles from all lifestyles: business, formal, casual, athletic, radical and elegant. Publications such as *Glamour, Cosmopolitan* and *Gentleman's Quarterly* (GQ) can give you for insight into the fashion world. These magazines reveal tips on how people dress, why they pick particular dressing styles and the impression the clothing they wear make. Read the magazines to spot the latest fashion trends and styles. Then notice what people around you are wearing to see if any magazine fashions filtered down it into everyday life.

3. **Study Peoples' Color Choices.** The colors people choose send a message about them. Whether it is the color of their car, clothes, furniture, walls, house, shoes, makeup or accessories such as handbags, each color reveals something about them. Experts say that the color a person chooses can reveal their mood, personality and character. It also reveals a stranger's judgment and style. For example, experts consider red a bold color. They associate it with an outgoing, confident personality. Practice watching people and observe the colors they chose. Are the colors coordinated? Are they bright, attention getting? Does the color convey a calm, relaxed personality or an aggressive, threatening one? Does the person wear dark colors such as black, blue, brown, or bright colors like yellow, orange or red? Read the following books to learn more about colors and psychology: *The Beginner's Guide to Color Psychology* by Angela Wright, *Color Me Beautiful* by Carole Jackson and *Color Your Style* by David Zyla. Go to the following websites to test your color personality: http://colorquiz.com/ and http://www.testcolor.com/.

Search on Google, Facebook for information on how colors affect people.

4. **Study Obscure Subjects.** Sherlock Holmes studied different types of dirt and mud from various parts of London so that he could tell where a stranger came from. Study shoe scuffmarks, rips on jeans, stains on shirts, hairs on coats and so forth to determine their origin or source. It is easy to spot dirt, scratches, stains, rips and other minor things on strangers. The hard part is to know what these minor indications mean. The only practical way to learn how to read these things is through trial and error. You have to study people as you go about your daily activities. Make it a habit to closely watch for obvious but minor things you see on strangers. Also, study yourself. How do you get stains on your shirt? Scuffmarks on your shoes? Rips on your clothes? The same way these things happen to you, they happen to other people. Use common sense and keep your analysis simple. Practice doing this as many times as necessary.

5. **Take Up a Hobby.** Sherlock Holmes had several hobbies, which directly related to his occupation. The hobbies he took up increased his ability to investigate crimes and study strangers. He studied different tobaccos to narrow down possible suspects. He learned about tracing footsteps to track down criminals. He learned how to read hands to tell a stranger's trade. Pick a hobby that you enjoy. Practice it and see if you can tie it into sizing up strangers. For example, you could learn lip reading. Lip reading is the technique of visually deciphering a person's speech from their mouth, tongue and face movements without sound. You could use it to obtain information from strangers without them realizing it. You can learn more about lip reading at websites such as www.lipreading.org or a book like *How To Read Lips for Fun & Profit* by Edward Nitchie. The important thing is

that you tie the hobby in some way to your particular field of interest like Holmes did. Practice doing this for as long as it takes.

6. **Study Tattoos.** Sherlock Holmes was a master at reading tattoos. In several cases, he reveals his ability to scan a tattoo and tell the stranger's past activities or occupation. Tattoos have come a long way since the 19th Century. People wear tattoos without the stigma society associates with them like in the past. Learn why people wear tattoos, where they place them on their bodies, the type of tattoos they get, how many they get and why they remove or cover them. For example, people get tattoos for religious, political and status reasons. They get tattoos to show affiliation with a gang, group or organization, to honor a family member, lover or friend. They get tattoos for attention, for good luck or to rebel. You can also go to a tattoo parlor and learn first hand how they do it. You can read *The Mammoth Book of Tattoos* by Lal Hardy, and *Russian Criminal Tattoo Encyclopedia* Volume 1 by Damon Murray. You can go to websites such as www.tattooarchive.com and www.vanishingtatto.com, to learn more about tattoos. Movies such as *Skyfall (2012)* and *Eastern Promises (2007)* show how characters size up people by their tattoos. You can also find tattoo videos on *YouTube* and learn more about tattoos on *Wikipedia.* The best way to learn, however, is to practice reading stranger's tattoos as you go about your daily activities. First, practice spotting tattoos on strangers you see. Then practice determining the kind of tattoo it is. Then practice sizing up a stranger based on the tattoo he or she is wearing. Finally, you can approach the stranger, strike up a friendly conversation, compliment him or her on the tattoo and ask why they wear it to verify your guess. The more knowledge and training you get on reading tattoos, the easier time you will have in sizing up a stranger who has them.

7. **Study Physical Symptoms.** Teach yourself to spot a stranger's health status. We all do this naturally. We are all armchair doctors, watching our family members, relatives, friends, neighbors', coworkers and strangers for good and bad health signs. Women and men do it when they are seeking partners. They look for the healthiest members of the opposite sex. They look at body built, skin condition and muscle tone among other things. Learn the basic physical symptoms for general medical conditions. You do not need to become a doctor, but develop general knowledge on what certain physical symptoms look like. Teach yourself to diagnose what certain cuts, blisters, burns, blemishes, rashes and marks on the skin mean. Train yourself to notice red eyes, cracked nails, dry lips, overweight, lost weight and so forth. People do this every day when they encounter strangers. When they see someone with a skin rash, they know the person has a skin problem, although they may not know exactly what it is. You can go to websites such as *www.webMD.com*, and *http://www.mayoclinic.org* to learn more about reading physical health symptoms. You can read technical books like *Handbook of Signs & Symptoms* by Lippincott Williams & Wilkins, *Symptom to Diagnosis: An Evidence Based Guide, Second Edition* by Scott Stern and *Geriatric Physical Diagnosis: A Guide to Observation and Assessment* by Mark E. Williams, M.D. You can watch medical videos on *YouTube* and discuss the topic on media websites like *Facebook* and *Twitter.* You can also search online and read health articles that discuss what people's health say about them. Practice doing this as long as necessary.

8. **Research/Study Profiling.** Study profiling techniques to understand the difference between sizing up a stranger based on facts and evidence and evaluating them based on stereotypes and bias. In the late 19th Century,

Sherlock Holmes profiled criminals based on the evidence he discovered at crime scenes. Modern day profiling encompasses assessing individuals from several fields. Research the profiling fields to understand how they work. The fields include but are not limited to criminal, traveler, behavioral, customer and psychological profiling. Some critics charge that many so-called behavioral detection programs are nothing more than racial, gender and cultural profiling. Other critics claim criminal profiling is unscientific and unproven. Know and understand the pros and cons regarding profiling individuals. You can research profiling on the Internet and at the library. You can search for online articles with *Google* or *Bing*. *The Skeptic's Dictionary* also discusses profiling at www.skepdic.com. You can read books such as *The Forensic Psychologist's Casebook: Psychological Profiling and Criminal Investigation* by Laurence Alison (Amazon) and *Criminal Profiling: An Introduction to Behavioral Evidence Analysis* by Brent Turvey. Watch old TV shows on DVD such as *Cracker* (in which a behavioral psychologist aids police in solving crimes). You can watch profiling videos on *YouTube* and discuss it on media websites like *Facebook* and *Twitter.* You can go to a website such as www.chasehughes.com to learn about *The Behaviorial Table of Elements* (use it with the memory temple technique from Chapter 7). Understand the techniques law enforcement uses to profile individuals and adapt the techniques to your everyday evaluations of strangers. Practice doing this as long as it takes.

9. **Research/Study Cold Reading.** Cold reading uses similar principles as the Sherlock Holmes Method. Learn cold reading to understand the difference between sizing up a stranger based on facts and evidence and evaluating them based on the supernatural and trickery. You can learn a lot about how to size up strangers by studying cold reading. Reject such techniques as the Barnum

statement (seemingly personal statements that apply to many people), the Shotgun (broad statements that relate to everyone) and the Rainbow Ruse (statements that say both good and bad things about people). Cold readers use these techniques to manipulate people into thinking they know about them. Instead, focus on the cold reader's ability to read body language, facial expressions and statistical knowledge. Cold readers use probabilities to guess a stranger's job, background, health, love life and financial status. They understand trends and human nature and use these things to con people. You can watch a movie such as *Leap of Faith (1992)*, to get an idea how cold reading works. In the movie, faith healing con man Jonas Nightengale cold reads a highway patrol officer. He then gets the officer to not write a speeding ticket plus give a donation. Go to websites that discuss cold reading such as http://www.psychicscience.org/coldread.aspx and http://www.skeptics.com.au /publications/articles/ guide-to-cold-reading-ray-hyman/. You can also study cold reading books such as Ian Rowland's *Full Facts Book of Cold Reading* (6th edition). Practice doing this for as long as it takes.

10. **Test Your Sherlockian Knowledge.** Go to www.gradesaver.com and test your Sherlockian knowledge. The website usually tests your knowledge about Sherlock Holmes from movies, TV and books. The more answers you get right, the higher your score. You simply type in 'Sherlock Holmes' on the search function. A list of Holmes related stories will appear. Pick a story to read. After you read the story, you can take the test.

11. **Use Technology Like Sherlock**. In the BBC series "Sherlock," the modern day Sherlock Holmes uses his smartphone and computer to gather facts and information. Practice using your smartphone, tablet or computer in sizing up strangers. For example, you could

use a smartphone to take pictures of stranger's shoes and study them. You could use a tablet computer to video record friends or family members to study their facial expressions or body language. You could use a laptop or desktop computer to use search engines such as *Google* or *Bing* to obtain information immediately. You could use apps such as *Psych Guide, PsycExplorer, Personality Types* and *The Questions* to learn about psychology and understand people. Incorporate technology to improve your skill in sizing up strangers.

12. **Practice Private Investigator Techniques.** Sherlock Holmes used PI techniques such as interrogation, surveillance, background checks and information searches. You can research PI techniques on the Internet and at the library. You can search for online articles with *Google* or *Bing*. You can read books such as *The Complete Idiot's Guide to Private Investigating, Third Edition* by Steven Kerry Brown and *The Everything Private Investigation Book* by Sheila L. Stephens. Watch detective TV shows on DVD such as *Murder She Wrote, Columbo and Ironside*. Watch detective movies such as *Chinatown (1974)* and *The Maltese Falcon (1941)*. You can watch PI videos on *YouTube* and discuss them on media websites like *Facebook* and *Twitter*. Professional Investigator Magazine covers every aspect of the PI field. You can go to the website at: http://www.pimagazine.com to learn about *PI techniques*. Practice the techniques private investigators use. The PI techniques rely on the same questions and principles found in this book. Do this for as long as it takes.

EXPERIENCE EXERCISES

The purpose of the following exercises is to help you develop your general knowledge and common sense. The exercises below will improve your practical everyday skills in dealing with people. Remember the third basic question: *"How can I verify it?"* as you do the exercises.

1. **Practice Studying Con Artists.** Whether they are seeking to steal your finances or your heart, con artists have one thing in common — they seek to establish trust. They want you to think they are your friends. They want you relaxed and comfortable. That way, they can steal your money, break your heart, lie to you and even hurt you. The techniques they use to fool people seem normal. They come across as non-threatening and harmless when you first meet them. But then they prey on your desire to help. They take advantage of your gullibility. The only way to defend yourself against them is to stay suspicious, be skeptical and gain knowledge. Learn how they operate and know the warning signs so they will not catch you off guard. Simply use your common sense when dealing with strangers so no one can use you for their own selfish ends. You can research con artists on the Internet and at the library. You can read books like *How to Become a Professional Con Artist* by Dennis M Marlock, *Catch Me If You Can* by Frank W. Abagnale and *The Big Con: The Story of the Confidence Man* by David Maurer. Watch movies such as *Elmer Gantry, (1960), The Hustler (1961), The Sting (1973)* and *House of Games (1987)* to get a sense how they operate. You can watch videos on YouTube and discuss it on media websites like *Facebook.*

2. **Practice Learning Job Descriptions.** Both Dr. Joseph Bell and Sherlock Holmes sized up strangers by their trades. One way you can do this is to learn about many different trades or jobs. It is harder today to tell a person by their trade than in Sherlock Holmes's time, but it still is possible. Practice taking educated guesses on the type of work people do as you go about your daily business. Look for specific clues in their physical appearance, behavior, speech and fashion. Then check your

inferences with the stranger to see if they are accurate. For example, one way to do this is to look at a stranger's hands. As a rule of thumb, a person with soft hands probably does some type of office work. A person with rough hands, probably does some type of manual labor.

Another way is to use the base rate factor to determine the probability that a stranger has a particular job. The key is to understand the base rate factor and know it for the particular trade you are seeking to estimate. The base rate relies on general rather than specific information. *Wikipedia.com* gives an example of a man who wears gothic inspired clothing, has long black hair and listens to death metal music. Is he more likely to be a Christian or a Satanist? Most people would say he is a Satanist. Why? The answer is because they ignore the fact that there are two billion Christians in the world while there are only a few thousand Satanists.

When you meet a stranger, know when to focus on general rather than specific information about them. To guess a stranger's trade accurately with the base rate factor, ask yourself: what is the probability of a stranger being in a particular trade? For example, a stranger who has a doctor's white coat, a stethoscope and prescribes medicine is probably in the medical field. Ask yourself: what percentage of the population is a police officer? A firefighter? A doctor? A lawyer? A postal worker? A transit worker? A sanitation worker? A union official? A soldier? You can find base rate statistics at government and private websites that do calculations on jobs such as www.fedstats.gov/ and www.governing.com. You can learn more about the base rate factor at Wikipedia.com and the FallacyFiles.com. Practice doing this for as long as it takes.

3. **Practice Speed Dating**. Speed dating tests your ability to make rapid judgments about a stranger in three minutes or less for romantic reasons. Companies such as *HurryDate* and *8MinuteDating* gather single men and women together for these on the spot romantic encounters. The participants converse quickly; making rapid judgments about the person, then move onto the next single stranger. At the end of the session, the organizers provide singles that are mutually interested contact information. If you are a single person looking for a partner, this may be one way to improve your Sherlockian skills while simultaneously finding a soul mate. Do this for once a day for 30 days.

LISTENING EXERCISES

The purpose of the following exercises is to help you become an effective listener. The exercises below will improve your ability to hear and listen to what people really say. Remember the second and third basic questions as you do the exercises.

1. **Practice Listening to the Way People Walk.** Practice identifying people from the sound of their footsteps. Some people walk fast. Some walk slow. Some people walk aggressively. Some walk casually. Some people make sounds with their heels as they walk. Some people walk quietly. In *The Adventure of Wisteria Lodge,* Holmes identified Scott Eccles from the sound of his footsteps as he came up the stairs to 221B Baker Street.

2. **Practice Listening to the Sounds People Make.** In *A Case of Identity*, Holmes stated he could tell when a man has seriously hurt a woman romantically because the symptom "is a broken bell wire." Practice identifying people from the sound they make when knocking on a door or pressing a doorbell. You can often tell a specific

person is approaching by listening to the sounds of their keys or coins in their pockets.

3. **Practice Listening for Jargon.** Often people say words that are specific to their job, hobby or special interest. Learn about different fields and study the terminology in each one. If you hear a person talking about a 'tell', that could mean they are a poker player. A person mentioning they are 'uploading data onto a server' could mean they work in the computer field.

4. **Practice Listening to People Over the Telephone.** Guess the person's age, gender, race, nationality, educational level, personality, mood, financial status and intelligence from what you hear. Then confirm with the person the facts you deduced from listening. While listening, focus on the pitch, volume, tone and other factors in the person's voice. Do this whenever you are on the telephone. Then verify your educated guess by asking the person, for example, how old they are or what level of education they have.

5. **Practice Listening To People Around You.** Keep your ears open as you go about your daily routine. Often you can overhear a stranger's conversation and gather clues to their personality from what you hear. When you are in the street or on the job walking towards strangers who are conversing, practice listening to what they say to hear any informational tidbits you can use later. For example, you might hear the stranger's name, age, destination and so forth. Cold readers do this when they are fishing for information about people to later use during a reading.

6. **Practice Listening to the Radio.** Each day turn on your radio and listen to the talk channels. The speakers on these channels are professionals. They receive

training on presenting their voices in the most positive light. Focus on each speaker's voice and what they say. Concentrate on their voice tone, pace, rhythm, inflection and vocabulary. Then listen to the guests. Some guests are professional speakers such as politicians. Others are average everyday people. Listen to what the speaker is conveying. Listen between the lines of conversation for unspoken messages and meaning. Imagine the person speaking. See if you can tell the speaker's gender, race, age, personality or education level from his or her voice.

7. **Practice Listening to Speech.** Whenever someone introduces you to a person, take time to listen. Concentrate on not only what they say but also the way they say it. Zero in on their specific way of expressing themselves. Listen for feelings and thoughts. Practice taking educated guesses on the person's background based on what you hear the stranger say. The more you listen to a stranger's speech, the better you will get at sizing them up.

8. **Practice Giving Feedback.** When you listen to people, let them know that you understand what they say. Each day for 30 days, practice giving signs that you hear them. At the appropriate time during the conversation, interject comments such as "I hear you", "Go on" or "I understand" to let a person know you are paying attention. You can also repeat back to the person what they said, to confirm that you understand them.

9. **Practice Listening for Accents.** You can usually tell where people come from by their accents. A New Yorker will have a different accent than a person who lives in Boston. Someone who lives in the South will speak differently than someone who lives in the North. Someone who lives in Scotland will speak with an accent different from someone who lives in Britain.

Make it a habit to focus on a stranger's accent when you meet them. Practice listening to TV programs from specific regions and areas so you can pick up the accents. All this may seem like common sense, but it is surprising how many people do not consider these obvious things when sizing up strangers.

10. **Practice Listening for Deception.** One study found that within the first ten minutes of meeting each other strangers told up to three lies. When you listen to someone who you believe is lying, change the topic. Practice closely watching their reaction to you unexpectedly changing the subject. Does the person go along with you changing the subject with no problem? Do they seem relieved that you started a new topic? This could be a sign that the person has lied. A stranger with nothing to hide will react surprised that you suddenly changed the subject. He or she will want to still talk about the issue. Liars are usually happy you changed the subject.

11. **Practice Listening to Recorded Conversations.** You can record telephone or in person conversations (with the person's permission) and listen to yourself. How does your voice sound? What feelings are conveyed in your voice tone? Did you interrupt the person? Did you miss anything the person said? Did you let the person know you were listening by giving verbal indicators? Did you understand what the person said? Were you distracted or not paying attention? Recording a conversation on the telephone or in person can help you listen more effectively.

12. **Practice Listening to Out of the Ordinary Sounds.** Most people do not listen to the sounds around them. They unconsciously tune out the sounds of life and their environment. Practices listening to things you do not

326

normally listen to. If you normally listen to gospel or country music, try listening to rap or rock music. Pay attention with your ears to sounds in the street — engines, horns, subway, etc. Practice listening to lectures, sermons, scientific speeches or congressional debates. Listening to sounds you do not normally hear can improve your ability to listen effectively.

13. **Practice Listening When It is Hard.** You will not be able to listen to every stranger you meet clearly. Some people have thick foreign accents. Some people stutter. Some people do not speak clearly, speak too loud or low or speak very fast. You can increase your ability to listen effectively by adjusting to each stranger you meet. When you meet someone whose speech is unclear, practice focusing on his or her voice. Let them know you are "all ears" and give them your full attention.

14. **Practice Your Listening Speed.** You can think faster than a stranger can talk. Most people speak from 120 to 180 words a minute. Most listeners can process up to 500 words a minute. As a stranger is speaking to you, focus on what he or she is saying. Do not let your mind wander or daydream. Use the difference in speed to analyze what the speaker is saying so you can accurately size up the person.

15. **Practice Listening in the Street.** As you are walking in the street, practice listening to the sounds behind you. If a stranger is walking behind you, try to deduce his or her gender, age, race, weight, height and other things from the sounds you hear. Then look back to verify your deductions. For example, see if you can guess how old a stranger is from the sound of his or her voice. The person's voice can reveal whether they are a man or woman, whether they are black, white, Latino and so forth. Try to tell from the sound of their footsteps

whether they are male or female, a child or senior citizen. The sounds of scrapes, bumps and screeching can tell you whether they are carry bags, knapsacks, luggage and so forth. The more you practice, the better you will get at guessing the sounds you hear. Do this once a day for 30 days.

IMAGINATION EXERCISES

The purpose of the following exercises is to help you develop your powers of visualization. The exercises below will improve your ability to put yourself in a stranger's shoes. Remember the fourth basic question: *"What Do I Conclude?"* as you do the exercises.

1. **Practice Visualizing Sizing Up People.** Before you go outside in the real world, take some quiet time and imagine yourself sizing up a stranger. Find a quiet place and relax your mind. Close your eyes. Then picture yourself looking at the stranger's facial expressions, body language and clothing. Imagine yourself hearing the stranger speaking. Listen in your imagination for their tone of voice, pitch, and so forth. Imagine any details on the stranger, such as tattoos, scars, scuff marks, stains, bulges in pockets and so forth. Imagine the person's height, weight, gender, age and race. Visualize yourself doing all these things before you actually do them and you will find it easier when you do it in real life with real people. Your brain finds it easy to create pictures. You dream in images. Therefore, when you study, visualize it. For example, picture in your mind the shoes, pants, shirt, hat, gloves, a stranger may wear. You can go online and read *"How to Use Your Imagination For Creative Visualization"* by Tania Kotsos from *Mind Your Reality.com.* You can read the article at: www.mind-your-reality.com/use_your_ imagination. Html # Part_2.

2. **Practice Putting Yourself In The Stranger's Shoes.** As you observe, speak or listen to a stranger, visualize what the person may be feeling or thinking. Closely watch the stranger's facial expressions, body language, gestures, posture and speech. Then practice feeling what the person is feeling. Adopt the same posture, words, facial expressions and body language as the stranger. Mirror their reactions to be in harmony with them. Draw a mental picture what the person is saying. Ask yourself questions that will help you understand and empathize with them. Why are you angry? Afraid? What is it like walking in the stranger's shoes? How would you feel if you were the person? Actors ask questions like this when they role-play. You can do this to help empathize with people. Do this once a day for 30 days.

3. **Practice Bringing Your Images to Life.** Practice imagining yourself meeting a person and scanning them for information. Visualize yourself making inferences about them. See yourself using the questions and principles on people you meet. Imagine yourself already deducing strangers. Visualize images in your mind's eye. Use your five senses. Relax. Close your eyes and stay calm. Conceive it and you will achieve it. Your thoughts will transform themselves into reality with the aid of your imagination. Make your images move like in a movie or dream. Make these images come alive in your mind. Make the images vivid and specific. You can do this by playing your favorite music as you think with your mind movies. Believe you can do it. Close your eyes and see it as if it is already happening. You can also use your emotions to add fuel to your imagination. The more you do this, the better your imagination will get and make it easier to size up strangers.

4. **Practice Imagining Different Possibilities.** Whenever you meet a stranger, keep in mind there are many

possible interpretations for their appearance and behavior. Imagine as many possible reasons for their facial expressions, gestures and actions as you can. Then narrow down the possibilities to the most probable or likely. You can do this in your mind while you are on the bus or subway, while you are waiting in line at a store or bank or while you are walking down the street. Look at people and try guessing the most-likely reasons for their appearance and actions. You do not have to verify these guesses because you are using your imagination. Once you start actually sizing up strangers, then you will seek to confirm what you deduce with them. This exercise is simply to let your mind run wild to see how many possibilities you can imagine. Do this exercise once a day for 30 days.

MEMORY EXERCISES

The purpose of the following exercises is to help you improve your memory. The exercises below will help you develop your memory like you would any other muscle. The more you use your memory, the better it will become.

1. **Practice Living Healthy to Improve Your Memory.** Simply keeping a positive mental attitude, following a healthy diet, regularly exercising and reading new and unusual subjects, will improve your recollection. Experts say nothing beats these four things when it comes to boosting your memory. Make a decision to change your lifestyle and make these four healthy memory-boosting tips a part of it.

2. **Practice Writing Things Down.** You can write down what you want to remember by creating to-do lists, using post-it notes or writing on a calendar. These simple techniques can help you remember important dates,

people and events in your life. The more things you write down, the more likely you will remember them.

3. **Practice Remembering Names.** Joshua Foer writes in the online article *"The Secret To Superpower Memory"* (*http://www.huffingtonpost.com*) that to remember names you must pay attention. Then visually associate the person's name and face in your imagination. Whenever you meet people, pay close attention when they say their name. Create an image in your mind and associate it with the person's name. In the article Mr. Foer writes: "To make a name memorable, try creating a visual association in your imagination between the person's name and face. If it's a woman named Abby, imagine a bee stinging her eye. If it's a guy called Bill, imagine him with a duckbill for a mouth. If it's someone named Barbara, picture a crown of barbed wire around her head. Create these images in your mind's eye with as much color, action and meaning as possible. For example, don't just picture a bee stinging Abby's eye. Hear the bee buzzing, imagine her eye swelling, and try to feel how painful it would be. The more senses you can use, the better." Practice this exercise whenever you meet a stranger. Your memory will improve as a result.

4. **Practice Remembering Through Association.** Each day for the next 30 days pick something about a person you want to remember. It could be their face, name or something they do or say. Then study it. Think about it and commit it to your memory. Visualize what you want to remember. Use your sense of hearing and say it out loud. You can also associate your sense of taste and smell with a memory. For example, you can associate perfume or food odors with people you know. A cologne or perfume smell could remind you of a boyfriend or girlfriend. A cake smell could remind you of your mother or grandmother baking in the kitchen. Doing this will

help make a sensory connection between what you smell and what you want to remember. The smell will then jog your memory. You can also touch or physically feel the person (shake their hand, pat them on the back, etc.) to help you remember them. Associate your sense of touch with something about the person. Telling a story, making a joke or simply exaggerating a situation can help you remember a person. Practice doing these things to improve your memory.

5. **Practice Taking Tests to Improve Your Memory.** Kendra Cherry in the online article *"10 Facts About Memory" (http://psychology.about.com)*, states that taking tests on information you learn is one good way to improve your memory. According to the article, researchers found that students who studied and then took a test had better recall. You can improve your memory by studying and then testing yourself on the topic. There are many memory tests on the Internet you can use such as the Pyschology.com test. It asks several questions and only takes five minutes to complete. Take the test at: http://psychologytoday.tests.psychtests.com /take_test.php?idRegTest=3360. You can also read memory books and take some of the practice tests. You can find memory books by searching the *Google* or *Bing.* The important thing is that you practice taking tests in the subject you find interesting. This one exercise will improve your ability to recall information dramatically.

6. **Practice Using Technology To Improve Your Memory.** Your smartphone, tablet, personal computer can aid in you remembering things and people. You can use these electronic devices to remember dates, telephone numbers, important to-do lists and so forth. You can also use memory apps such as *Evernote*, *Lastpass* and *Remember The Milk* to aid you in recalling important information (you can find these apps on *iTunes*). But do

not depend on technology so much that you cannot remember a phone number or face without it. Use technology to supplement your memory, not replace it.

7. **Practice Using Memory Triggers.** A memory trigger is something that helps you recall something else you want to remember. Make a mental note of something you want to recall. For example, you constantly forget your house keys when you leave in the morning for work. Place your keys on the bedroom table in the evening and associate the keys with the table. When you think about the bedroom table, it will jog your memory about the house keys. You can use this simple technique to remember almost anything. Simply practice taking a mental inventory of the things you need to recall. Then look around your room. Memorize where specific things are located. Think about what you want to remember and associate it with the items in your room. When you think about the items in your room, you will recall the items you need to remember.

8. **Practice Remembering Through Repetition.** You can recall information easier if you repeat it over in your mind. For example, if you are studying, go over the information slowly. Then separate the information into different sections. Then read each section repeatedly until you know it by heart. Once you read each part individually, go back over everything and read the entire thing. See how much you can recall. Repetition is one of the techniques you can use to remember something quickly or to learn a long list in a short time.

9. **Practice Playing Black Jack.** You can improve your memory skills by playing a card game such as Blackjack. Learn about basic strategy and counting cards. These two techniques rely on you memorizing basic rules to improve the chance you will hit 21. You can also read

books such as *Big Book of Blackjack* by Arnold Snyder, *Professional Blackjack* by Stanford Wong and *Blackjack Attack* by Don Schlesinger, which focus on improving your memory through card playing. Websites such as www.blackjack.com and http://www.bj21.com have many articles on basic strategy and card counting. *YouTube* has many videos that explain card counting and basic strategy. You will find apps such as *21 Pro* and *Black Jack* that you can play to practice your card playing skills. You can also watch movies such as *21 (2008)* that reveal how an MIT professor and students used their memories to count cards. They then went to Las Vegas and won thousands of dollars playing blackjack. You can search online for articles on how to play Blackjack. Social media such as *Facebook* and *Twitter* have forums where you can socialize with like-minded card players to improve your memory.

10. **Practice Listening to Music.** Practice memorizing things along with the musical sounds you hear. Listen to your favorite songs. Associate what you want to remember with a song. Then when you hear the song, it will trigger the subject you want to remember. This technique makes use of your natural hearing ability.

11. **Practice with a Memory Community.** The website mnemotechnics.org has many exercises you can use to improve your memory. The community website offers different forums, tips, videos, clubs, blogs, books and techniques for you to use. For example, you can join a memory club. The club usually meets once a month. The members ask memory related questions, share tips and network with other clubs. The club can meet online or in person. The clubs practice memory techniques and take tests to improve their recall skills. The members also train for competitive events all the way up to the *World Memory Championships.* You can sign up at

http://mnemotechnics.org/. You can also use the use the Wiki memory resource. This website is a community written source of information that promotes memory training. The site lists memory tips and techniques, information on how to start a memory club, the different types of memory systems, memory challenges, competitions and various other types of memory related information. You can find and review it at http://mnemotechnics.org/wiki/Main_Page.

12. **Practice Playing Memory Games.** In the online article *"Top 5 Unforgettable Memory Games,"* writer Jacob Clifton lists games that improve your hand to eye coordination and sequential memory. He states you can practice improving your memory with games such as the board game "Concentration," exercise game *"Wii Fit,"* dance game *"Just Dance,"* chess and Rubic's cube. Each game focuses on a specific type of memory. For example, the *"Wii Fit"* games focus on physical memory and the *Concentration* game focuses on sequential memory. You can buy these games and practice them to improve your own memory. In addition, he discusses how in the memory championships, judges request competitors match hundreds of face photos to peoples' names. You can also find and read the memory game article at http://entertainment.howstuffworks.com/leisure/brain-games/5-memory-games.htm#page=4.

13. **Practice the Look, Snap & Connect Technique.** In the online article: *"5 Experts Answer: What's the Best Way to Improve My Memory,"* writer Amanda Chan (www.livescience.com) interviews one of five experts, Dr. Gary Smalls. Professor Smalls recommends following three simple memory steps: Look, Snap & Connect. Practice using this technique when you need a reliable way to remember something. You can learn these three basic memory skills in the online article at:

http://www.livescience.com/35580-5-experts-answer-improve-memory.html.

INTUITION EXERCISES

The purpose of the following exercises is to help you follow your gut when sizing up strangers. The exercises below will help you improve your intuitive ability.   Remember the third and fourth basic questions: *"How can I verify it?* and *"What do I conclude?"* as you do the exercises.

1. **Practice Having Faith in Your Intuition.**   When you believe in a sixth sense it is more likely to work for you. Your intuitions are a natural part of you. They come from your instincts and experiences. Trust in your gut feelings and hunches and they are more likely to turn out right. Practice thinking positive thoughts. Pay attention to any feelings or spontaneous thoughts that flash within your mind. Ask yourself a question such as: "Does this feel right?" whenever you want to tap into your sixth sense. It will communicate with you through a symbol, image, feeling or physical sensation.

2. **Practice Improvising**. Your intuitive ability gets better the more you use it. Do not be so rigid when dealing with people.   Stay flexible and make it up as you go along. Practice thinking on your feet when you meet strangers. Go by your instincts. How does the person make you feel? What is your first impression of the stranger? Often your job can help you to think on the fly. For example, a police officer must often make split second decisions under pressure. These stressful situations will often force the officer to think off the top of his or her head. The officer learns through experience to play it by ear and follow his or her gut feelings. The more you practice, the better you will be at adlibbing. Practice winging it until you can do it without thinking.

3. **Practice Freeing Your Mind.** You can free your mind to receive intuitions by relaxing your mind. Practice asking yourself questions. Then take your mind off what you are thinking or trying to do. Do something else. Then come back to it. Listen for the first answer that comes from within your mind. Whatever pops from within your mind will usually be the answer you are seeking. Listen to your feelings. The more you know yourself, the easier it is to tap into your intuitive nature.

4. **Practice Looking for the Big Picture.** When you meet someone ask yourself who does he or she remind you of. Does the stranger have similar facial expressions, body language and personal tics? Do they dress the same? Do they speak the same? Practice looking for similarities and patterns in the strangers you meet to develop your intuitive ability. The more you practice, the easier you will find it to intuitively pick up on things about strangers. Always check your intuitions for possible mistakes.

5. **Practice Meditation.** Relax your mind and tune into your inner self. Meditate for at least 15 minutes a day. Use music, a quiet area and comforting accessories (pillow, soft couch, etc.) to increase your receptiveness to the mediation experience. You can attend meditation classes or obtain meditation instructional DVDs or CDs at a website such as (http://www.gaiamtv.com/spiritual-growth/meditation). You can also read books on meditation such as *The Book of Secrets* by Osho or *Wherever You Go, There You Are: Mindfulness Meditation in Everyday Life* by Jon Kabat-Zinn.

6. **Practice Paying Attention to your Body.** Sweating hands, a pounding heart or a funny feeling in your stomach are often cues that your intuition is trying to tell

you something. Pay attention to these physical signs in yourself and others. Any raise in your stress level while you are doing something could be a sign that your intuition is flashing an alarm. Are you feeling nervous for no reason? Is your mouth suddenly dry? Do you feel nauseous about something? Pay attention to these signs. Then act on them. Without realizing it, you may have a reason to be concerned about a stranger.

7. **Practice Sleeping On It.** You can tap into your intuition when you have a problem by sleeping on it. Your unconscious mind will work even while you sleep. Before you lay your head down, put a notepad and pen on the nightstand next to you. Write down what the problem is and think about it while you are falling asleep. Your unconscious will work on the problem as you sleep. It may give you an answer in the morning through an inspiration or flash of thought. Whether you wake up in the middle of the night or the morning, pay attention to any flashes of insight you get and write them down.

8. **Practice Intuitive Guessing.** When you meet a stranger for the first time, practice using your sixth sense to get a 'feel' for them. Watch the stranger's eyes, facial expressions and body language. Estimate the stranger's mental state by their moods or feelings. Ask yourself is the stranger a 'friend' or 'foe.' Use your intuition to make a guess about the person. Try to guess their motives, goals or intentions. Will they help you? Hurt you? These thoughts are usually unconscious and instinctual. What you are doing now is making yourself consciously aware of them. Start a friendly conversation to see if your inferences are correct. Write down your intuitive guesses on a notepad. After a month or two, review the notepad to see how many impressions you got right and wrong about the people you met.

338

9. **Practice Intuition Exercises.** You can learn a skill that requires you to think creatively such dancing, playing music or painting. You can do physical exercise to stimulate your intuition. Watch intuition videos clips on *YouTube.com.* Take the time to practice the activities above to improve your intuition. Use your intuitive ability or it will slowly become less effective.

10. **Practice Writing an Intuition Journal.** You can keep track of your flashes of insight about people with an electronic journal. Look for a pattern with your intuitions. Do the intuitions come while you are working? Eating? Sleeping? Interacting with strangers? Studying? Exercising? You do not have to do anything with it. Simply record it. For example, I keep track of my intuitions on my smartphone under my memo feature. Whenever I get a flash of insight, I type it into my smartphone. I note the date; briefly describe when I received the intuition and what it is about. I also note if it was an image, a feeling or a physical sensation. I then go back periodically to review them to see how many are right or wrong.

11. **Practice Intuition Techniques.** Writer Karen Horan discusses the red light/green light technique in *"4 Ways to Tap Into Your Intuition."* She states professional spiritual and medical intuitive Marla Mitchell advises you to first use the technique in situations where you already know the answer. First, Mitchell says to visualize a traffic light system that is green and red. Green means, "yes" and red means "no." Ask yourself questions that you already know are true or false. In your mind's eye look to see if the color changes based on your answer. Once you get the hang of it, use the technique in situations where you do not know the answer. This exercise teaches you to trust your intuitions. You can review the article at: http://life.gaiam.com/article/4-ways-tap-your-intuition.

READING PERSONAL ITEMS EXERCISES

In the BBC Series *Sherlock*, Actor Benedict Cumberbatch as Holmes deduces information about Watson's brother from a mobile phone.[77] Holmes observed the model, age, scuff marks, scratches and engraving on the device. He then infers from the facts that the phone belonged to Watson's alcoholic brother, who separated from his wife.

First, practice with your own personal item. Look at it to see if you can deduce anything from it. Since it is your phone, you can verify it immediately.

Second, ask a friend to lend you his or her phone and do the same. Ask the friend to verify any deductions you make.

Third, ask a co-worker or neighbor to let you analyze their phone. You can use this book as an excuse to analyze the phone. Do this with all the personal items listed below.

The purpose of the following exercises is to help you develop the ability to read a stranger's personal belongings. The exercises below will improve your ability to analyze inanimate objects. Remember the first, second and third basic questions as you do the exercises.

Practice With Everyday Items:

1. **Smartphone.** Practice analyzing a smartphone to see if you can determine the owner's personality and characteristics. Look at it to see if you can deduce anything from it. Note the wear and tear on the phone, look for any fingerprints, dents, scratches or engravings.

---

[77] Benedict Cumberbatch's reading Watson's cellphone is based on Watson's pocket watch and Holmes's reading of it in *The Sign of Four*.

Note the model, features, whether its password enabled, the phone case and other characteristics. Try to guess the owner's age, gender, right or left handedness, financial status, education level, whether the phone is used for business or personal reasons and so forth. The more you practice, the better you will get at deducing devices such as tablets and smartphones.

2. **Umbrella.** Look at it to see if you can deduce anything from it. Try to guess the owner's age, gender, race, right or left-handedness and financial status, education level. Note the wear and tear on the umbrella, look for any marks, stains, dents, scratches or engravings. Is it wet or dry? Does it have any damage? Note the style, color, age, whether its manual or push-button and whether it has a wood, plastic or metal handle.

3. **Pocketbook.** Note the wear and tear on the purse, look for any marks, stains or scratches. Note the style, color, model, age and whether it has a designer label. What size is it? Small? Medium? Large? Does it have straps? What type of purse is it? Does the woman use it for business? Personal? Is it for dressing up? Casual? Is it a practical handbag? Take an educated guess on what type of woman would purchase and use it. Can you guess her age, race, personality or financial status?

4. **Gloves.** Note the wear and tear on the gloves, look for any marks, stains or rips. Note the size, style, color, gender and whether it has a designer label. What type of material is it? Leather? Suede? Cotton? Cloth? Does it have fur on the inside? Does the person wear it for work? Personal? Is it for dressing up? Casual? Is it a sports glove? Take an educated guess on what type of person would purchase and use it. Can you guess person's gender, age, race, personality or financial status?

5. **Backpack.** What type of backpack is it? Does the person use it for school? Work? Business? Recreation? Sports? Note the wear and tear on the backpack, look for any marks, stains or rips. Note the size, style, color, gender and whether it has a designer label or not. Does it have straps? A handle? Wheels? What type of material is it? Leather? Suede? Cotton? Cloth? What is inside it? Books? Clothes? Sneakers? Laptop computer? Take an educated guess on what type of person would purchase and use it. Can you guess person's gender, age, race, personality or financial status from looking at the backpack?

6. **Hat.** What type of hat is it? Work hat? Cap? Derby? Dress hat? Casual? Business? Does it belong to a man, woman or child? Note the wear and tear on the hat, look for any marks, stains or rips. Note the size, style, color, and whether it has a designer label or not. What type of material is it? Leather? Suede? Cotton? Cloth? Take an educated guess on what type of person would purchase and use it. Can you guess person's age, race, personality or financial status from looking at the hat?

7. **Eyeglasses.** What type of eyeglasses is it? Does the person use the eyeglasses for school? Work? Business? Fun? Note the wear and tear on the eyeglasses; look for any dirt, marks or damage. Note the style, color, gender and whether it has a designer label or not. Does it have straps? What type of metal is it? Plastic? Chrome? Take an educated guess on what type of person would purchase and use it. Can you guess person's gender, age, race, personality or financial status from looking at the eyeglasses?

8. **Watch.** What type of watch is it? Does the person use it for school? Work? Business? Fun? Sports? Note the wear and tear on the watch, look for any marks, dirt or

damage. Note the style, model, color, gender and whether it has a designer label or not. Does it have a monogram or initials? What type of metal is it? Plastic? Titanium? Steel? Iron? Take an educated guess on what type of person would purchase and use it. Can you guess person's gender, age, race, personality or financial status from looking at the watch?

9. **Jewelry.** What type of jewelry is it? Diamonds? Pearls? Silver? Gold? Does the person wear it to work? Entertainment? Casual? Note the wear and tear on the jewelry, look for any marks, dents or scratches. Note the style, color, gender and whether it is real or fake. Is it designer jewelry? Take an educated guess on what type of person would purchase and use it. Can you guess person's gender, age, race, personality or financial status from looking at the jewelry?

10. **Footwear.** What type of footwear is it? Boots? Shoes? Sandals? Sneakers? Are the toes square, round, open or pointy? Does the person wear it to school? Work? Business? Sports? Entertainment? Is it a medical shoe? Is the footwear casual? Dress up? Note the wear and tear on the footwear. Look for any dirt, stains or scuffs marks. Note the size, style, color, gender and whether it is designer footwear or not. Does the footwear have straps? Buttons? Buckles? Laces? How does the person tie the laces? What type of material is it? Leather? Suede? Cotton? Cloth? Canvas? How high is the heel? Does it have a heel? Is the footwear cheap or expensive? Take an educated guess on what type of person would purchase it. Can you guess person's gender, age, race, personality or financial status from looking at the footwear?

HANDWRITING EXERCISES

The purpose of the following exercises is to help you analyze handwriting in a practical way. The following exercises do not rely on association or magical thinking. They rely on the four basic questions and eight principles. Keep them in mind as you do the exercises below:

1. **Practice Making Educated Guesses.** When you analyze a stranger's handwriting, make an educated guess regarding the person's age, gender or educational level. Look for signs in the writing that give hints. Practice looking at the writing and guess how old the person is or whether they are male or female. For example, a person who writes about events or people from the 1970s and 1980s is probably in their late thirties or forties. Pay attention to the words the stranger uses in the writing. People no longer use certain words or phrases from the 1970s or 1980s when they speak. You will find this is one possible clue to a person's age. If a writer continually expresses female-oriented terminology in the writing, you may reasonably infer the writer is female. For the most part, sloppy people tend to have sloppy writing and neat people tend to have neat writing. Deduce the handwriting based on what you see. For example, look at the writing surface, whether they are right or left handed, type of writing device used, when they wrote it, where they wrote it and so forth.

2. **Practice Comparing Handwriting Samples.** Go to *the science of email* website at www.csiro.au/helix/ sciencemail/ attitudes/handwriting.html. Read the tutorial on handwriting analysis, and then follow the instructions for doing an actual handwriting comparison. You will need materials such as paper, a pen and ruler. The exercise will have you comparing letter tops and slants. The purpose of the exercise is to help you identify

a specific person's handwriting or detect someone's fraudulent handwriting. The exercise has several handwriting samples for you to use.

3. **Practice Looking for Handwriting Elements.** Train yourself to look for elements in handwriting not personality traits. The handwriting elements are the characteristic way a person writes. In other words, the shape, alignment, spacing and style in writing are similar. You will need the tools of the trade to do a good handwriting examination — a ruler, a document, a protractor and magnifying lenses. David A. Katz has an online article entitled *"Handwriting Analysis"* that discusses how to analyze handwriting to detect authenticity or fraud. For example, one exercise in the article instructs you to write your signature five times. Then write your signature exactly from the fifth sample. Ask a friend to write your signature exactly as you did in the fifth sample. Then he instructs you to use the data and results checklist in the article. You can review the online article at http://www.chymist.com/ handwriting %20analysis.pdf.

4. **Practice Deducing Mobile Technology.** Scientists state that you can tell a lot about a person from how they use e-mail, text messages and twitter. In a recent study from *Brigham Young University*, researchers found that people who lie take longer to write responses to text messages. The researchers also discovered that people become more deceitful when they do not have face-to-face communications. The same practical techniques you use to analyze handwriting, you can use to analyze text messages, emails and twitter messages.

5. **Practice Examining Documents.** An online article discusses how to analyze handwriting using the technique of document examination. The article

describes the materials you need, the procedure and handwriting characteristics to look for when doing it. It also has handwriting samples and a form for you to complete. You can see the article and practice examining documents at the website: http://www.chymist.com /handwriting%20analysis.pdf. The National Archives website also has a form that their educational staff department help create. The *written document analysis worksheet*' lists factors (document type, characteristics, dates, etc.) you can use to analyze documents. Review the worksheet and print it at http://www.archives.gov /education/lessons/worksheets/. Watch a movie such as *Zodiac (2007)*, to get in the mindset of questioning documents. The movie discusses question document analysis at length and it is crucial to the storyline. Go to websites such as http://www.asqde.org/ and http://www.aafs.org/ to learn more about question document analysis. You can also study question document related books such as *Scientific Examination of Questioned Documents, Second Edition* by Jan Seaman Kelly and Brian S. Lindblom. In addition, check out *Handwriting Identification: Facts and Fundamentals* by Roy A. Huber and A.M. Headrick.

6. **Listen To Radio Talk Shows.** Several talk shows such as *The Steve Harvey Morning Show* on 107.5 WBLS, discuss love letters received from listeners. The listeners send the letters in asking for advice about their romantic situations. Mr. Harvey and his co-hosts read the love letters on air and decipher the letters' meaning through common sense and reason. Listen to the radio talk shows to see if you can figure out how the radio hosts analyze the letters to give advice to the listener.

Sherlock Scan Checklist

1. WHAT DO I OBSERVE?

Physical Characteristics (Look for Pressure Marks, Indentations, Appearance Changes)

Height: _____ Weight: _____ Age: _____ Race: _____ Gender: _____
(Short, Tall, etc.) (In Pounds)   (From 1 to 115) (Asia, White, etc.) (Male, Female, Gay)
Body Type: _____ Posture: _____ Complexion: _____
(Muscular, Thin, Heavy) (Erect, Stoop, Slump, Loose) (Pale, Rough, Shallow, Florid, etc.)
Head: _____ Hair: _____ Mustache/Beard: _____
(Broad, Narrow, etc.)   (Short, Long, Black, Blonde, Bald, etc.)   (Thick, Thin, Trim, etc.)
Mouth: _____ Torso: _____ Hands: _____
(Teeth, Lips, Jaw, etc.) (Hips, Chest, Arms, etc.)   (Calluses, Nails, Rough, Soft, Bony)
Walk: _____ Feet: _____
(Fast, Slow, Aggressive, Casual, Unnatural)   (Small, Medium, Large, Calluses, Bruises)
Face:_____
(Eyes Color, Eyebrows, Ears, Nose, Forehead, etc. Look at the muscles around the face.)
Distinctive Marks/Behavior: _____
(Scars, Birthmarks, Tattoos, Bruises, Scratches, Habitual Mannerisms, Irrational Actions)
Speech: _____
(Tone, Pitch, Talk Fast, Slow, Stutter, Accent, Slang, Jargon, Verbal Tics, etc.)

Appearance (Look for Scuff Marks, Stains, Bulges, Dirt, Rips, Wear & Tear, Holes, etc.)

Neat: _____ Sloppy: _____ Sporty: _____ Casual: _____ Sexy: _____
Expensive: _____ Business: _____ Cultural: _____ Dressy: _____
Designer: _____ Work: _____ Party: _____ Sleeves: _____
Trouser Knees: _____ Pockets: _____ Creases: _____ Cuffs: _____
Outerwear: _____ Footwear: _____
(Coats, Jackets, etc.)   (Boots, Sneakers, Shoes, Sandals, Pumps, etc.)
Headwear: _____ Accessories: _____ Jewelry: _____
(Hats, Caps, Scarves)   (Gloves, Handbags, Canes, etc.)   (Rings, Necklaces, Bracelets)

Behavior (Details, Patterns, Anything Missing, Not Fitting, Obvious, Inconsistencies, etc.)

Facial Expressions: _____
(Look For Facial Expressions: Joy, Anger, Sadness, Fear, Disgust, Surprise, Contempt, etc.)
Eye Movements: _____
(Look At The Direction The Eyes Are Moving To Gauge The Stranger's Interests, etc.)
Micro Expressions: _____
(Look For Split Second Facial Expressions: Joy, Anger, Sadness, Fear, Disgust, Surprise, etc.)
Body Language: _____
(Look at how the Stranger is Standing, Sitting, Walking, Moving, Gesturing with Hands, etc.)

First Impression: _____
(Look At Overall Appearance & Behavior, Cluster Of Details, Gestures, Speech, Fashion, etc.)

2. WHAT CAN I DEDUCE?

What do you infer from the details, facts and evidence you see? Try to determine the following from the data you have gathered:

Personality: _____ Health: _____
(Outgoing, Shy, Shrewd, Emotional, Logical)   (Smoker, Drinker, Physically Fit, etc.)
Financial Status: _____ Martial Status: _____
(Poor, Middle-Class, Wealthy, etc.)   (Single, Married, Divorced, Widowed, etc.)
Education: _____ Job/Career/Business: _____
(Junior High, High School, College, etc.)   (Manual Labor, Office Worker, Entrepreneur etc.)
Background: _____ Hobby/Recreation: _____
(Family, Neighborhood, Political, etc.)   (Sports, Dancing, Singing, Writing, Painting, etc.)
Prior Activities: _____
        (Determine What The Stranger Did Before Meeting You: shopping, working, eating, etc.)

3. HOW CAN I VERIFY IT?

Always confirm your results. As Doctor Joseph Bell stated: "Observe carefully, deduce shrewdly and confirm with evidence."

Make A Statement: _____
                        (Observe The Stranger's Reaction To What You Say)
Ask A Question: _____
                (Listen For The Answer. Were You Correct?)
Check Sources: _____
            (Check With A Friend, Witness, Website, Directory, Expert For Corroboration, etc.)
Make A Prediction: _____
                (Do A Simple Test, Conduct An Experiment, etc.)

4. WHAT DO I CONCLUDE?

Always look for the result. Check your conclusion to make sure it is correct.

Did You Consider All Possibilities? _____
Did You Interpret Anything Wrong? _____
Did You Have All Information? _____
Did You Commit A Logical Fallacy? _____
Were You Bias In Any Way? _____
Were You Right? Yes _____ No _____ Partially _____ Why? _____
If Wrong, Did You Recheck Your Conclusions? _____
What Is Your Final Conclusion? _____
_____

Books For Further Reading

You can find many of the books or eBooks listed below online through *Amazon.com* or other digital booksellers.

Questions

Liebow, M., Ely, March 2007. *Dr. Joe Bell,* Popular Press.

Sobel, Andrew, February 2012. *Power Questions: Build Relationships, Win New Business, and Influence Others,* Wiley.

Browne, Neil, M. & Keeley, Stuart, July 2011. *Asking the Right Questions: A Guide to Critical Thinking,* 10th Edition, Pearson.

Fadem, Terry, December 2008. *The Art of Asking: Ask Better Questions, Get Better Answers,* FT Press.

Leeds, Dorothy, September 2000. *The 7 Powers of Questions: Secrets to Successful Communication in Life and at Work,* 1st Edition, Perigee Trade.

Observation

Smith, Denis, O, January 1998. *The Chronicles of Sherlock Holmes, Volume 2,* Calabash Press.

Fast, Julius, January 1970. *Body Language,* Pocket Books.

Gosling, Sam, May 2009. *Snoop: What Your Stuff Says About You,* Basic Books.

Tieger, Paul & Barron-Tieger, Barbara, February 1999. *The Art of SpeedReading People: How to Size People Up and Speak Their Language*, Little, Brown and Company.

Rowland, Ian, March 2014. *The Full Facts Book Of Cold Reading*, Ian Rowland Limited.

Tradecraft, 2002. *Tradecraft: The Art & Science of Mentalism Cold Reading*, eBook, Trickcraft.com.

Laurence, Alison, March 2011. *The Forensic Psychologist's Casebook: Psychological Profiling & Criminal Investigation*, Willan.

Bandler, Richard, Grinder, John, Andreas, Steve, 1979. *"Frogs into Princes: Neuro Linguistic Programming (NLP)*, Real People Press.

Driver, Janine, 2014. *You Can't Lie To Me: The Revolutionary Program to Supercharge Your Inner Lie Detector and Get to the Truth*, reprint edition, HarperOne.

Meyer, Pamela, September 2011. *Liespotting: Proven Techniques to Detect Deception*, St. Martin's Griffin.

Darwin, Charles R. 1872/1998. *The Expression of the Emotions in Man and Animals*, 3rd ed., Oxford University Press.

Ekman, Paul, January 2009. *Telling Lies: Clues to Deceit in the Marketplace, Politics and Marriage*, W. W. Norton & Company, revised.

Ekman, Paul, March 2007. *Emotions Revealed, Second Edition: Recognizing Faces and Feelings to Improve Communication and Emotional Life*, Holt Paperbacks.

Ekman, Paul and Wallace V. Friesen, 1975. *Unmasking the Face: a Guide to Recognizing Emotions from Facial Clues*, Prentice-Hall.

Ekman Paul & Erika L. Rosenberg, eds., 1997. *What The Face Reveals: Basic and Applied Studies of Spontaneous Expression Using the Facial Action Coding System (FACS)*, Oxford University Press.

Morris, Desmond, 1979. *Manwatching: A Field Guide to Human Behavior,* Harry N Abrams.

Morris, Desmond, 2002. *Peoplewatching: The Desmond Morris Guide to Body Language.* London: Vintage Books.

Navarro, Joe, 2011. *Clues to Deceit: A Practical List*, Amazon Kindle.

Navarro, Joe, 2009. *The Psychology of Body Language*, Amazon Kindle.

Navarro, Joe, 2008. *What Every Body Is Saying*, New York, Harper Collins.

Pease, Allen & Barbara, July 2006. *The Definitive Book of Body Language*, Bantam.

Walters, Stan, May 2000. *The Truth About Lying: How to Spot a Lie and Protect Yourself from Deception,* Sourcebooks, 1st edition.

Laird, Dr. Donald & Eleanor, 1951. *Sizing Up People,* McGraw-Hill. Read it free online at: http://www.archive.org/stream/ sizingup people00lairrich/ sizinguppeople00lairrich_djvu.txt.

Jung, Carl, Hull R., Baynes H, October 1996. *Psychological Types (The Collected Works of C. G. Jung, Vol. 6), (Bollingen Series XX),* Princeton University Press.

Logical Thinking

Smith, Daniel, October 2013. *How to Think Like Sherlock: Improve Your Powers of Observation, Memory and Deduction,* Michael O'Mara.

Konnikova, Maria, December 2013. *Mastermind: How to Think Like Sherlock Holmes,* Penguin Books.

Louise Blackwood, *The Deduction Guide*, August 2014. Amazon.com

Taz, Rai, 2013, *The Art of Deduction, ebook.* Find it at: *http://www.artofdeduction.com.*

Young, Gregg, 2010. *Reasoning Backwards: Sherlock Holmes' Guide to Effective Problem Solving*, Atlas Books.

Carroll, Robert Todd, August 2003. *The Skeptic's Dictionary: A Collection of Strange Beliefs, Amusing Deceptions, and Dangerous Delusions*, Wiley.

Carroll, Robert Todd, July 2012. *Becoming a Critical Thinker: A Guide for the New Millennium (2nd Edition),* Pearson Learning Solutions.

Burton, Robert. 2008. *On Being Certain: Believing You Are Right Even When You're Not.* St. Martin's Press.

Dawes, Robyn M. *Everyday Irrationality: How Pseudo-Scientists, Lunatics and the Rest of Us Systematically Fail to Think Rationally* (Westview Press 2003).

Gilovich, Thomas. *How We Know What Isn't So*: *The Fallibility of Human Reason in Everyday Life* (New York: The Free Press, 1993).

Kida, Thomas, 2006. *Don't Believe Everything You Think: The 6 Basic Mistakes We Make in Thinking.* Prometheus.

Clark, Theo & Jef, 2005. *Humbug! The Skeptic's Field Guide to Spotting Logical Fallacies in Thinking,* Nifty Books.

Sherlock Holmes (author), W. Lambert (editor). The Whole Art of Deduction, Scot & Siliclone. Free eBook. You can read it at: http://siliclone.tripod.com/books/whole1.html.

Specialized Knowledge

O'Brien, James, January 2013. *The Scientific Sherlock Holmes: Cracking the Case with Science and Forensics,* Oxford University Press.

Wagner, E. J., 2007. *The Science of Sherlock Holmes: From Baskerville Hall to the Valley of Fear, the Real Forensics Behind the Great Detective's Greatest Cases*, Wiley, 1st edition.

Brent Turvey, 1999. Criminal Profiling: An Introduction to Behavioral Evidence Analysis, Academic Press, 451, pp.

Dutton, Tim, 2006. *Streetwise Guide to Conducting Hardball Investigations,* Thomas Investigative Publications.

Crewse, Donald, 2002. *The Business of Private Investigations: How to Develop The Cases, The Clientele and Conduct the Investigations,* Thomas Investigative Publications.

McMahon, Rory, August 2012. *Practical Handbook for Professional Investigators, Second Edition,* CRC Press.

Experience

Carnegie, Dale, October 1998. *How to Win Friends & Influence People,* Pocket Books.

Reid, Rebecca, Kindle Edition. *Self-Discipline - How to Develop Good Habits, Self-Control, Beat Procrastination and Live an Exceptional Life,* Amazon Digital Services.

Weinzimmer, Laurence & McConoughey Jim, October 2012. *The Wisdom of Failure: How to Learn the Tough Leadership Lessons Without Paying the Price,* 1st Edition. Jossey-Bass.

Hallinan, Joseph, T., February 2010. *Why We Make Mistakes: How We Look Without Seeing, Forget Things in Seconds, and Are All Pretty Sure We Are Way Above Average,* Reprint Edition. Broadway Books.

Covey, Stephen, R., November 2013. *The 7 Habits of Highly Effective People: Powerful Lessons in Personal Change,* Deluxe Edition, Simon & Schuster.

Listening

Nirenberg, Jesse, S., December 2011. *Getting Through To People,* Literary Licensing, LLC.

Ekman, Paul. 1985. *Telling Lies: Clues to Deceit in the Marketplace, Politics and Marriages.* New York: W.W. Norton & Co.

Ford, Charles V. 1996. *Lies! Lies! Lies!: the Psychology of Deceit.* Washington, D.C.: American Psychiatric Press, Inc.

Inbau, Fred E. et. al. 2001. *Criminal Interrogation and Confessions, 4th. Ed.* Gaithersburg, MD: Aspen Publishers, Inc.

Schafer, John R. and Joe Navarro. 2004. *Advanced Interviewing Techniques.* Springfield, Il. Charles C. Thomas Publisher.

Vrij, A, 2008. *Detecting lies and deceit: Pitfalls and opportunities (2nd ed.).* New York, NY: John Wiley & Sons.

Imagination

Liu, Eric, Noppe-Brandon, Scott, April 2011. *Imagination First: Unlocking the Power of Possibility,* 1st Edition, Jossey-Bass.

Carson, Shelley, September 2012. *Your Creative Brain: Seven Steps to Maximize Imagination, Productivity and Innovation in Your Life,* Jossey-Bass.

Ciaramicoli, Arthur & Ketcham, Katherine, April 2000. *The Power of Empathy: A Practical Guide to Creating Intimacy, Self-Understanding and Lasting Love in Your Life,* Dutton Adult.

McLaren, Karia, October 2013. *The Art of Empathy: A Complete Guide to Life's Most Essential Skill,* 1st Edition, Sounds True.

Jacoboni, Marco, June 2009. *Mirroring People: The Science of Empathy and How We Connect with Others*, 1st Edition, Picador.

Memory

Foer, Joshua, February 2012. *Moonwalking with Einstein*, reprint edition. Penguin Books.

Yates, Frances, April 2001. *The Art of Memory* by Frances Yates, reprint edition, University of Chicago Press.

Green, Cynthia, January 2001. *Total Memory Workout: 8 Easy Steps to Maximum Memory Fitness,* Bantam.

Arden, John, July 2002. *Improving Your Memory For Dummies, 1st. Edition*, For Dummies.

O'Brien, Dominic, January 2014. *How to Develop a Brilliant Memory Week by Week: 52 Proven Ways to Enhance Your Memory Skills,* Watkins Publishing.

Allen, Robert, September 2004. *Improve Your Memory*, Collins & Brown.

Smile, Lewis, The Memory Palace: Learn Anything and Everything. Kindle edition, Amazon Digital Services, Inc.

White, Ron, November 2011. *Memory Improvement: How To Improve Your Memory In Just 30 Days.* Kindle Edition, Laurenzana Press.

Vaughn, Dean, *April 2007. How to Remember Anything: The Proven Total Memory Retention System,* St. Martin's Griffin.

Intuition

CUNY philosophy professor Massimo Pigliucci explores in a chapter of *Answers for Aristotle: How Science and Philosophy Can Lead Us to A More Meaningful Life.*

Chabris, Christopher, Simons, Daniel, June 2011. *The Invisible Gorilla: How Our Intuitions Deceive Us,* reprint edition, Harmony Press.

Gladwell, Malcolm, April 2007. *Blink: The Power of Thinking Without Thinking,* Back Bay Books, 1st edition.

Kahneman, Daniel, April 2013. *Thinking, Fast and Slow,* reprint edition, Farrar, Straus and Giroux.

Klein, Gary, June 2004. *The Power of Intuition: How to Use Your Gut Feelings to Make Better Decisions at Work,* Crown Business.

Pigliucci, Massimo, October 2012. *Answers for Aristotle: How Science and Philosophy Can Lead Us to A More Meaningful Life,* Basic Books.

Sadler-Smith, Eugene, November 2009. *The Intuitive Mind: Profiting from the Power of Your Sixth Sense,* Wiley.

Ickes, Williams, November 2003. *Everyday Mind Reading: Understanding What Other People Think and Feel, First Edition,* Prometheus Books.

Handwriting Analysis

Santoy, Claude, August 2005. *The ABCs of Handwriting Analysis: The Complete Guide to Techniques & Interpretations,* Da Capo Press.

Beyerstein, Barry, 1992. *The Write Stuff,* Prometheus Books.

Dresbold, Michelle, 2008. *Sex, Lies and Handwriting: A Top Expert Reveals the Secrets Hidden in Your Handwriting,* Free Press, reprint edition.

Lowe, Sheila, January 2007. *The Complete Idiot's Guide to Handwriting Analysis, second Edition, Alpha.*

Seifer, Marc, October 2008. *The Definitive Book of Handwriting Analysis: The Complete Guide to Interpreting Personalities, Detecting Forgeries and Revealing Brain Activity Through the Science of Graphology,* Career Press.

Amend, Karen Kristen, Mary Ruiz, August 2011. *Handwriting Analysis: The Complete Basic Book,* Pentagon Press.

Rodgers, Vimala, March 2000. *Your Handwriting Can Change Your Life,* Touchstone.

D'Gabriel, Treyce, August 2011. *The Only Handwriting Analysis Book You Will Ever Need,* Center of Forensic Profiling.

McNichol, Andrea, Nelson, Jeff, 1991. *Handwriting Analysis: Putting It to Work for You,* Contemporary Books.

References, Sources & Citations

The following is a list of articles and sources the author consulted, reviewed and relied on during his research in writing the book:

Introduction

Information from the short Sir Arthur Conan Doyle biography came from an online biographical sketch written by Daniel Stashower entitled *"Such is the life I have led: Arthur Conan Doyle and his World"* for the Conan Doyle Estate Ltd. Website. The author, according to Jon Lellenberg from the Conan Doyle Estate website, wrote the best Conan Doyle biography in recent decades, *Teller of Tales: The Life of Sir Arthur Conan Doyle* (2000). You can view the brief biography at http:// www.conandoyleestate.co.uk/ index.php/biography. You can also find a great biography of Conan Doyle at *The Wide World of Sherlock Holmes* from *The Sherlock Holmes Society of London.* You can review the Sir Arthur Conan Doyle biography at http://Sherlock-holmes.org.uk/world/conan_doyle.php.

Chapter 1: Questions

"How to Ask Intelligent Questions With Impact" is an online article by Gary Lockwood www.bizsuccess.com/articles/ask.htm.

The *"Questioning"* Section on the *Changing Minds* website has 26 subsections on various kinds of questions.www.changingminds.org /techniques/questioning/kipling_questions.htm.

The *"Questioning Techniques"* page on the Mind Tools website has an excellent description on how to ask questions. See it at the website: www.mindtools.com/pages/article/newTMC_88.htm.

PhD Anne Marie Helmenstine writes about the steps of the scientific method on the about.com website. See it at the website: www.about.com/od/sciencefairprojects/a/Scientific-Method-Steps.htm.

Scientific Buddies has an excellent graph of the steps in the scientific method at the website: www.sciencebuddies.org/ sciencefairprojects /project_scientific_method.shtml#overviewofthescientificmethod.

The Scientific Detective, Sherlock Holmes, Solves the Case of the Sign of Four is an article written by Carl L. Heifetz. He seeks to establish that Sherlock Holmes's personality and the methods he used were similar to a research scientist. Article was published in *The Wigmore Street Post Office, Issue No. 11, spring, 1998, p 3-9; published in The Hounds Collection, Vol. 4, April 1999, p 5-12.*

Morelli, Freud and Sherlock Holmes: Clues and Scientific Method is an article written by Carlo Ginzburg (with an introduction by Anna Davin). It seeks compare three different fields (art, psychoanalysis, detection) and establishes how they relate to the scientific method and knowledge. *Ombre Rosse (Red Shadows) 39, June 1979.*

Chapter 2: Observation

The online article *The Real Sherlock Holmes* gives a brief synopsis of Dr. Joseph Bell and his influence on Sir Arthur Conan Doyle. You can review it at the website Sherlock Holmes and Watson: http:// www.sherlockandwatson.com/the%20real%20sherlock%20 holmes.html.

Sherlock Holmes and Dr. Joseph Bell is an online article from the website *The Chronicles of Sir Arthur Conan Doyle.* You can review it at http://www.siracd.com/work_bell.shtml.

Dr. Joseph Bell, A Model for Sherlock Holmes is an online article written by Tom McQuain. It gives a brief summary of Dr. Joseph Bell's influence on Conan Doyle. You can review it at http://www.diogenes-club.com/joebell.htm.

The Straight Dope website answers a fan mail about whether Sherlock Holmes actually existed. www.straightdope.com/ columns/read /2088/did-sherlock-holmes-really-exist.

Observe Carefully, Deduce Shrewdly: Dr. Joseph Bell is an online article from Dr. Katherine Ramsland. It discusses Joseph Bell's methods and his impact on the forensic field. You can review it on the *American Board of Forensic Dentistry* website at the website: http://www.abfd.us/ articles/news/3/15/Observe-Carefully-Deduce-Shrewdly-Dr-Joseph-Bell.

"How to Increase Your Powers of Observation" by Laurel Ahnert. This article outlines five steps to improve your observational skills while investigating people and situations. See it at the website: www.ehow.com/ how_8237706_increase-powers-observation.html.

"Observation Still Matters" by Ronald L. Mendell. This article discusses the how to improve your observational skills during an investigation. www.pimall.com/nais/n.obser.html.

Improving Crime Observation Skills is an online article written by Lt. James Perez for the crime watch section of *Connecticut News*. It gives common sense citizen tips for improving your observational skills during a crime. You can review it at the website: http://blog.ctnews.com /crimewatch/2011/11/28/improving-crime-observation-skills/.

7 Ways To A More Observant Life is an online article written by Susheel Chandrahdhas. The article gives seven tips photographers can use to be more observant. You can review it at the website: http://www.beyondphototips.com /2008/11/28/7-ways-to-a-more-observant-life/.

Powers of Observation and Concentration is an online article written by Sheila L. Stephens for private investigators. It outlines steps you can take to improve your ability to observe people, places and things. You can review it at http://www.netplaces.com/private-investigation/do-you-have-the-right-stuff/.

How to Begin People Watching is an online article from *wikihow.com*. It outlines steps you can take improve your people watching skills. You can review it at: http://www.wikihow.com/Begin-People-Watching.

At *Businessballs.com*, Alan Chapman has a detailed section devoted to body language. Although he provides no scientific citations, the informative is interesting. http://www.businessballs.com/body-language.htm#body-language-introduction.

The *Wikipedia* section on observation lists the various kinds of observation (such as confirmation bias, processing bias, etc.). It briefly discusses the scientific method and gives links to other sources of information. http://en.wikipedia.org/wiki/Observation.

"What is Your Body Language Saying" by Susan Smith (*RealSimple.com*) lists the various facial expresses and gestures people use to read each other.http://www.cnn.com/2011/LIVING/01/06/rs.body.language/index.html?hpt=Sbin.

"How to Read People: Preparing to Read" by Life Training compares reading people to a four layered onion. It also discusses the barriers to reading people effectively. You can learn more at the website: http://www.lifetrainingonline.com /blog/how_to_read_people.htm.

"How to Develop Sherlock Holmes Like Powers of Observation and Deduction." This article discusses Holmes observation, deduction, knowledge and memory techniques. It also draws from *Mastermind: How to Think Like Sherlock Holmes* by Maria Konnikova. You can read the article at the website: http://lifehacker.com/5960811/how-to-develop-sherlock-holmes+like-powers-of-observation-and-deduction.

"How to Pick a Plaintiff Jury by Nonverbal Indicators" by Constance Bernstein discusses how to pick an 'open' jury through body language. The discussion on sizing up jurors by their shoes, clothing and accessories is particularly interesting. You can find the article at: http://www.plaintiffmagazine.com /Oct07%20articles/Bernstein_How%20to%20pick%20a%20plaintiff%20jury%20by%20nonverbal%20indicators_Plaintiff%20magazine.pdf.

"Body Language: Explained" by Annie Finnigan. This article discusses communicating non-verbally at: http://www.womansday.com /life/etiquette-manners/reading-body-language.

"Understanding Body Language" by Kendra Cherry breaks down the different ways people used body language to send messages to each other. You can find the article at the website: http://psychology.about.com/od/nonverbalcommunication /ss/understanding-body-language.htm.

"Using Body Language" at the *Changing Minds* website has over 75 pages of body language information. Find it at: http://changingminds.org /techniques/body/body_language.htm.

"Body language vs. Micro-Expressions," by Joe Narrivao discusses body language. He draws from his 25-year experience as a former FBI agent and research in the field to give a precise overview of micro-expressions and how people use them. You can find the article at: http://www.psychologytoday.com/blog/spycatcher/201112/body-language-vs-micro-expressions.

The website *readingbodylanguage.com* has a detailed section devoted to body language. Although it provides no scientific citations, the informative is interesting. You can find it at http://readingbodylanguagenow.com.

"Why Are We So Bad at Detecting Lies" by Bella De Palo, PhD in an online *Psychology Today* article, discusses why most people are not good at detecting lies. She gives her arguments at: http://www.psychologytoday.com/blog/living-single/201305/why-are-we-so-bad-detecting-lies.

"Don't Believe The Lie to Me Hype" in a online *Washington Post* article, staff writer Neely Tucker interviews experts Paul Ekman and Maureen O' Sullivan (among others). The conclusion draw is that most people cannot tell lies from the truth. Read the article at: http://www.washingtonpost.com /wp-dyn/content/article/ 2009/02 /12/AR2009021204220 .html?hpid =artsliving.

"How to Detect Lies" is from a website named *'blifaloo,'* which means beautiful. The online article gives a basic introduction about lie detection. Another article on the website discusses the principles of eye movement and lying, based on NLP principles and experiments. Go to http://www.blifaloo.com/info/lies.php.

"Detecting Deception" a 2004 article by Rachel Adelson published online in the APA website discusses lie detection with several experts. According to the article, studies and research link pupil size and lip pressing to lies and not posture or blinking. Review the article at: http://www.apa.org/monitor/julaug04/detecting.aspx.

"The Truth about Lie Detection" is a pull no punches online article by Joe Navarro published by *Psychology Today*. In the article, he argues convincingly against several lie detection myths and beliefs. He argues for example, that people are no better than chance at catching lies. He asserts that DNA evidence freed many innocent people that judges, prosecutors and juries truly believed were guilty. He also argues against lie detection by so-called experts, studies, television, micro-expressions and lie detection machines. Find the article at: http://www.psychologytoday.com /blog/spycatcher /201112/body-language-vs-micro-expressions.

The Eyes Don't Have It: Lie Detection and Neuro-Linguistic Programming. Wiseman R, Watt C, ten Brinke L, Porter S, Couper S-L, et al. (2012). PLoS ONE 7(7): e40259. doi:10.1371/journal.pone. Five researchers conducted three studies to test the claims of Neuro-Linguistic Programming (NLP) that certain eye-movements are reliable indicators of lying. The studies found no significant support to the NLP claims. See it at the website: http://www.plosone.org/ article /info%3Adoi%2F10.1371%2F journal.pone.0040259.

Looking for Clues is an online article from the *Inspector Insight* website that discusses Sherlock Holmes's observation and deductive skills. It draws from the modern BBC version of *Sherlock* when giving examples and making its points. You can review the article at: http://www.inspectorinsight.com /insight/looking-for-clues/.

Chapter 3: Deduction

The *"Types of Reasoning"* Section on the *Changing Times* website has 17 subsections on various kinds of reasoning. I found especially interesting the sections on induction, deduction, abduction and if-then condition reasoning. You can check out the website at: http://changingminds.org/ disciplines/argument/types_ reasoning /types_reasoning.htm.

The *"Fallacy List"* from the website *Skeptics Field Guide* lists 48 logical fallacies people use in arguments and thinking. The site also has a paperback and free eBook version of the eBook version of *Humbug! The skeptics' field guide to spotting fallacies in thinking.* You can view the website at: http://www.skepticsfieldguide.net/2005/01/fallacy-list.html.

Regina Pacelli is an author who has written three books. Her website links to several resources such as critical thinking, creatively, decision making and intuition. I used her website to find other links to topics I needed to research. You can check it out at the website: http://www.reginapacelli.com/create-solve-decide-resources/ detective-investigation-knowhow.html.

"You Know My Method": A Juxtaposition of Charles S. Pierce and Sherlock Holmes written by Max H. Fisch. It analyzes how Philosopher Charles Pierce and Sherlock Holmes are similar in abduction. Read it at: http://www.visual-memory.co.uk/b_resources/abduction.html

"How to Think Like Sherlock Holmes" is an article written by Michael Parker on his blog *Dreamspear.* Check it out at: http://www.dreamspear.co.uk/blog/how-to-think-like-sherlock-holmes/.

Charles King has an interesting article entitled *"How to Think."* He discusses argumentation and reasoning at the website: http://www9.georgetown.edu /faculty/kingch/How_to_Think.htm.

Sherlock Holmes and Probabilistic Induction is a paper presented by Soshichi Uchii to the *Center for Philosophy of Science.* The paper discusses Sherlock Holmes's skills as a logician and the various ways he reasoned using induction, the method of elimination, hypothesis formation, analytical and synthetic reasoning and the balance of probabilities. I reviewed it before writing the ten rules of deduction in chapter three. You can review the paper at http://philsci-archive.pitt.edu/167/1/holmes.html.

Why the Sherlock Holmes Approach to Problem Solving is Wrong is an online article written by Luke Houghton. He that argues Sherlock Holmes jumped to conclusions and guessed even though he claimed he did not. You can review the article at the website: http://problemsolvingcourse.com.

How Deductive Reasoning Can Lead Us To Stupid Conclusions is an online article written by Carolyn Thomas for *The Ethical Nag.* Ms. Thomas cites an essay called *Deductive Mis-Reasoning* to show flawed deductive reasoning. She makes the point that people who use a logical deduction often fail to consider alternative conclusions consistent with the premise. You can review the article at: http://ethicalnag.org/2010/09/21/e3eudtive-reasoning/.

A Sherlock Holmes Logical Fallacy by Steven Novella is an online response posted on *The Rogues Gallery* (skeptic blog) to a reader's question. Mr. Novella provides an interesting answer to the reason by elimination rule's limitations. You can view the response at: http://theness.com   /roguesgallery/index.php/logicphilosophy/a-sherlock-holmes-logical-fallacy/.

Scientific American published a series of articles on Sherlock Holmes by author Maria Konnikova. In one article, Ms. Konnikova discusses Holmes ability to keep two lines of thought separate and not focus on unrelated information. You can find the series at the website: http://blogs.scientificamerican.com/guest-blog/2011/09/16/lessons-from-sherlock-holmes-dont-tangle-two-lines-of-thought/.

"A Practical Guide to Critical Thinking" by Grey R. Haskins presents a concise introduction to critical thinking. He describes it as a handy tool to help anyone evaluate or develop sound reasoning and arguments. You can study it at the website: *http://www.skepdic.com /essays/haskins.pdf.*

Butte College has a tip sheet for the various logical thinking processes such as induction, deduction and abduction. The tip sheets are short and to the point. See the tip sheets at: http://www.butte.edu /departments/cas/tipsheets/thinking/reasoning.htl.

The blog common sense atheism has an *Intro to Logic* index that lists 12 subjects on critical thinking. Blogger Luke Muehlhauser created the index and you can study the subjects at the website: http://commonsenseatheism.com/?p=3703.

Professor Alan Macfarlane has an interesting analysis of the Sherlock Holmes Method. I reviewed it before writing the ten rules of deduction in chapter three. You can see it at the website: http://www.alanmacfarlane.com/TEXTS/holmes.pdf.

"The Advantages and Disadvantages of Induction Reasoning" by James Jordan on the eHow website gives a basic summary of reasoning by

induction. You can view the online article at: http:// www.ehow.com/ info_8491871_advantages- disadvantages-inductive-reasoning.html.

Chapter 4: Specialized Knowledge

"Think and Grow Rich" by Napoleon Hill discusses how to obtain specialized knowledge in Chapter 5. Dr. Hill's writings influenced chapter four in this book. See it at the website: http://www.sacred-texts.com/nth/tgr/tgr10.htm.

Russian Criminal Tattoos: Breaking The Code by Will Hodgkinson discusses the secret tattoo language of Russian prisoners. He reveals the hidden meaning behind several tattoos they wear. See it at: http://www.theguardian.com/artanddesign/2010/oct/26/russian-criminal-tattoos.

"Sherlock Holmes Codes the Social Body" is an online article written by Rosemary Jann, which explains the various ways Holmes complies with the social codes of his day. See http://courses.wcupa.edu /fletcher/special/jann.htm.

Offender Profiling is an online section from *Wikipedia* that defines criminal profiling. It describes the history of profiling, explains profiling methods and controversy surrounding the subject. Review the article at: http://en.wikipedia.org/wiki/Offender_lprofiling.

"Whodunnit?" an online article by Jon Ronson details how psychological profiling is no longer held in high esteem. See http://www.guardian.co.uk/uk/2010/may/15/criminal-profiling-jon-ronson.

"Psychological Profiling 'Worse Than Useless," an online article by science correspondent Ian Sample for *The Guardian.com*. The article states experts contend profiling of killers has no real-world value, wastes police time and risks bringing the profession into disrepute. http://www.theguardian.com/science/2010/sep/14/psychological-profile-behavioural-psychology.

"Effectiveness of Criminal Profiling" by Flourish I. Abumere presents the pros and cons of criminal profiling. http://www.academia.edu /2333675/Effectiveness_of_Criminal_Profiling.

"Seeing The Invisible" is an online article on the *Science of Strategy* website, which explains how experts see things that novices cannot. You can review the article at: http://scienceofstrategy.org/main/content/seeing-invisible.

Chapter 5: Experience

"Common Sense is Neither Common Nor Sense" is an online article written by Jim Taylor, PhD for Psychology Today.com. See it at: http://www.psychologytoday.com/blog/the-power-prime/201107/common-sense-is-neither-common-nor-sense.

"Cold Reading: How to Convince Strangers You Know All About Them" is an online article written by Ray Hyman. It reveals the truth about cold reading. See it at: http://www.skepdic.com/Hyman_cold_reading.htm.

Chapter 6: Listening

"Ten Listening Tips for Better Communication" is an online article from Teachthought.com. The tips are common sense and practical (although I do not agree with Tip#3: men only use half their brains while listening. The author gave no scientific studies to back up the claim but did give a link to another writer who also did not give any supporting evidence). See it at: http://www.teachthought.com/learning/10-listening-tips-for-better-communication/.

"Listening effectively" is an online book written by John A. Kline. The author takes a 'how-to' approach to listening and states anyone can improve their listening skills. It has many practical tips and suggestions for listening better. You can view it online at the website: http://www.au.af.mil /au/awc/awcgate/kline-listen/b10ch5.htm.

"Ten Tips for Effective Listening" is an online article written by Diane Schilling for Forbes.com. The tips are common sense and practical. You can review them at the website: http://www.forbes.com/sites/womensmedia/2012/11/09/10-steps-to-effective-listening/.

Improve Your Listening: 15 Tips to Improve Your Listening by Tony Valdes posted on the Art of Manliness.com. Review it at:

http://www.artofmanliness.com/2012/05/08/listen-up-part-ii-15-techniques-to-improve-our-listening/.

Listen Up! 10 Great Tips for Better Listening from the *Work Awesome.com* website. You can see it at: http://workawesome.com/communication/10-great-tips-beter-listening/.

10 Tips to Effective & Active Listening Skills is an online article by Susie Michelle Cortright. You can see it at: http://powertochange.com/students/people/listen/.

The experts at *Changing Minds* have a section just for Listening. The section lists 16 subsections with information on various styles and types of listening, how to listen, listening habits and much more. You can view the listening section at: http://changingminds.org/techniques/listening/listening.htm.

"Airport Profilers: They're Watching Your Expressions" by Paul Shukovsky, P-I, Reporter discusses the technique TSA behavior experts use to spot deception. You can view it at the website: http://www.seattlepi.com/local /article/Airport-profilers-They-re-watching-your-1259789.php.

"Faces, Too, Are Searched at U.S. Airports" by Eric Lipton for the *New York Times.com*. The online article discusses the listening technique airport security personnel use to spot terrorists before they have a chance to strike. You can review the article online at the website: http://www.nytimes.com/2006/08/17/washington/17screeners.html?ei=5090&en=8636975a2f266b72&ex=1313467200&adxnnl=1&partner=rssuserland&emc=rss&adxnnlx=1187518129-3DxGpQM/SqCalK8gYa2eMQ &pagewanted=all.

"Airport Security Arsenal Adds Behavior Detection" by Thomas Frank for *USA Today.com*. The online article discusses the questioning technique developed from the Israeli method of deception detection and used at various airports in the United States. You can review the article at: http://usatoday30.usatoday.com/travel/flights/2007-09-25-behavior-detection_N.htm.

Micro-expressions: The New Face of Security? Professor Paul Ekman wrote this online article. He argues for airports to use behavioral

369

detection techniques to screen travelers and detect potential threats to airport security. You can review the article at the website: http://archives.californiaaviation.org/airport/msg38987.html.

Airport Security: Intent to Deceive? This online article by Sharon Weinberger discusses the pros and cons of deception detection. You can review the article online at the website: http://www.nature.com /news/210/100526/full/465412a.html.

Airport Security Arsenal Adds Behavior Detection by Thomas Frank is an online article from the *USA Today* website. It discusses the pioneering Israeli security techniques that airports implemented to stop potential terrorists. You can review the article at: http://usatoday30.usatoday.com/travel/flights/2007-09-25-behavior -detection.

Dangerous Minds is an online article by Malcom Gladwell posted by *The New Yorker in 2007.* It outlines the criminal profiling the FBI uses and gives several examples why it does not work. Read it at: http://www.newyorker.com/magazine/2007/11/12/dangerous-minds.

10 Tips for Active Listening by Barbara Bray. You can review it at http://barbarabraynet/2012/01/10/10-tips-for-active-listening/

Active Listening: Hear What People are Really Saying is an online article from the *Mind Tools* website. Review it at http://www.mindtools.com /CommSkll/ActiveListening.htm.

Chapter 7: Imagination

"The Empathy Machine" is an online article written by author Maria Konnikova for *Aeon Magazine.* She discusses the perception of Sherlock Holmes being unemotional and how new research supports his detached mind view of understanding others. See the article at: http://www.aeonmagazine.com/being-human/maria-konnikova-empathy-sherlock-holmes/.

Chapter 8: Memory

"Why Sherlock Holmes was Wrong and What You Should Do About it" by Chris Wondra argues that Sherlock's concept of the 'mind attic' is wrong. He argues that the mind is elastic and advocates that the way to improve memory is to read more. See his article at: http://www.weteachwelearn.org/2013/07/why-sherlock-holmes-was-wrong-and-what-you-should-do-about-it/.

"Trust Your Memory? Maybe You Shouldn't" by Jacque Wilson for *CNN.com* discusses the different ways memory can be unreliable. You can read the online article at: http://www.cnn.com/2013/05/18/health/lifeswork-loftus-memory-malleability/index.html?hpt=hp_c4.

"The Study of Human Memory" is online article from *human memory.net*, which outlines the chronological history of research on human memory from Aristotle to present day. The website also has other memory related articles such as *"What is Memory?"* etc. See it at: http://www.human-memory.net/intro_study.html.

"Ten Facts About Memory" is an online article on *About.com* by Kendra Cherry. The article discusses various interesting facts about human memory. You can review it at: http://psychology.about.com/od/memory/ss/ten-facts-about-memory.htm.

"Superior Memory of Experts and Long Term Working Memory" is an online paper by K. Anders Ericsson. The updated version details how experts are superior in what they do than average individuals but only in their specific fields of expertise. You can review it at the website: http://www.psy.fsu.edu/faculty/ericsson/ericsson.mem.exp.html.

"Introduction to Memory Techniques" is a section on the *mindtools.com* website that helps to improve your memory skills. The website discusses the various ways you can improve your memory by using the same mnemonic techniques memory experts use. You can see it at: http://www.mindtools.com/memory.html.

How To Improve Your Memory is an online article from *wikiHow.com*. It lists several mnemonic techniques that can help you remember. You can view the article at http://www.wikihow.com/improve-your-memory.

Intelligence Intensification Memory Techniques is an online article from wikiBooks website. It lists mnemonic techniques such as linking, peg words, memorizing playing cards and the Method of Loci to improve your memory. You can review the article at: http://en.wikibooks.org/wiki/Intelligence_Intensificaiton/Memory_Techniques.

"8 Tips to Improve Your Memory" is an online article written by John H. Grohol, Psy.d., for *pyschcentral.com*. See it at: http://psychcentral.com/blog/archives/2010/09/03/8-tips-for-improving-your-memory/.

"5 Experts Answer: What's the Best Way to Improve Your Memory?" is an online article written by Amanda Chan for *livescience.com*. Each expert gives tips for improving memory: http://www.livescience.com/35580-5-experts-answer-improve-memory.html.

"Is My Memory Normal?" is an article from author Lisa Davis published in AARP magazine. The article explains the brain's ability to grow and shrink in response to the world around it. She also offers steps to a stronger memory. *AARP, June/July 2013 issue, pages p45-47, 66.*

"How to Improve Your Memory" is an online article written by Melinda Smith, M.D. and Lawrence Robinson for *helpguide.org*. You can review the article at: http://www.helpguide.org /life/ improving_memory.htm.

Pimp Your Memory: How to Build a Mind Palace like Sherlock Holmes is an online article written by Davinia Hamilton. It explains how to build a memory palace to improve your ability to recall specific people, places and things. You can see the article at the website: http://daviniahamilton.com/2013/05/20/pimp-your-memory-how-to-build-a-mind-palace-like-sherlock-holmes/.

Sherlock Holmes Photographic Memory Technique is an online article by Enoch Gawain. This article explains six steps to creating a mind palace that anyone can use. See it online at the website: http://www.empowernetwork.com/overclockedeg/blog/ sherlock_holmes_photographic_memory.

Sherlock Holmes & His Mind Palace is an online posted by Rebecca Hughes on the Cognitive Psychology website. The article explains how

Sherlock Holmes uses the memory technique of categorization to consolidate and retrieve long-term memories to solve a mystery. See the article at http://psychinlife.blogspot.com/2013/04/sherlock-holmes-and-his-mind-palace.html.

Chapter 9: Intuition

The *Intuition (Psychology)* section on *Wikipedia* discusses the perception regarding women having a higher intuitive ability then men. According to *Wikipedia:* "...research by William Ickes has shown that women are susceptible to stereotypes, and try harder in situations where they would expect to do better. In situations where they are unaware that this is expected, no improved performance is found." You can review it at the website: http://en.wikipedia.org/wiki/Intuition_(psychology).

Mind Reading is an online article on by Annie Murphy Paul. It gives a brief history of intuition, discusses the pros and cons of using it and describes how we accomplish everyday 'mind reading.' You can review the article on the *Psychology Today* website at: http://www.psychologytoday.com /articles/200708/mind-reading.

The *Skeptic Dictionary.com* analyzes the *"Myers-Briggs Type Indicator."* It traces the history of type psychology from Carl Jung to Isabel Briggs Myers. It takes a cynical view of the MBTI, stating in sum: "...no behavior can ever be used to falsify the type, and any behavior can be used to verify it." You can see the review online at the website: http://www.skepdic.com/myersb.html.

"Gut Almighty" is an online article written for *Psychology Today.com* by Carlin Flora. The article discusses intuition and when best to rely on it and when not to rely on it. You can see it online at the website: http://www.psychologytoday.com/articles/200704/gut-almighty.

"The Powers & Perils of Intuition" is an online article written for *Psychology Today.com* by David G. Myers. It discusses the pros and cons of using intuition. You can review it online at the website: http://www.psychologytoday.com /articles/200212/the-powers-and-perils-intuition.

"Relying On Intuition - Should You Always Trust Your Gut Feelings?" By John Morrish discusses business leaders and experts use their intuitions to make decisions. Read it at the website: http://www.managementtoday.co.uk /news/1155928/.

"Going with Your Gut Feeling: Intuition Alone Can Guide the Right Choice, Study Says." This online article discusses how intuition can work in many situations. The article relies on a study from *American Friends of Tel Aviv University.* You can read it at *Science Daily.com*: http://www.sciencedaily.com/releases/2012/11/121108131724.htm .

"The Trouble With Intuition" is an online article on *The Chronicle of Higher Education* by Daniel Simons and Christopher Chabris. The article discusses the pitfalls of using intuition. You can review it at: http://chronicle.com/article/The-Trouble-With-Intuition/65674/.

"Trust Your Gut: Intuitive decision-making based on expertise may deliver better results than analytical approach" is an online article that discusses research which shows experts tend to make more accurate intuitive decisions than novices. See the online article at: http://www.sciencedaily.com/releases/2012/12/121220144155.htm

In March 2005, the online magazine *Monitor on Psychology* presented the theme of *"Intuition."* It provided several articles that covered humanity's natural intuitive ability. You can view the articles on the *American Psychological Association* website at: http://www.apa.org/monitor/mar05/.

"How to Develop the Sherlock Holmes Intuition" is an online line article from *wikihow.com.* It outlines several ways you can increase your intuitive powers as Sherlock Holmes did. You can view it at: http://www.wikihow.com/Develop-the-'Sherlock-Holmes'-Intuition.

"How to Use Intuition More Effectively" is an online article from Ben Newell that discusses the way we use intuition. It draws from the books *"Blink," "Thinking Fast & Slow"* and research from psychologists Adriaan De Groot and William G. Chase regarding how experts use intuition. You can review it at http://www.lifehacker.com.au /2013/05/how-to-use-intuition-more-effectively/.

Chapter 10: Personal Belongings

The source for this chapter originates from the five stories in the Canon that Arthur Conan Doyle wrote. The five stories: *The Sign of Four, The Adventure of the Blue Carbuncle, The Yellow Face, The Adventure of the Golden Pince-nez,* and *The Hound of the Baskervilles,* describe how Holmes made deductions from the items presented to him such as a hat and watch.

Chapter 11: Handwriting Analysis

Handwriting Analysis Tips by Lee Johnson. This online *eHow.com* article gives tips on analyzing several handwriting elements such as slants and pressure. See http://www.ehow.com/info_ 8026039 handwriting-analysis-tips.html.

What Your Handwriting Says About You is an online article from the website Real Simple.com. Writer Amanda Armstrong discusses handwriting tips such as reading loops, letter size, alignment and legibility. See the article at: http://www.realsimple.com/work-life/life-strategies/handwriting-101-00000000015886/page11.html.

Methods For Handwriting Analysis by eHow Contributor Scott Wolfenden discusses two types of handwriting analysis. He distinguishes between question documentation examination and Graphology. He then briefly discusses identifying handwriting strokes. You can review the article at the website: http://www.ehow.com /info_8148992_methods-handwriting-analysis.html.

"Sherlock Holmes Methods of Deduction" is a blog that discusses how Sherlock Holmes used Graphology in books and films. Review it at: http://shdeduction.blogspot.com/2012/06/1-graphology.html.

PBS interviewed scientist Barry Beyerstein, asking him several questions regarding Graphology. http://www.pbs.org/ safarchive /3_ask/archive/qna /3282_bbeyerstein.html.

"Graphology: Your Writing Style and Your Personality" by a member on the *desitwist.com* website, discusses the different elements of Graphology. You can review it at: http://www.desitwist.com/ general-

knowledge   /graphology   -your-writing-style-your-   personality-8085.html.

The *Handwriting Analysis* website lists dozens of techniques and definitions for analyzing handwriting. It discusses strokes, slants, word spacing, size, signature, pressure, zones and many other handwriting elements. You can review it at online at the website: http://handwritinglense.com/tag/55-handwriting_analysis_techniques.html.

The *Handwriting Analysis Insights* website analyzes the various elements of Graphology. It gives a detailed description of zones, writing styles, slants, spacing, margins, letter size, loops and many others. The article has many sample writings and illustrations. You can review it at: http://www.handwritinginsights.com/terms.html.

"The Lowdown on Handwriting Analysis" is an online article written by Matthew Scanlon and James Mauro for *Psychology Today.com*. The article describes a meeting with Graphologist Andrea McNichol. It also discusses Graphology basics and its' standing in the scientific community. See it at the website: http://www.psychologytoday.com/articles/200910/the-lowdown-handwriting-analysis.

Statement Analysis Field Examination Technique: A Useful Investigative Tool by Gene Klopf and Andrew Tooke. This article examines a study that reviews two elements of statement analysis to determine whether it can identify deception in written statements. You can see the article (scroll down to article) at: http://leb.fbi.gov/2003-pdfs/leb-april-2003.

Statement Analysis: New Investigative Process to Help You Uncover the Truth by Ralph Thomas. This online article outlines the specific techniques used in statement analysis to determine whether a subject's statement is truthful. You can review it at the website: http://www.pimall.com/nais/n.intera.html.

What Is Statement Analysis by Mark McClish. This online article discusses statement analysis and gives definitions and rules for using it during investigative interviews. You can review it at the website: http://www.statementanalysis.com/explain/.

The *Southeastern Association of Forensic Examiners* website is an informative source for document examination. It gives document examination definitions, the scope of the examination, handwriting identification and various other ways (forgery, typewriter identification, etc.). It also has workshops, lists the qualifications of an examiner and career paths to take. You can check out the website at: http://www.safde.org/whatwedo.htm.

Chapter 12: Practice and Train

"You Can Judge 90 Percent of People's Personalities by Their Shoes, Researchers Say" is an online article by Eric Pfeiffer for *Yahoo News.com*. The article describes how a study conducted at the *University of Kansas* and published in the *Journal of Research in Personality,* found people can deduce personality traits from the shoes you wear. You can review the article at the website: http://news.yahoo.com/blogs/sideshow/judge-90-percent-people-personalities-shoes-researchers-192903995.html.

"Top 10 Brain Teasers" is an online article written by Jamie Frater for *ListVerse.com.* Mystery #2 came from this article. You can see the other nine brainteasers at: http://listverse.com/2007/09/21/top-10-brain-teasers/.

"Sherlock Holmes Riddles with Answers" is an online blog at Daily Brain Teasers.com. Mystery #3 came from this blog. You can see the other brainteasers at: http://dailybrainteaser.blogspot.com /2013/10/ sherlock-holmes-riddles-with-answers _26.html.

"10 Websites for Puzzles, Brain Teasers and Riddles" is an online article written by Saikat Basu for *Make Use Of.com.* Riddle #1 came from this article, as did the suggestions for best websites for riddles. You can review the complete list of riddle websites at: http://www.makeuseof.com/tag/10-websites-puzzles-brain-teasers-and-riddles/.

"Practical Reasoning Puzzles" is an online practical reasoning riddle from the website *Rink Works.com.* Riddles #2 & 3 came from the Brain Teaser Section. You can see the other practical reasoning riddles at: http://www.rinkworks.com/brainfood/p/practical1.shtl.

39369026R00215

Made in the USA
San Bernardino, CA
24 September 2016